Mediaeval Sources in Translation 43

Peter Lombard, The *Sent*

Book 2: On Creation

TRANSLATED BY GIULIO SILANO

Peter Lombard's major work, the four books of the *Sentences*, was written in the mid-twelfth century and, as early as the 1160s, the text was glossed and commented on in the schools. There is hardly a theologian of note throughout the rest of the Middle Ages who did not write a commentary on the *Sentences*. Yet in spite of its importance in Western intellectual history and its capacity to excite many generations of students and teachers, the *Sentences* has received little attention in more recent times. Indeed, it has been called "one of the least read of the world's great books."

This volume makes available for the first time in English a full translation of Book 2 of the *Sentences*. It consists of forty-four Distinctions, in the first of which Peter sets out a definition of creation and ponders the reasons which God may have had for engaging in it. Angels, their creation, nature, fall, ranks, and ministries are the subject of Distinctions 2-11. Distinctions 12-15 set out an hexaemeron, or an account of the six days of creation as described in Genesis. The next three Distinctions concentrate on the creation of man and woman, and the following two discuss the state of human beings before their sinful fall, including their manner of procreation. Distinctions 21-29, organized around the fall, are devoted to human psychology, freedom of choice, and grace. In Distinctions 30-33 the focus is on original sin, its transmission by the current mode of procreation, its remission in baptism. And the Book concludes in Distinctions 34-44 with a detailed analysis of actual sin and how it occurs by free choice in the diminished condition of human freedom after the fall.

The volume contains an introduction to Book 2, a list of the major chapter headings, and a bibliography.

Saint Michael's College Mediaeval Translations

General Editors

Mediaeval Sources in Translation 43

PETER LOMBARD

THE *SENTENCES*

BOOK 2: On Creation

Translated by

GIULIO SILANO

PONTIFICAL INSTITUTE OF MEDIAEVAL STUDIES

This book has been published with the help of a grant
from the Canadian Federation for the Humanities and Social Sciences,
through the Aid to Scholarly Publications Programme,
using funds provided by the Social Sciences and
Humanities Research Council of Canada.

Library and Archives Canada Cataloguing in Publication

Peter Lombard, Bishop of Paris, ca. 1100-1160
The Sentences / Peter Lombard ; translated by Giulio Silano.

(Mediaeval sources in translation, ISSN 0316-0874 ; 42-43)
(Saint Michael's College mediaeval translations)
Translation of: Sententiae in IV libris distinctae.
Includes bibliographical references and index.
Bk. 1. The mystery of the Trinity – bk. 2. On creation.
ISBN 978-0-88844-292-5 (bk. 1).–ISBN 978-0-88844-293-2 (bk. 2)

1. God–Early works to 1800. 2. God–Attributes–Early works to 1800.
3. Trinity–Early works to 1800. 4. Catholic Church–Doctrines–Early
works to 1800. 5. Theology–Early works to 1800. I. Silano, Giulio, 1955-
II. Pontifical Institute of Mediaeval Studies III. Title. IV. Series. V. Series.

B765.P33S46 2007 231 C2006-907006-7

Reprinted 2012
Pontifical Institute of Mediaeval Studies
59 Queen's Park Crescent East
Toronto, Ontario, Canada M5S 2C4

PRINTED IN CANADA

Contents

Peter Lombard, The *Sentences*
Book 2: On Creation

To Stefano

Ed elli a me: “Se tu segui tua stella,
non puoi fallire a glorïoso porto,
se ben m'accorsi ne la vita bella”

'n la mente m'è fitta, e or m'accora,
la cara e buona imagine paterna
di voi quando nel mondo ad ora ad ora
m'insegnavate come l'uom s'etterna

(*Inferno*, 15.55-57, 82-85)

Introduction

As noted in the Introduction to the translation of Book 1 of the *Sentences*, it is our view that Peter Lombard's work is best read as if it were analogous to a legal casebook intended for the training of experts.[1] A few of them would become academic theologians, though most would become leaders in the Church. The varied functions to which they would be called would normally include some preaching and teaching, but they would also be deeply involved in the governance of their communities, whether ecclesiastical or secular. They might rule directly, as pastors, abbots, presiding officers of communities, episcopal and papal officials, or even as bishops and popes, or they might assist ecclesiastical and secular rulers as their advisors. In all these varied roles, the kind of disciplined reflection on the Christian tradition which the *Sentences* of Peter Lombard canonized was increasingly thought to be useful and necessary. An understanding of the great diversity of functions which medieval students of the *Sentences* fulfilled may help the modern reader to cultivate a better appreciation of the work itself.

In the first book of his *Sentences*, Peter Lombard had undertaken to explore in a stammering way, as he himself indirectly acknowledged, the mysteries of God's unity and trinity;[2] with less hesitation, in this second Book he turns to the consideration of creatures. The Book comes to us divided into forty-four Distinctions, in the first of which Peter sets out a definition of creation and ponders the reasons which God may have had for engaging in it. Angels, their creation, nature, fall, ranks, and ministries are the subject of Distinctions 2-11. Distinctions 12-15 set out an

[1]That Introduction also contained a brief overview of Peter's life and work, a discussion of the nature and purposes of the *Sentences* as a whole, and a summary of the contents of Book 1. The serious reader of Peter Lombard in English will want to consult the magisterial study of Marcia L. Colish, *Peter Lombard*, 2 vol. (E.J. Brill: Leiden, New York, Cologne, 1994). If in the notes below I disagree with a few readings of Peter by Colish, this ought not to be taken as denial of the great value of her study, particularly in setting Peter's teachings in the context of the school debates of his time. Her pioneering and thorough examination of Peter's thought is an indispensable reference work for the English reader. A useful and engaging introduction to Peter's life and thought, which complements Colish's more substantial work, is Philipp W. Rosemann, *Peter Lombard* (Oxford University Press: Oxford and New York, 2004).

[2]See Book 1 p. 54.

hexaemeron, or an account of the six days of creation as described in Genesis. The next three Distinctions concentrate on the creation of man and woman, and the following two discuss the state of human beings before their sinful fall, including their manner of procreation. Distinctions 21-29, organized around the fall, are devoted to human psychology, freedom of choice, and grace. In Distinctions 30-33 the focus is on original sin, its transmission by the current mode of procreation, its remission in baptism. And the Book concludes in Distinctions 34-44 with a detailed analysis of actual sin and how it occurs by free choice in the diminished condition of human freedom after the fall.

In a Book devoted to creatures, it is perfectly sensible for Peter to begin by presenting his view of creation itself. In a work meant for people of faith, it is equally unsurprising that he should distance himself from philosophers and their ponderings on this issue, particularly insofar as these seem to detract from the clarity of Scripture's description of the Creator's free, unique, and sovereign initiative. And so he begins with a rejection of Plato's view of creation as inconsistent with divine creation *ex nihilo* (dist. 1 c1). Creation from nothing is what distinguishes God from men and angels; were God simply an artificer, he would not be qualitatively different from other artificers (c2). Furthermore, artificers make things by a motion or change in themselves, which cannot be predicated of the unchangeable God. Hence it is improper even to speak of God creating things as if anew; by divine creation, things come to be because it has always been in God's eternal will that it should be so (c3 nn1-4). And this happens because of the goodness of God's will, which has decreed from all eternity that others ought to become sharers in that blessedness which is God's from all eternity and which can be shared without diminution (c3 n5). Because it can only be shared through the intelligence, God created the rational creature, able to understand the highest good, to love it by understanding, to possess it by love, to enjoy it by possession (c4 n1).

Rational creatures are either incorporeal or corporeal, that is, angels or human beings, both of whom were created by God's goodness so that they might praise, serve, and enjoy God (c4 nn2-4). And this service is for their own utility, since God has no need of it (c4 n5). The world, in turn, was made to serve man (c4 n6). Such is the dignity of human persons that all things (including God) might be said to be theirs, and even the angels are sometime said to serve them (c4 n7). As for the view that man was made to make up for the fallen angels, Peter does not approve of it—at least not in the sense that humans would not have been created, if some of the angels had not fallen (c5).

In regard to why God joined the soul to a body, thereby seeming to place it in a less worthy state, Peter asserts that the first cause of this is simply that God willed it, and his will is not to be queried (c6 nn1-2). The second cause was to hearten humankind by providing an example of the union which is between God and his creature in eternity (c6 nn3-4). Furthermore, to serve God in a body is more demanding in this life and so deserving of a greater crown in the next (c6 n6).

On Angels and the Works of the Six Days

For all the dignity which Peter ascribes to the human condition, angels remain "the worthier creature" (c6 n6), and so they will be considered before man. And yet, perhaps continuing his bid for the assertion of human dignity, and despite (because of?) conflicting authorities on the subject, Peter insists that angels were created together with primordial matter and in time (dist. 2 cc1-3), and both were formless upon creation. Primordial matter would be formed in the course of the six days of creation; the angels became fully formed only by their conversion toward God in love (c5).

At their creation, angels received a simple essence, personhood, a creaturely rationality, and a free will, by which, as soon as they were made, they might turn toward good or toward evil (dist. 3 c1). Although they all received these endowments, it is not to be held that they all received them equally; as there is difference in the bodies of corporeal beings, even before the fall, so it seems plausible that angels were different from one another in a manner suitable to their state. And so they differ in the fineness of their nature, the perspicacity of their knowledge, and the freedom of their will. On these initial differences of endowment would be grounded the eventual hierarchy of angels (c2 nn4-5), but the less endowed are not thereby made weak, ignorant, or unable to choose freely (c2 nn4-5). The discernment of these differences can be properly exercised by God alone (c3).

Angels were created good and did not become good by their free choice. They were just by the innocence of their nature, and not by the practice of virtue. But they were made with the ability to sin and not to sin, and it was by the exercise of free choice that some fell and some remained steadfast (c4). They were all endowed with sufficient natural wisdom and love to make this choice (cc5-6).

At their creation, the angels were neither blessed, nor miserable, since there can be no misery without sin, and no one can be truly blessed without certainty or hope regarding the lasting nature of beatitude (dist. 4 c1). As to whether they were perfect at their creation, they were perfect in the sense that they were endowed with all that they required when they were created, but their nature would not be entirely fulfilled until after their confirmation. Even then, their perfection could not approach the divine nature (c1 nn5-6).

Those angels who, by the exercise of their free will, turned toward God in love immediately fulfilled all their potentialities, becoming, as it were, mirrors of God's wisdom (dist. 5 c1). Others chose to turn away from God in envy and hatred, wishing to become equal to God; by their choice, their gifts were perverted and they were made blind. A good choice was made by those on whom God's grace was conferred, an evil choice by those to whom no grace for conversion was given. But all chose with a free choice, now defined as the free power and aptitude of the will to choose what it pleases and make rational judgements (c2). The angels who converted were assisted to make a good choice by the divine conferral of co-operating grace, without which the rational creature cannot make progress and gain merit (c3). By this grace, the good angels were turned to a perfect love of God; because they were already good, they did not require the aid of operating grace, by which an evil person is made good. But co-operating grace was kept from those who fell (c4). Not unreasonably, this gives rise to the question of whether the fallen angels ought to be blamed for their fall, since it was not by their fault that co-operating grace was not given to them. Peter's answer is that, although the good angels had not merited grace, the evil ones had deserved its withholding because, by their free choice, they had chosen not to stand firm until grace should be conferred on them (c5).

Although the good angels are granted blessedness at the time of their confirmation, the question remains of whether they merited it or whether it came to them entirely by grace. Peter's graceful conclusion is that, although either view has merit, "the angels merit what they received at that time as a reward for the service which they render to us in obedience and reverence to God; and so the reward preceded the merit. And I confess that this latter view is more pleasing to me" (c6 n2). This charming statement obviously flows from a thoughtful reflection on the dynamism of love; it also rejoices in the community which exists between angels and humankind and, not incidentally, confirms once more Peter's high view of the dignity of human persons.

Among both good and evil angels are to be found members of the higher and lower reaches of the angelic hierarchy. Indeed, Lucifer, the highest of them all, was among those who fell for desiring to be like God not by imitation, but in equality of power (dist. 6 c1). For their depravity,

Lucifer and the other fallen angels were cast down from the empyrean heaven into the cloudy atmosphere next to us in order to test human beings (cc2-3). In this way, even after their fall, the demons do not cease to be subject to God's providential design and the link between angels and human beings finds another unexpected confirmation.

The perversion of their gifts does not mean that the demons do not preserve a hierarchy among themselves which echoes the hierarchy of the good angels and will remain until every form of rule is done away with (c4). In the meantime, under Lucifer's leadership, demons harry and tempt men here on earth, and some of them may already be in hell to hold prisoner and torment the souls of evil people (c5). It seems probable that Lucifer is bound in hell, from where he will emerge to become an even more powerful tempter in the time of Antichrist (c6). And lest one think that the warfare which the saints wage upon the demons is exclusively personal to them, the view is reported that individual demons defeated by the saints are rendered unable to tempt other human beings (c7).

If, as an irremediable consequence of their original choice, the evil angels cannot will the good, even when what they do turns out to be good, the good angels are unable to will evil (dist. 7 c1). This ought not to be taken as evidence that angels no longer have free choice. In the case of the good angels, the effect of divine grace is to perfect their freedom of choice so that they freely love more and more fully; in the evil angels, their abandonment by divine grace leaves them to their own malicious free choice and unable to rise to the good (c2). The good angels' inability to will evil confers upon them a freer choice, and this fuller freedom comes to them not from nature, but from grace; it follows that no confusion can occur between even the good angels and God, since God alone in unable to sin by nature (cc3-4).

As for demons, despite their malicious obstinacy, they are able to acquire powerful knowledge because of their nature and experience, and through revelation (c5), but only because God has allowed them knowledge and power so that they may become his instruments in the testing of human beings (c6). The magical arts are a telling sign of demoniacal power and its limits (c6). Although the exercise of magic can make it seem as if visible matter obeyed the demons and their power extended to creation, it is not so. God alone is the creator. But demons know the laws of creation much more thoroughly than human beings; they understand the seeds of things, which God has placed in creation, and they can manipulate them to produce the effects which are sometimes observed in the exercise of the magical arts. And yet they cannot do these things without God's permission, for whose service these things are allowed to occur (cc7-10).

From Scripture and authority, it appears that angels have bodies. At any rate, they take bodily form when, at God's bidding, they appear to human beings. Although Peter professes himself unable to settle the various questions which excite human curiosity regarding these subtle matters (dist. 8 cc1-2), the one point he holds with firm certainty is that God has never appeared to human beings in the form of his divine essence (c3). In this way, Peter encourages his students to bow humbly before the divine transcendence. The point is reiterated by the assertion that, in cases of demonic possession, demons do not enter human beings substantially. God alone, who created the human creature, is capable of being received substantially by that same creature; demons exercise their power by deception, by "drawing the soul to a disposition for wickedness (c4)."

As for the angelic hierarchy, Scripture affirms that it is distinguished into nine orders, which seems entirely fitting, since this trinity of threes is a wonderful sign of the divine Trinity (dist. 9 c1). The angels are grouped in these orders by their gifts of nature and grace (c2), but their names were given for our sake, since they know each other directly through contemplation without need of names (c3). These names come from the pre-eminence, and not the uniqueness, of the gifts which the names denote, since in heaven all is shared and nothing is possessed singularly (c3 nn1-2). The most pre-eminent of these gifts is love, and so the Seraphim, whose predominant characteristic is a burning love, are higher than the Cherubim, who are characterized by knowledge (c3 nn3-4). The superiority of love over knowledge is not a pointless thing for master and students to ponder!

It does not seem plausible that the angels were distinguished in rank from the moment of their creation: if they had already possessed the gifts which distinguish them in their ranks, none of them would have fallen. It seems safer to say that, from the moment of creation, they were distinguished by a different degree of fineness of nature and discernment of form; in this sense, some could be called superior, others inferior (c4). These distinctions presumably continue even now within each order (c5).

As for the assertion that a tenth order of angels is to be completed from human beings, Peter is loath to support the view that the creation and salvation of humankind might have been contingent upon the fall of the evil angels (c6). He prefers the interpretation "that what fell in the case of the angels will be restored from men, and that so many fell from among the angels that a tenth order could be made" (c6 n3). That this is the sounder view seems confirmed by the fact that the human beings to be saved will correspond in number to the angels who remained steadfast rather than to those who fell away (c7 n1).

Since angels are so named from their being messengers of God to men, Peter next asks whether it is characteristic of all angels that they are sent (dist. 10 c1 n1). He seems to think this is plausible, but that the greater ones are sent more rarely and for the more signal tasks, as was the case with Michael, Gabriel, and Raphael (cc1-2).

Peter receives the traditional doctrine regarding the assignment of individual angels and demons to guard and test human beings, but he regards it as more plausible that each angel carries out the function for more than one human being, either sequentially or contemporaneously (dist. 11 c1).

This consideration of the work which angels do for the benefit of humankind fittingly introduces the concluding question of Peter's little treatise on angelology and prepares the way for his account of creation: it concerns whether angels make progress in merit or reward. After reporting an apparent conflict of authorities on the matter, Peter comes down firmly in favour of the view that they do for the work which they perform on behalf of human beings and that their progress and reward consist in the increase of love and knowledge. Even angels profit, as it were, from the existence and mission of the Church, through which they gain an increased knowledge of the divine mysteries, even if such an increase is not necessary for their blessedness (c2).

So concludes Peter's discussion of angels. Aside from the subject's intrinsic interest, the student has learned from it how to interpret the various references to angels in Scripture and in the Christian tradition and, not incidentally, has already met issues and topics which will arise again in the coming discussion of the creation and fall of the human person. Aside from having the undoubted merit of following chronology, the placement of angelology at the beginning of Book 2 has also allowed Peter to raise issues such as the freedom of the will and the role of grace in salvation in a less heated context than that of human creation and salvation. The numerous reaffirmations of divine transcendence and sovereignty also provide a useful context within which to discuss those aspects of creation which more closely touch his listeners and readers. But before he broaches these issues, he outlines the scriptural account of the creation of the universe and some of the heated disputes which have arisen in the course of Christian reflection on that account.

The creation account begins with the reiteration of the fact that, in the beginning, God created angels and formless matter (dist. 12 c1). By this restatement, Peter takes sides already on the issue of whether God created everything at once: he does not think so (cc2-3). With the angels, God created the matter of the four elements, which is called formless because it did not yet have any clear, distinct, and beautiful form. For Peter, then, the work of the six days can be described as the imposition of the form of beauty on matter (c5 n2).

The work of the first day is the formation of light, which may be understood both as spiritual and corporeal light (dist. 13 cc1-2). This act of creation and those of the rest of the six days are described in Scripture as if they occurred by God speaking. This is not to be understood literally, as if God used speech, since this would imply mutability and the existence of language. The expression makes sense, if it is referred to the coeternal Word, "through whom all things were made" (c6). But neither ought one to make the mistake of considering the work of creation as the Father's work, carried out in and through the Son, as if he were an instrument. Reiterating a characteristic concern of his, Peter insists that the work of creation is to be understood as the work of the whole Trinity (c7).

Peter next makes short shrift of the works of the second, third, and fourth day, which include the creation of the firmament, the separation of the waters above from those below, and the making of the sun, moon, and stars (dist. 14 cc1-11). The straightforward presentation of the Genesis account is punctuated by the occasional interjection of items of interest. Bede's reference to the creation of the starry heaven implicitly confirms Peter's rejection of the view that all things were created simultaneously (c2). The failure of Genesis to refer to the work of the second day as good is taken not as a sign of divine ambivalence, but as a warning that twoness can be the origin of otherness and division (c6). One of the reasons for making the heavenly luminaries is "that the night should not remain devoid of beauty, and that those men who find it needful to work at night should be consoled by the moon and stars" (c10), so confirming the view that creation is the imposition of the beauty of forms upon formless matter and remembering that God creates for the sake of persons.

A brief account of the creation of animals and a preliminary sketch of the creation of humankind serve as preparation for a much fuller consideration of the state of the human person at creation (dist. 15 cc1-5). Once more, the bare-bones account is enlivened by the interjection of some issues of particular interest. Did the creation of animals extend also to dangerous and poisonous ones? Whether it did or not, such animals would not have been harmful to man, if he had not sinned; they became harmful to punish vices and test virtues (c3). Even in this, one finds confirmation that creation is for the sake of persons. And here, again, Peter returns to the question of whether the world was created all at once, giving the arguments of the other side, but making it clear that he regards it as the less probable view as being the less well-supported by Scripture and the Church's tradition (c5 n2–c6).

God's resting on the seventh day provides the occasion to ponder God's unceasing creative activity; although God stopped producing new creatures, creation could not continue in its existence and order, except for the Trinity's ceaseless activity (c7).

The Creation and Fall of Man

Beginning with Distinction 16, Peter turns to the treatment of the creation of man, his state before the fall, the fall itself, and the work of human restoration (c1). Reflection on human nature begins with the emphatic assertion that its creation is the work of the whole Trinity (c2), and that it is in the image and likeness of the whole Trinity that the human person is created (c3 n1).

It is in human rationality that the image and likeness of God are discerned, "in his image according to memory, intelligence, and love; in his likeness according to innocence and justice, which are naturally in the rational mind" (c3 n5). One might also discern the divine image in the human apprehension of truth, and likeness in the human love of virtue. Lastly, "image pertains to form, likeness to nature," that is, to the very essence of the immortal and invisible soul. And yet the usage of image as applied to man is not to be confused with the sense of the term when applied to the Son, who "is image, but not in the image, because he was born, not created, equal and in no way unlike" (c4 n1). But even the body of the human person, by its erect posture, points toward heaven and so in some way points to the divine likeness (c4 n2). It is notable that, in all that has been said about the human soul, no distinction has been drawn according to gender; in this, Peter has been said to avoid the subordinationism expressed by some of his contemporaries in their differentiation of male and female nature.[3]

Distinction 17 discusses the creation of Adam, the first man. First, Peter offers a warning: in reading the Genesis account, one is not to forget that God is pure spirit, and so his forming man and breathing life into him are not to be taken in an anthropomorphic sense (c1 nn1-3). A proper reading of the text of Genesis will help to avoid the heretical conclusion

[3]Colish, *Peter Lombard*, 1.366-67; 2.731.

that the human soul is consubstantial with God (c1 nn4-5). As for the subtle and controverted question of whether Adam's soul was created before his body or in his body, Peter declines to choose between the contending views; he is certain, on the other hand, that subsequent human souls are created in the body.[4] Unlike other men, however, Adam was created in the fullness of his maturity. That such should have been the case, and without the violation of nature, is taken to be another manifestation of the sovereignty of God's good pleasure, "whose will is necessity" (c3 n2).

Adam was not created in paradise; he was transferred there by God's grace (c4). And this paradise of delights is to be understood neither as a merely corporeal place, nor as a merely spiritual one, but as both, so that it is both itself and a sign of the Church (c5). This garden was rich in beautiful trees, among which were the tree of life and the tree of the knowledge of good and evil (c6). Nor was the latter true evil; its name derives from what happened afterwards, when the human creature would learn the difference between the good of obedience and the evil of disobedience by transgressing God's command not to eat of the fruit of that tree. By his transgression, man, who had known evil only in the abstract, now came to know it also by experience (c7 n1).

The creation of woman occurred in paradise and from the substance of the man (dist. 18 c1 n1). She was created after Adam so that humankind should recognize its common paternity in him and so be united by the loving bond of common filiation (c1 nn2-3). And the woman was created from the man's side, and not from his head or feet, so that it should be clear that the two are called to union in the fellowship of love (c2). That her formation from Adam's side should be experienced entirely as a good thing explains why it was done with Adam asleep and untroubled and serves as prefiguration of the Church's formation from the side of Christ on the cross (c3 n2).

Peter rejects the view that anything other than the man's substance was used in the creation of the woman; at the same time, he firmly re-

[4]On this question, Colish, *Peter Lombard*, 1.367, claims that Peter "cannot resolve the question of whether there was a time lag between the creation of Adam's body and of his soul." Rosemann, *Peter Lombard*, p. 106 and n37, asserts that "the Lombard distances himself from Augustine's position according to which the human soul was initially created without body," and that Colish's assertion is unambiguously rebutted by Peter's statement in dist. 17 c2 n4. Colish seems to have read Peter's unwillingness to take sides as an implicit admission of inability to do so; Rosemann seems to have missed Peter's careful distinction, in the text cited, between whatever may have been the case in Adam's creation and what happens in all other instances.

proves the opinion that the woman's soul was derived from the man's (c4 n1, c7 n1). Linked to these issues is a brief discussion of causation, distinguishing direct divine causation and causation through secondary causes (cc5-6). Furthermore, the reflection on the creation of Eve's soul leads to the affirmation that human souls are not derived from one another, nor were they all created at once; each soul is created and infused into the newly formed body in the womb, so attesting to God's tender and ever-present providence (c7).

In Distinction 19, Peter turns to the question of the state of the human person before the fall, which is in part described by comparison to the same state after the fall and to how it will be at the resurrection. In the first state, there was the power to die and the power not to die; in the second state, after sin, there is the power to die and no power not to die; in the third state, there shall be the power not to die and no power to die (c1). But even in the first state, the human body was an animal one, requiring the sustenance of food; at the resurrection, the body shall become entirely spiritual and the need for food will disappear (c2). The most marked effect of the fall on the human body is the transition from the possibility of death to its necessity; the most marked effect of the resurrection upon the body shall be the impossibility of death (c3). The possibility of immortality, which the human body enjoyed before the fall, came from grace; the possibility of death came from the body's own nature (c4).

Perhaps even more revealing of the changes wrought in the human body by the fall is human sexuality and the procreation of offspring. Peter briskly rejects the view that there would have been no sexual joining without sin because sexual intercourse cannot happen without stain; he holds that it was possible, but would have occurred with the parties enjoying complete control over all their members. Lust, a consequence of sin, has brought about loss of this control (dist. 20 c1). If the first parents did not engage in stainless union before the fall, it was perhaps due to the speed with which they fell, or because God had not yet commanded them to become so joined (c3).

If the fall had not happened and procreation had occurred in paradise, children would not have succeeded to their dying parents, since there would have been no necessity for the latter to die, but perhaps they would have been transferred to a better state after the just fulfilment of their duties. And yet one should not be tempted by the view that, if there had been no fall, human beings would have been born fully grown and without the need to make physical progress, or even to take food. These things are not flaws, but the human condition, and so would have been the case even if there had been no fall (c4). What changes as a result of the fall is the immoderate nature of the appetites; without the fall, there would have been no hunger (c4 n6). Similarly, Peter favours the view that human beings would not have been born with fullness of knowledge, but would have made progress in the use of their senses and intellect. Nor would they have failed to know what they ought to know. Such ignorance occurs from the darkening of the intellect which is brought about by sin (c5).

Such was the state of the human person before sin; the faculties with which humans had been endowed would have been used to obey the divine command and these glorious creatures would have received an eternal spiritual reward (c6). The fall, cause of so many changes, finds its root in the devil's envy of the possibilities that the practice of humility opened up for human beings, and so he tempted them by pride (dist. 21 c1 n1). The timid malice of the devil looked for weakness in our first parents and found it in Eve's less vigorous rationality (c1 n2).[5] That the devil's power is bounded and subject to God's is shown even by the form of a serpent which he was allowed to take in tempting Eve. Although he was permitted to practice deceit on Eve by taking animal form, he was only allowed a form through which his malice was detectable (c2). The fraud which the devil perpetrates is sufficiently thin that the punishment that follows is fully justified; this is the case, even though the serpent became, for the occasion, the most cunning of all the beasts (c3).

Peter next examines the rhetoric of the serpent's address to Eve, which provides evidence of its great cunning. Questions are the tempter's effective device to discover and exploit the weaknesses in Eve; she proves willing to doubt God's warning and to believe the devil's promise of divinity and of the knowledge of good and evil (c5 nn1-5). The chinks in Eve's defenses are gluttony, vainglory, and avarice; the last is understood to extend also to an immoderate desire for knowledge, which gives new

[5]Colish, *Peter Lombard*, 1.377 and 2.732, reads this as an assertion that Eve was less rational than Adam and sees it as an inconsistent and unwitting departure by Peter from his view of their equality of nature in Adam and Eve. But Peter's language is quite nuanced on the matter: he does not say that Eve was "less rational" than Adam, but that in her "reason was less vigorous than in the man." Rosemann, *Peter Lombard*, p. 109, more attentively points out that Peter seems to hold that reason is less developed in Eve. This is explainable by Eve's more recent creation, and so by her lesser practice of the rational faculty, rather than by any intrinsic and permanent inferiority of female rationality. Such a reading is entirely consistent with Peter's views (dist. 20 cc4 and 5) about the gradual development of physical and moral faculties even if the fall had not occurred.

point and weight to Peter's frequent warnings to his students and readers about the unsuitability of not respecting bounds in the desire to know.

That the account of Eve's temptation is not merely historical, but is meant to instruct about temptation in the here and now, is made clear by a brief description of human temptation, which is distinguished into an exterior and an interior one. Exterior temptation comes exclusively from the tempter suggesting an evil by some word or sign. Interior temptation occurs invisibly and can arise from the devil or from our own corrupt flesh. The second does not occur without sin; in the first, there is no sin, unless there is consent on our part (c6). It was because humankind fell by exterior temptation that forgiveness is possible; since the angels who fell did not do so in the same way, forgiveness is not open to them (c7 n1).

This brief excursus leads to the consideration of whether there was pride in the human person before the serpent's temptation. How else does one explain Eve's willingness to be convinced by the serpent? Or Adam's yielding to Eve's words? (dist. 22 c1 nn1-5). But if this were the case, then our first parents would have sinned by their own pride and their fall would have been irremediable. And so pride is said to have arisen in Eve after the serpent's suggestion that great power was available for the taking (c1 nn6-8).

In Eve and Adam, pride appears to have been gender specific. Eve was so undone by the serpent's temptation that she wished to become God's equal (c2). Adam was not taken in by the devil's mendacious assertions, but he misjudged the severity of the disobedience; since nothing untoward had yet happened to Eve after her eating of the forbidden fruit, he concluded that the offense was not serious and so yielded to his own desire to eat it (c3).

The comparison of the different kind of guilt in Eve and Adam appears to have been a standard school exercise.[6] This is sometimes read as a discussion of who sinned more grievously of the two, with Eve coming out the loser in the comparison. Peter has been said to side with those who convict Eve of being the more guilty party.[7] If Peter shares this view, he does not state it explicitly here. Under the rubric of 'Who sinned more, Adam or Eve,' he sets out the various arguments, first outlining the case for Eve's greater guilt, which is grounded in her greater pride, the greater number of persons against whom she sinned, and her more severe punish-

[6]Colish, *Peter Lombard*, 1.373-376, on the school debates regarding this subject, and 1.378-379 on Peter's supposed position on this topic.

[7]Ibid., 1.378; Rosemann, *Peter Lombard*, pp. 109-110.

ment (c4 nn1-5). The arguments are then outlined which posit Adam's greater guilt, but each of these appears to have an adequate response (c4 nn6-12). At the conclusion, the case for Eve's greater guilt remains standing, while the one for Adam's appears to have adequate answers. And yet Peter avoids a formal determination of the question. Indeed, he will return to the question in a short while in order to argue once more, and on a somewhat different basis, for Adam's greater culpability (dist. 24 c4 nn6-12).[8] As that discussion makes even clearer, the question of degree of culpability is useful in order to canvass exhaustively the mechanics of temptation and the conscious decision to sin as they apply to all human beings.

In line with this task, the discussion of Eve's guilt becomes an occasion for outlining the various kinds of ignorance and whether they excuse a sinner. Ignorance is first distinguished between vincible and invincible (dist. 22 c5 n1). It is then further differentiated in three ways. The first concerns those who are able to know, but do not wish to do so; this is itself a sin. The second ignorance relates to those who wish to know, but are unable; this is punishment for sin and excuses the sinner. The third is the ignorance of those who simply do not know, and have no inclination to learn; this may make for a lighter punishment, but does not fully excuse the sinner (c5 n2). It is notable that, although it was Eve's possible defense of ignorance that gave rise to this discussion, there is no explicit reference to Eve, thereby making clear that Eve's case is simply an occasion for reflection on concerns which affect all human beings and their responsibility for their own choices.

The careful analysis of the temptation and fall of the first parents is followed by the question of why God allowed them to be tempted, knowing that they would fall, or why God did not make man unable to sin (dist. 23 c1 nn1-4). The glory of choice appears to be the answer, and God's ability to draw good even out of evil. But here, too, ultimately the most adequate response is to bow down before the mystery of divine knowledge (c1 n5). Presumably, this injunction ought to have all the more force now that the student has contemplated the role of presumption to excessive knowledge in the fall of Eve.

The mention of divine knowledge leads to a consideration of human knowledge before the fall, which was threefold in respect to its objects,

[8] Colish, *Peter Lombard*, 1.378. Rosemann, *Peter Lombard*, p. 235 n52, has already pointed out that Adam's greater culpability is to be inferred from Peter's discussion here; it is not clearly stated. This seems consistent with what we have just said concerning the question of Eve's greater guilt.

namely God, nature, and man himself (cc2–3 n1). The knowledge of God was not so perfect as that which the saints shall have when they will see God face to face, but neither was it as opaque as our own is now. God's presence was more accessible to the first man than it is to believers now, who seek the absent God (c3 n4). As for other creatures, man knew them sufficiently as to be able to give names to each of them and assume responsibility for their care; human knowledge regarding creatures survived the fall, as did the knowledge by which to provide for the needs of the body (c3 nn2-3). As for self-knowledge, the first man knew his own place and responsibilities in creation; had he not had such knowledge, he could not have been guilty of transgression (c3 n5). But he had no foreknowledge of his own fall (c4).

Peter next begins to address the tangled question of the relationship of grace and nature, or of grace and freedom, in man before the fall. The crucial concern here is to safeguard both divine sovereignty and the dignity of human freedom. Just like the angels, man was created with a sufficient endowment of divine grace that he was able not to fall. By this grace, he was able to live in accordance with natural goods, but not to live spiritually unto salvation. Had he not had this grace, he would not have merited punishment for the fall (dist. 24 cc1-2).[9] And yet, had he resisted temptation, he would not have gained merit since there was no impulse to evil in him which needed to be resisted (c2 nn7-8).

Free choice—the faculty by which the good is chosen with the aid of grace and evil without its aid—is said to reside in will and reason. It is called free because the will can bend either to good or evil; it is called choice because of the power of reason to discern between the two (c3 n1). This faculty of free choice is what distinguishes human beings from brute animals, which have only sensual appetites (c3 n2). As for reason, it is said to have two parts, one higher and the other lower, namely wisdom and knowledge. Wisdom applies to the contemplation and observation of the highest eternal things; knowledge looks to the proper use of temporal things. Wisdom is entirely severed from, while knowledge is close to, the sensuality which humans share with the beasts (c5).

These reflections on free choice, reason, and sensuality occur here because they serve to clarify the fall of Adam and Eve and the way in which human beings sin now (c6). In effect, the story of the fall, which has been read carefully and literally for what it says about Adam and Eve,

[9]For useful comments on this difficult issue, see Rosemann, *Peter Lombard*, pp. 111-112.

now is read explicitly for what it says about all human beings. In them, sensuality is the serpent, knowledge is the woman, and wisdom is the man (cc7-8). Sensuality presents the attraction of sin to knowledge which, if it consents to it, then suggests it to wisdom (c9 nn1-2). If sensuality alone is drawn to sin, then the sin is slight (c9 n3). If wisdom consents to it, the temptation to sin is actualized and the sin is mortal (c11). If the inclination to sin is not held for long in the pleasure of thought and wisdom intervenes to curb it, then the sin is venial. But if knowledge revels for too long in the prospect of sin, and wisdom does not intervene, then the sin is mortal (c12 n1). Ever mindful of the responsibility to teach his students to read Scripture attentively and prudently, Peter closes this discussion with the textual note that, in Scripture, the term sensuality is not confined to that part of the soul we share with animals, but is also used to refer to the lower part of human reason (c13).

The brief definition of free choice which has just preceded the account of temptation is reiterated and expanded (dist. 25 c1). Choice is a free judgement concerning one's own will, its exercise, and its movement toward good or evil things (c1 n2). Free choice applies neither to past, nor to present things, but only to future ones, and only those whose occurrence is dependent on that choice (c1 n3). This description of free choice is not suitable to describe God's exercise of his own free will, but that is no reason to assert that God does not have free choice because of the divine inability to choose evil things. The ability to choose such things is rather a disability from which God does not suffer: thus, the divine choice is not subject to necessity and is entirely free to do all things as it wills, and all those things are good (c1 nn4-5, c2). Similarly, the angels and saints, who cannot and do not wish to turn to evil, enjoy free choice. Indeed, the saints have a freer choice than the one which Adam enjoyed before the fall since he was able not to sin, but they are unable to sin (c3). Theirs is a freer choice "because, without compulsion or necessity, it is able to desire or elect what it has decreed by reason" (c4 n2).

Combining these considerations on free choice with the earlier reflections on the fall, Peter sets out a perspective in which free choice is greater or lesser according to the different time frames in which it is exercised. Before the fall, human freedom was greater than it is now, since reason was then free to sin and not to sin. Our own state is much depressed in comparison, since we are able to sin and not able not to sin, and our sin was mortal before our restoration in Christ and is at least venial after that restoration. Finally, in glory, human beings will be able not to sin and will not be able to sin (c5). This perspective is also restated in terms of four states of free choice. In his first state, before the fall, man was not impelled to do evil or impeded from doing good, so that evil was easier to avoid and the good easier to achieve. After the fall and before Christ's reparation, man was pressed down and overcome by concupiscence; his freedom was so profoundly weakened by evil that he was unable not to sin, even mortally. After restoration in Christ, the will remains weak and the propensity to sin strong, but the human will aided by grace can now resist concupiscence and at least avoid mortal sin. In glory, this weakness toward evil will be entirely removed, and grace will be so perfected in man that his freedom of choice will have reached its highest state, the inability to sin (c6).

As if what has been said so far had not already made it abundantly clear, Peter proceeds to tell us explicitly that the limitation and corruption of free choice was a most awful consequence of the fall. As a result of sin, "natural goods became corrupt in man and the goods of grace were taken away" (c7 n1). Freedom survives the fall, but in a greatly reduced state, now consisting only in the natural freedom from necessity, that is, from absolute compulsion to evil; insofar as the will survives, of necessity freedom does also, because a will is not such if it is not in some degree free.[10] But two other kinds of freedom, namely freedom from sin and from misery, were lost at the fall because they belong to grace, and not to nature (c9 n1).

Freedom from sin "frees us from the servitude of sin and renders us servants of justice" (c8 n3). This freedom is restored in some measure in those on whom Christ confers his grace to the point that they are not dominated and ruled by sin (c8 n4). Freedom from misery and trouble was enjoyed by man before the fall and will be enjoyed even more fully in glory, but not in this life because, even after Christ's coming, the lack of this freedom continues as punishment of sin (c8 n9). Despite the survival of free choice in the human will after the fall, it remains the case that the will cannot raise itself toward the good, or actually fulfil it, without the

[10]Rosemann, *Peter Lombard*, p. 236 n62, has noted that Colish, *Peter Lombard*, 1.383, seems to misread Peter here, when she states that "[f]reedom from any necessity at all was a feature of the human will before the fall. This mode of free will ... now applies to no one but God." Colish's misreading becomes more egregious and indefensible in her more emphatic and unnuanced later restatement of her view (at 2.733): "While the Lombard staunchly holds that man still possesses a conscience ..., he argues that fallen man is no longer free from necessity. The freedom to choose without violence or constraint has gone by the boards." This is quite clearly and flatly contradicted by what Peter says in dist. 25 c8 n2.

aid of divine grace. Indeed, without prevenient grace, man would not even be able to beg for God's co-operating grace, the necessary aid for achieving the good which he now wills (c9 n2).

Divine grace may also be distinguished into operating and co-operating grace; the first goes ahead of the will and prepares it, while the second assists the same will to do what it has willed (dist. 26 c1). The point remains that, without God's mercy, a man may neither will, nor act in any way that does him any good (c1 n3). As for the will itself, it is defined, in Augustine's terms, as "a movement of the spirit, without the compulsion of anyone, toward not committing something or toward gaining it" (c2 n1). It cannot achieve the avoidance of evil, or the gaining of the good, without the aid of divine grace, but it is also true that even such grace will be fruitless without the consent of the will. Nothing good can happen without divine initiative and aid, but human freedom and effort do not thereby lose their dignity, since they also remain necessary (c2 nn2-3).

The grace which precedes the will is the faith of Christ, which alone is the cause of justification; this faith goes first, freeing the will from the servitude of sin, so that a man may live in loving piety (c3). And yet, this faith itself proceeds from the will. A loving faith can only be such, if it comes from a free will that freely receives the gift of faith which God freely confers (c4). Once more, divine sovereignty and human dignity are presented in a creative tension in which neither undoes, and each confirms, the other.

The problem of whether good will precedes faith is resolved by saying that faith does so "not in time, but according to cause and nature" (c4 n3). Whatever precedes temporally, whether good will or good thought, can only make for righteousness if accompanied by faith and charity, which cannot be present apart from grace (c4 n5). Consideration of the good may precede faith, but not that faith by which one may live righteously. The latter comes about as follows: our reason shows us the good and the usefulness of God's judgements, but our affection is slow in embracing them; we begin to wish that we might love these judgments and, with the assistance of grace, begin to delight in their operation (cc5-6). For a pious life, then, one must first seek understanding of the good and conclude that it is from God, and not from oneself; then delight in works must follow, once the will has been made good by faith and charity (c6).

For all man's radical inability to achieve righteousness apart from grace, one ought not to hold that nothing good can be done apart from co-operating grace. Free choice alone is sufficient for the achievement of such good things as the cultivation of fields and the building of houses (c7 n2). But within the hierarchy of goods, those which can be achieved by free will alone are the least important since it is possible to live righteously without them. The highest goods are those by which one lives righteously and which cannot be used evilly; the middle kind are those without which one cannot live righteously, but which may be used well or evilly. The virtues are highest goods; they cannot be used evilly and other goods are used well when they are subject to them. The powers of the soul, which may be used well or evilly, are middle goods (c10). Since free choice may be used well or evilly, it falls in this middle group (c11 n1). But its good use is a work of virtue, and that is the sense in which it is sometimes called a virtue, even if somewhat improperly (c11 n2).

To distinguish virtue from its work, Peter restates Augustine's definition of virtue as "a good quality of the mind by which we live righteously and of which no one makes an evil use; God alone works virtue in man" (dist. 27 c1 n1). On scriptural authority, it seems evident that the virtues of justice and faith are from God; the same is to be understood of all other virtues (c1). Human merit comes from grace and free will. From these, a good disposition, such as belief, follows, and this constitutes the first merit; in like manner, from charity and free choice, one begins to love. The same is true of all virtues from which merit flows (c4). But the acts of the virtues could not be meritorious, or deserve justification, in the absence of that charity which is the Holy Spirit (c5). Once again, Peter's conclusion points to the beauty and the fruitfulness of the co-operation of human freedom with the divine initiative.

As a fence against too high a view of the role of human freedom in the work of redemption, Peter next turns to a discussion of the Pelagian heresy, which had made divine grace dependent on human merit (dist. 28 c1 n1). The Pelagians are described as holding that human beings can fulfil the divine mandate without divine grace, which, they say, only serves to make such fulfilment easier. The heresy is also said to deny all value to the prayers which the Church offers for the conversion of the infidel and the perseverance in faith of the faithful; the heretics deny, too, that children are born with original sin (c1 n2). The quick assertion of these views is followed by a dossier of Augustinian passages which the Pelagians had been able to claim in support of their own opinions (c2); Peter then adduces other texts of Augustine in which he shows that his earlier assertions had been misunderstood by the Pelagians (c3). The effect is to deepen and extend the earlier discussion of grace and freedom while providing the students with a further example of the method by which apparent contradictions may be resolved, as well as of the humility which a student of these matters (even an Augustine!) ought to practice in addressing these challenging questions, about which one ought to be ever ready to become further instructed and to correct oneself accordingly.[11]

Concluding the extended discussion on grace and free choice and related issues, Peter returns to the subject which had been occasion of the discussion itself, namely the state and condition of the human person before the fall. Given the terminology which his readers have acquired from the preceding discussion, they can now be asked to ponder whether operating and co-operating grace were needed by man before the fall (dist. 29 c1 n1). The answer is that both kinds of grace were necessary even then, although operating grace was not needed then for every reason which makes it necessary now. It was not needed for liberation from sin, for example, since man was not yet subject to sin, but it was required for the efficacious willing of the good. Furthermore, even before the fall there would have been no merit without grace, since free choice alone, without divine aid, would have been insufficient for the having and retaining of justice (c1 n2).

On the question of whether man had virtues before the fall, it had seemed evident to some that the fall itself proved the lack of such virtues; Peter takes the view that the fall proves that, by his sin, man had lost the virtues which he used to have (c2), not to mention paradise itself, and the prospect of immortality (cc3-4). Indeed, Cherubim with a flaming sword were placed before paradise so that man might not return there; this signifies that a return to paradise is only possible through the fullness of knowledge, which is charity (and which the Cherubim signify), and the bearing of the sufferings of this life (c5).

After the Fall

A humble profession of the inadequacy of his account of the first sin precedes Peter's discussion of the transmission of sin and death to Adam's posterity (dist. 30 c1). The Pelagians had described Adam's sin as actual, rather than original, and had asserted that it descends to Adam's progeny by imitation (cc2-4). It seems fair enough to say that all men imitate Adam when they sin willingly, but this does not account for the fact that all are born with sin. It follows that Adam's sin was transmitted by both imitation

[11]For example, at dist. 28 c3 n4, Augustine is quoted as saying: "Undoubtedly, I would not have said those things, if I had already known that faith itself is also included among the gifts of the Holy Spirit."

and propagation and origin (c4 n2). Original sin is transmitted to all who are "begotten with concupiscence through [Adam's] vitiated flesh" (c5).

Peter acknowledges frankly that there is little clarity or agreement among the ancient and modern doctors on the nature of this sin (c6 n1). Some say that it is a liability to punishment, but not a fault or a punishment *per se* (c6 n2). For Peter, Scripture and the Fathers make it undeniable that original sin is both a punishment and a fault of all who are born through concupiscence (c7). Because it is not actual sin, original sin is not an act; it is the incentive to sin, namely concupiscence or the law of the flesh (c8). This concupiscence, with which human beings battle their whole life long, is present even in children (c9). Since all human beings were materially present in Adam, they all acquired the corruption of this sin and can even be said to have all sinned in him (c10). From Adam's actual disobedience, carnal concupiscence arose in Adam and proceeds to all his offspring, so that they are all born sinners (cc11-12).

The objection has been raised that all human beings past and present could not have been contained physically in Adam, since their number exceeds even the number of atoms in Adam's body (c14 n1). But this objection is not cogent because all humans were present in Adam materially and causally, but not formally. They descend from him by the law of propagation, not by some sort of subdivision, and so they can rightly be said to have been present in him by seminal reason (c14 nn2-3).

In addressing the question of whether original sin is transmitted via the soul or the flesh, Peter firmly rejects the view that the soul is transmitted to offspring through their parents; it follows that original sin must be transmitted through the flesh (dist. 31 cc1-3). That the flesh has become corrupt is shown by the fact that even married couples cannot engage in sex without lustful concupiscence; the flesh procreated in such lust and concupiscence is itself subject to the vice of concupiscence. This is the original sin which the flesh transmits to the soul that comes into contact with it (cc4-6).

As for the difficulty posed by the fact that children born to baptized parents are afflicted by the original sin from which their parents had been cleansed, Peter responds to it with Augustine's analogies to circumcision and winnowed wheat. Circumcised fathers beget uncircumcised children; wheat from which the chaff has been removed does not produce wheat without chaff. In the same way, baptized parents beget children who are themselves in need of baptism (c6 n3).

And yet we should not hold that we derive original sin simply from Adam's flesh, for then Christ himself, who was also formed from flesh that descended from Adam, would have been subject to original sin. Instead, it should be clear that original sin is so called from the vicious law of our origin, which is the lust of the flesh. Since Christ's conception occurred by the work of the Holy Spirit, and not by lust, he was not subject to original sin (c7 n1).

But if original sin is concupiscence, and the sin is removed by baptism, how is it that concupiscence survives baptism? (dist. 32 c1 n1). It is true that concupiscence survives baptism, but in a diminished state, so that it can now be resisted; furthermore, after baptism, concupiscence is no longer imputed as a sin, but only as a punishment of sin (c1 nn2-6). As for whether this concupiscence comes from God, Peter holds that, insofar as it is a punishment for sin, God is its author; insofar as it is a fault, it is to be attributed to the devil or to man (c3).

The last large question which Peter raises as to original sin asks why God joins a soul without stain to a corrupt body, thereby exposing it to corruption and the risk of damnation. The best answer to the question is that this is a case of God's hidden justice at work. But it is perhaps also the case that Adam's sin and its consequences are not sufficient reasons for God to change the manner of human creation or the propagation of humankind (c6). This discussion closes with brief reflections on the effect on the soul of being created in a corrupt body and on the variety and different degrees of natural gifts conferred on souls at their creation and the irrelevance of such differences to their final reward or punishment (cc7-8).

If Adam's progeny inherits his sin, is it also the case that the sins of all parents are transmitted to their children? This question in part arises from certain scriptural statements and in part from the Church's practice of baptizing even children 'for the remission of sins' (dist. 32 c1). The use of the plural can be explained in part by the fact that several sins were involved in Adam's actual sin (c2 nn2-3). It is also possible to entertain the opinion that God, in his mercy, regards children as bound only by the sins of their own parents, but not of all their ancestors since Adam; Augustine had been willing to expound such a view, but only by way of opinion (c2 nn4-5). And yet the same Augustine says elsewhere that unbaptized children will be subject only to the mildest punishment because they have added no other sin to the original one; it follows that the sins of their parents are not imputed to them (c2 nn4-5). Furthermore, the plural is often used in the Bible for the singular (c2 n6).

Holding the question in suspension, Peter moves next to whether Adam's sin is graver than all other sins. It seems to be so because it changed all human nature and did the gravest harm, making man subject to bodily and spiritual death (c3 nn1-3). And yet Peter is not certain that Adam's sin is graver than the irremissible sin against the Holy Spirit which anyone may commit (c3 n4). At most, Adam's sin can only be called the gravest in view of the faults that emanated from it, but not as to its punishment since, even in our first parents, it was forgiven by their subsequent penance (c3 n5, c4).

This apparent digression seems to have been intended to blunt the glumness which one might have been tempted to bring to the resolution of the earlier question. The mention both of the irremissibility of one's own actual sin against the Holy Spirit and of the remissibility of original sin even in Adam has the effect of lifting the sense that one is burdened under the unbearable mass of inherited sin. Once more, the effect is to focus attention on one's own freedom and responsibility. And so it turns out that all those texts which speak of children being burdened by their fathers' sins can be read as referring to children who have freely chosen to imitate those same sins (c5). If readers are not satisfied with this interpretation, they can always engage in a metaphorical reading of some of the relevant texts (c5 n5).

After disposing of these preliminary issues, Peter next turns to an extended treatment of actual sin, its origin and first cause, in what it consists, what it is, and how it is contracted (dist. 34 c1). Since all that existed before sin was good, it must follow that sin originated in a good thing, namely, the angelic or the human nature, which God had created good, but in which arose an evil will from which all evil deeds are done (c2). Peter could not be clearer in tying the origin of sin to the free deliberation and intention of angels and men. This intentionalist view of sin will colour his whole discussion of the matter.

All subsequent evils flow from that original evil will of angel and man (c3). But since evil is nothing other than the privation of the good, it can only occur by corrupting a good nature, "and so sin cannot exist in other than a good thing" (c4 n2). It follows that even an evil man can be called an evil good, since one would hardly speak of sin occurring in such a man, if there were not still some good in him that was subject to corruption (c4 n3). And so, in this case, the rule of the dialecticians which denies the coexistence of opposites is shown to fail (c5).

As for definitions of actual mortal sin, Peter cites at least three from Augustine and Ambrose: every word, or deed, or desire against the law of God; the will to retain or obtain what justice forbids; transgression of the divine law and disobedience of heavenly commands (dist. 35 c1). These definitions present sin as consisting in some action; while Peter does not doubt this, he emphasizes that "sin exists primarily in the will, from which, like evil fruits from an evil tree, proceed evil deeds" (c2 n3). The parable of the good Samaritan is invoked to exemplify the effect of sin on the soul. The man drawn into the power of the devil by sins is like the man left half-dead by robbers, as he is deprived of both virtues and natural goods (c4 n2). Furthermore, through sin, man diminishes his own likeness to God and deprives himself even of the goods of the body (c5).

As for the variety of sins, a basic distinction is drawn between those which are also punishment of sin and those which are both cause and punishment of sin (dist. 36 c1). All sins which are not quickly removed through penance fall into one of these categories and entangle the sinner more and more (c1 n2). A sin is said to be a cause of sin with respect to a subsequent sin and a punishment by reference to a preceding one. When penance does not intervene to remove a sin, then that sin leads to another, which is not only a sin, but also a punishment for the unrepented one. By a just judgement, God darkens the heart of the unrepentant sinner so that, because of the earlier sin, the sinner falls into the next one. And yet the cause even of this sin is not from God (c2 n3).

Despite the fact that this discussion is firmly anchored in biblical texts and school debates, it is difficult not to discern in it Peter's profound curiosity about the psychology of sin. The use of terms of art and the discussion of technical issues does not obscure the plausibility of the moral and psychological picture being painted and the dynamism which Peter sees as underlying human decision-making.

In what sense God may or may not be said to be the author of sin had been the subject of much clever debate in the schools. Peter summarizes the various positions in what is essentially a logician's game (dist. 37 cc1-2). It is clear that, insofar as man is made worse by sins, God is not the author of sin; insofar as sin is just punishment, God may well be called its author (cc1-2).

Since sin resides primarily in the will, it is of some relevance to consider the will itself. Free will is weighed and judged by the end which it freely sets before itself. A good will is one which turns toward blessedness, eternal life, and God himself; an evil will is one which turns toward an evil pleasure (dist. 38 c1 n1). Charity is the briefest and best description of a righteous end for the will, and it ought to inform the fulfilment of every mandate, since every mandate is referred to it (c1 n2). Anyone who has charity as his end can properly be said to have as his end God or Christ or the Holy Spirit, from whom is all perfection (c2). In this quite beautiful manner, Peter reminds us, as he has not done in a while, of the Trinity as the horizon of everything.

To say that charity is the end of a good will is not to deny that such a will may also have other ends, but all of these are to be referred to the one end, if the will is to remain good (c3). I wish to prepare food to feed the poor, but for the end of pleasing God and having eternal life, which is the end of all ends. Put another way, it is my end to feed the poor and it is my intention to have eternal life. Put in yet another way, it may be said that it is my will to feed the poor, and it is also my will to have eternal life; there is no contradiction here, so long as the first is referred to the second. Delight remains the end concern; insofar as blessedness or life with God is the ultimate delight, all lesser ones ought to be referred to it. Nor is it useless for a reader of texts, and especially of the Bible, to be reminded that intention may sometimes be taken for the will itself and sometimes for its end (c4).

Mention of the possibility of an evil will may have puzzled the reader. Since the will is a natural gift, like memory and intellect, how can it ever be evil? The answer is that evil will does not refer to the natural power by which we will, but to its act when it is disordered (dist. 39 c1). In this, the will is not unlike memory and intellect; if I remember or ponder evils in order to do them, then I engage in the evil use of these good powers (c2).

If the will is judged by its end, is the same true of actions? Generally, this is indeed the case, except for some actions which are so evil in themselves that for no reason can they be called good. Theft, rape, blasphemy, adultery cannot be made good by a good intention. And yet, even in the case of such obviously evil deeds, the role of intention is not to be entirely dismissed, since their gravity may differ depending on the intention with which they are done (dist. 40 c1).

If actions are judged by intention, and the intention is directed by faith, ought one to conclude that all actions of those who lack faith are evil? (dist. 40 c1 n1). If there cannot be charity without faith, that would indeed seem to be the case (c1 n3). But the term 'good' may be taken in several ways. When it is taken to mean 'worthy of reward for life,' then a thing cannot be good which is done without faith and charity, even if it is useful and worthy for other reasons (c1 nn7-8, c2). As for the assertion that all sin is voluntary, and that sin is nowhere other than in the will, this is true of mortal and actual sin (cc3-6).

If an evil will is followed by an evil action, is there one sin or several? The will is the first cause of sin; a will and its deed constitute one sin because they spring from the same contempt. But the contempt is less when it is limited to the will and greater when it results in action (dist. 42 c1 nn1-2).

If someone committed a sin, but now has ceased to do so and no longer intends to commit it, can the sin be said to be still in him? A sin can be said to be in a person by action or by liability. In the case mentioned, the sin is no longer in the person by action, but it remains in him by liability (c2). In Scripture, this liability is described as a fault, punishment, or the obligation of punishment, eternal punishment in the case of mortal sin, temporal punishment in the case of venial sin (c3 n1). The first is so called because it makes one deserving of eternal death; the second is easily forgiven (c3 n2).

Different authorities have held that sin arises either from cupidity or from fear. Others distinguish sins by whether they are committed in thought, word, or deed. Yet others yet distinguish sins as being either against God, or against neighbour. All these taxonomies have their usefulness (c4). Among all sins, seven have been termed capital. As listed by Pope Gregory I, these are vainglory, anger, envy, sloth or sadness, avarice, gluttony, lust. All other sins emanate from these (c6). And yet, these too arise from pride which, according to Gregory, is the root of all evil (c7 nn1-2). But Paul seems to attribute this pivotal role to cupidity (c7 n3). The contradiction between these two views is apparent, not real, and only arises if one forgets to examine them by reference to types of sins, rather than to individual ones. All types of sins arise at times from pride and at other times from cupidity. At times, pride itself arises from cupidity, and cupidity from pride (c8).

A particularly noteworthy sin is that against the Holy Spirit, of which Christ says in the Gospel that it is not remitted (dist. 43 c1 n1). This sin is said to consist either in obstinacy in wickedness leading to impenitence, or in a despair by which one believes one's own wickedness to be greater than divine goodness (c1 n2). This sin is said not to be remitted not because it would not be, if the sinner acknowledged it in repentance, but because it keeps the sinner from penance and the hope of mercy (c2 nn3-6). And yet one ought not to cease praying for the obstinately impenitent while they are in this life (c2 n8).

To conclude his discussion of sin, Peter asks whether the very power to sin comes from the devil or from God (dist. 44 c1 n1). He rejects contrary views in order to assert unambiguously that God is the source of all powers, and so also of the will (c1 nn2-3). As has been the case throughout Book 2, Peter makes this assertion by adhering to a close and faithful reading of Scripture. It is hard to think what better, humbler, and more useful lesson he could have taught his students and readers.[12]

A loose understanding of power may lead one to conclude, from the previous discussion, that, since all power comes from God, one ought not to resist any power, even when it is wielded by the devil or a tyrant. Consistently with all we have seen him say regarding divine sovereignty and the dignity of human freedom, Peter ends this Book with the injunction to obey no power which commands evil things (c2).

* * *

In letting go of this second book of the *Sentences,* it pleases me to renew the expression of my gratitude to Fr. Ignatius Brady, O.F.M., editor of the work, and to Fr. Romain Georges Mailleux, O.F.M., Director of the Frati Editori di Quaracchi, for the "placet" to translate the *Sentences* from Fr. Brady's edition. Professor Joseph W. Goering, of St. Michael's College and the University of Toronto has continued his unfailing support of the enterprise and his testing of the translation in the most various and surprising of teaching venues.

My debt of obligation toward the staff of the Department of Publications of the Pontifical Institute of Mediaeval Studies becomes more and more inexpressible as they continue to shower the project with their patient interest and unboundedly generous efforts. Jean Hoff has not yet surrendered before my dilatoriness and appears to continue to delight in improving the work. Fred Unwalla is to be thanked once more for applying his great gifts to the form of the book.

In dedicating this second book of the *Sentences* to Stefano, the second of my children, I am anxious to make clear that he has shown no more interest in the work than any of his siblings; the dedication, and the occasion to reflect with Dante and Brunetto, are entirely affectionate gift.

Giulio Silano
St. Michael's College, Toronto
Ash Wednesday 2008

[12]See the useful comments in this same sense of Rosemann, *Peter Lombard*, p. 117.

Chapter Headings

HERE BEGIN THE CHAPTERS OF THE SECOND BOOK

[DISTINCTION XVII]

Ch. 1 (96) On the creation of the soul, whether it was made from anything; on the [manner of] God's breathing and blowing forth [of the soul].
2 (97) When the soul was made, whether in the body or out of it.
3 (98) At what age of life was man made.
4 (99) Why man, created outside paradise, was placed in paradise.
5 (100) In what ways is paradise taken.
6 (101) On the tree of life.
7 (102) On the tree of the knowledge of good and evil.

[DISTINCTION XVIII]

Ch. 1 (103) On the formation of woman.
2 (104) Why she was formed from man's side and not from some other part of his body.
3 (105) Why the rib was taken from man while asleep and not while awake.
4 (106) That she was made from that rib multiplied in itself, without the addition of anything extrinsic.
5 (107) On the higher and lower causes.
6 (108) On the causes which are simultaneously in God and in creatures, and of those which are only in God.
7 (109) On the soul of the woman, which is not from the man's soul, because souls do not derive from one another.

[DISTINCTION XIX]

Ch. 1 (110) On the state of man before sin, what he was like in respect to the body, and what he was like after sin.
2 (111) How man is said to have been made into a living soul.
3 (112) The body of man before sin was mortal and immortal; after sin, it was dead.
4 (113) Whether the immortality which he then had was from the condition of nature, or from a benefit of grace.
5 (114) If God had not commanded that he eat of that tree, and he had made use of other trees and not of the tree of life, whether man would have been able to live forever.
6 (115) On the first and second immortality of the body.

[DISTINCTION XX]

Ch. 1 (116) On the manner of procreating children, if the first humans had not sinned.
2 (117) Why they did not have sexual intercourse in paradise.
3 (118) On the manner of transferral to a better state, if they had not sinned.

The *Sentences*, Book 2

On Creation

HERE BEGINS THE SECOND BOOK

On the Creation and Formation of Corporeal and Spiritual Things, and Several Other Matters Pertaining to Them.

Insofar as we have been able, we have diligently treated those things which are known to pertain to understanding, if *only in part*,[1] the mystery of the divine unity and trinity. Now let us proceed to the consideration of creatures.

DISTINCTION I

Chapter 1

1. HE SHOWS THAT THERE IS ONLY ONE PRINCIPLE [OR BEGINNING] OF THINGS, AND NOT MANY, AS SOME HAVE HELD.—BEDE. Scripture, indicating the creation of things, shows at its opening that God is the creator and origin of time and of all creatures, visible and invisible, saying: *In the beginning, God created heaven and earth.*[2] By these words, Moses, inspired by the spirit of God, reports that the world was made by God the Creator in a single beginning, destroying the error of some, who hold that there have been many beginnings without beginning.

2. STRABUS: PLATO ASSERTED THREE PRINCIPLES [OR BEGINNINGS]. For Plato held that there were three first principles [or beginnings], namely God, the archetype, and matter; and that these were uncreated, without beginning, and that God was, as it were, an artificer, not a creator.

Chapter 2

BY WHAT REASON A CREATOR IS PROPERLY CALLED SUCH, AND WHAT IT IS TO CREATE AND WHAT TO MAKE. For a creator is one who makes some things from nothing, and, properly speaking, to create is to make some-

[1]Cf. 1 Cor. 13, 9.

[2]Gen. 1, 1. Cf. ordinary gloss, on Gen. 1, 1, quoting Bede, *Libri quatuor in principium Genesis* 1, 1.

thing from nothing; but to make is to produce something not only from nothing, but also from matter. And so, a man or an angel is said to make some things, but not to create them; and he is called a maker or an artificer, but not a creator. For this name is properly suitable only for God,[1] who makes some things from nothing and others from something. And so, he is creator and artisan and maker. But he has retained the name of creation properly for himself, while sharing the others also with creatures. And yet, in Scripture creator is frequently taken in the sense of maker, and to create in the sense of to make, without distinction of meaning.[2]

Chapter 3

1. THAT THESE VERBS, NAMELY TO MAKE AND TO DO AND SUCHLIKE, ARE NOT SAID OF GOD FOR THE SAME REASON AS THEY ARE SAID OF CREATURES. And yet it is to be known that these verbs, namely to make, to create, to do, and suchlike, cannot be said of God for the same reason as they are said of creatures. For when we say that he makes something, we do not understand that there is in him any motion in working, or any suffering in labouring, as usually happens to us. Instead, we signify some new effect of his sempiternal will, that is, that by his eternal will something newly exists.

2. IN WHAT SENSE GOD IS SAID TO MAKE SOMETHING. For when he is said to make something, it is as if one said that something is newly happening or existing according to his will, or by his will. Not that something new is happening in him, but that something new is made as it had been in his eternal will, without any motion or change on his part. We, however, are said to be changed by our labour because we are moved: for we do not do anything without movement.—And so God is said to make or do something, because he is the cause of things which are newly existent, when new things which did not exist before begin to be by his will, without motion on his part; and so it cannot properly be called an action, since any action consists of motion, but in God there is no motion at all.

3. HE SHOWS IT BY ANALOGY. Therefore, just as it happens that some things are made by the heat of the sun, but without any motion or change in the sun or in its heat, so new things have their being from the will of God without change in their author, who is the one and only principle of all things.

4. ARISTOTLE [ASSERTED] THREE PRINCIPLES.—STRABUS. But Aristotle asserted two principles, namely matter and form, and a third which he called 'operatory' [or efficient]; also, that the world always is and was.

[1]Cf. Augustine, *De Trinitate*, bk 3 c9 nn16-18.
[2]See, e.g., Gen. 1, 26 and 27; Gen. 2, 7; Eccli. 17, 1.

5. He teaches what is Catholic.—Bede. The Holy Spirit, to purge the errors of these men and others like them and teach the discipline of truth, "signifies that God created the world at the beginning of the ages, and that he existed eternally before all ages. He commends the eternity and omnipotence of the one for whom to have willed is to make,"[3] because, as we have said,[4] new things exist by his will and goodness.—Augustine, in the *Enchiridion*. And so let us believe "that the cause of created things, both celestial and earthly, visible and invisible, is nothing but the goodness of the Creator, who is the one and true God."[5] So great is his goodness that he, as the most highly good, wanted others to be sharers in his blessedness, by which he is eternally blessed: he saw that this could be shared and suffer no diminution at all. And so by goodness alone, and not by necessity, he willed to share that good, which he himself was and by which he was blessed, with another because it pertained to the most highly good to want to do good, and to the most omnipotent not to be able to be harmed.

Chapter 4

1. Why the rational creature was made. But no one can be a sharer in his blessedness, which is had so much more fully the more it is understood, except through intelligence. And so God made the rational creature, which might understand the highest good, and love it by understanding it, and possess it by loving it, and enjoy it by possessing it.

2. How the rational creature is distinguished. And he distinguished it in the following way, so that part would remain in its purity and not be united to a body, namely the angels; part would be joined to the body, namely souls. For the rational creature was distinguished into the incorporeal and the corporeal; and the incorporeal is called angel, but the corporeal is called man, who consists of a rational soul and flesh. And so the condition of the rational creature had God's goodness as its first cause.

3. Why man or angel is created. And so if it is asked why man or angel is created, it can be briefly answered: because of God's goodness. Hence Augustine, in the book *On Christian Doctrine*: "Because God is good, we are; and insofar as we are, we are good."[1]

4. For what is the rational creature created. And if it is asked for what is the rational creature created, answer: to praise God, to serve him, to enjoy him. By these things, the creature profits, not God. For God,

[3]Bede, *Libri quatuor in principium Genesis* 1, 1.
[4]Above, Bk 1 dist. 45 c4.
[5]Augustine, *Enchiridion*, c9.

[1]Augustine, *De doctrina christiana*, bk 1 c32 n35.

who is perfect and filled with the highest goodness, can be neither increased nor diminished. And so God's making of the rational creature is to be referred to the Creator's goodness and to the creature's utility.

5. VERY BRIEF ANSWER TO THE QUESTION OF WHY OR FOR WHAT THE RATIONAL CREATURE HAS BEEN MADE. And so, when it is asked why or for what the rational creature has been made, it may be answered most briefly: because of God's goodness and for its own utility. For it is useful for it to serve God and enjoy him. And so the angel or man is said to have been made for God: not because the creator, God and most highly blessed, needed the service of another, since he does not need our goods;[2] but so that the creature might serve and enjoy him, to serve whom is to reign.[3] For in this it is the servant who benefits, and not the one who is served.

6. AS MAN WAS MADE TO SERVE GOD, SO THE WORLD WAS MADE TO SERVE MAN. And just as man was made for God, that is, to serve him, so the world was made for man, namely to serve him. And so man was placed in the middle, so that he might serve and be served; that he might take from both and all might redound to the good of man: both the obedience which he receives and that which he extends. For God willed to be served by man in such a way that it would not be God, but the servant man, who would benefit by that service; and he willed that the world serve man, and by that too man might benefit.

7. HOW ALL THINGS ARE OURS. And so all was a good for man, both what was made for him, and that for which he was made.—AUGUSTINE. For, as the Apostle says, *all things are ours*,[4] namely the higher, the equal, and the lower ones. The things superior to us are ours to be enjoyed, as God the Trinity; the equal ones are for the sharing of life with them, namely the angels, who, although they are now superior to us, in future will be our equals. Even now, they are ours because they are ours to use, just as the possessions of lords are said to be their servants', not by right of ownership, but because they are theirs to use. And the angels themselves, in some passages of Scripture,[5] are said to serve us when they are sent to minister for our sake.

Chapter 5

HOW IT IS SOMETIMES SAID IN SCRIPTURE THAT MAN WAS MADE IN REPARATION FOR THE FALL OF THE ANGELS. Concerning man, it is also sometimes found in Scripture[1] that he was made in reparation for the fall of the

[2]Cf. Ps. 15, 2.
[3]Gregory, *Liber sacramentorum*, collect of mass for peace.
[4]1 Cor. 3, 22.
[5]See Hebr. 1, 14; Ps. 90, 11-12.

[1]Col. 1, 12; Deut. 32, 8.

angels. This is not to be understood as if man would not have been made if the angel had not sinned; but that among the other principal causes, there is even in some small way this one.—And so superior and equal things are ours; but lower things are also ours because they were made to serve us.

Chapter 6

1. WHY THE SOUL WAS UNITED TO THE BODY. It is also usual to ask, since the soul would appear to be of greater dignity if it had remained without a body, why it has been united to the body.

2. FIRST CAUSE. To this it may first be answered: because God willed it, and the cause of his will is not to be sought.[1]

3. SECOND [CAUSE]. Secondly, it may be said that God willed it to be united to the body so that he might show forth in the human condition a new example of the blessed union that is between God and spirit, in which he is loved with *the whole heart*[2] and is seen *face to face*.[3] For the creature might think that it could not become united with its Creator with such closeness as to love and know him with its whole mind, if it did not see the spirit, which is a most excellent creature, united in such love to such a base creature as is the flesh that it cannot be pressed to wish to leave it behind. The Apostle shows this by saying: *We do not wish to be stripped of the body, but to be clothed anew*:[4] by this it is shown that the created spirit is united in ineffable love to the uncreated Spirit.

4. As an example of the future fellowship which was to be achieved between God and the rational spirit in its glorification, God joined the soul to corporeal forms and earthly resting places, and he caused muddy matter to come to life so that man would know that, if God was able to join together such disparate natures as that of body and soul into one union and in such great friendship, then it would not at all be impossible for him to raise up the lowliness of the rational creature, although far inferior, to participation in his glory.—And so, as an example, the rational spirit was in part humbled even to being joined to an earthly body; [but] lest it seem exceedingly lowered by this, God's providence added that afterwards it would be raised with that very same, glorified, body to the fellowship of those who had remained in their purity. In this way, whatever it had received by the dispensation of its Creator as less in its creation, it would afterwards receive in its glorification by the grace of the same. And so the creating God assigned rational spirits to different lots, according to the discretion of his will. He established a heavenly resting

[1]Cf. above, Bk 1 dist. 45 c4 n2.
[2]Mt. 22, 37.
[3]1 Cor. 13, 12.
[4]2 Cor. 5, 4.

place for those whom he left above in their purity, and an earthly habitation for those whom he joined to earthly bodies below. He set before each the rule of obedience, so that the former should not fall from the place where they were, and the latter should be able to ascend from the place where they were to the one where they were not. And so God made man from a double substance, shaping the body from the earth, but making the soul from nothing.

5. THIRD [CAUSE]. Souls were also united to bodies so that, by serving God in them, they might deserve a greater crown.

6. AFTER THE MYSTERY OF THE TRINITY, WE MUST TREAT THE THREE-FOLD CREATURE, AND FIRST THE WORTHIER ONE, THAT IS, THE ANGELIC. From the foregoing, it appears that the rational creature is distinguished into the angelic and the human, of whom the first, that is, the angelic one, is wholly spiritual; the second, that is, the human one, is in part spiritual and in part corporeal.—And since we must treat these, namely the spiritual and corporeal creature, and the rational and the non-rational one, it seems that we must first treat the rational and spiritual one, that is, the angels, so that our reason may move from gazing upon the Creator to a knowledge of the worthier creature. Afterwards, it will descend to a consideration of the corporeal creature, both the one which is rational and the one which is not, so that the teaching regarding the three-fold creature and whatever shapes and touches it may follow the mystery of the uncreated Trinity.

DISTINCTION II

Chapter 1 (7)

1. WHAT THINGS ARE TO BE CONSIDERED CONCERNING THE ANGELS. Concerning the angelic nature, these things are to be considered first: when it was created, and where, and the qualities it had when it was first made; then how it was affected by the defection of some and the conversion of others; also some things are to be said about their excellence and orders and the difference of their gifts, and their functions and names and several other matters.

2. FIRST HE SAYS WHEN THE ANGELS WERE MADE, ON WHICH THE AUTHORITIES SEEM TO CONTRADICT EACH OTHER. Some authorities appear to indicate that angels were created before any other creature. Hence the statement: *Wisdom was created first of all things*,[1] which is understood to refer to the angelic nature, which in Scripture is often called life, wisdom,

[1]Eccli. 1, 4.

and light.[2] For that wisdom which is God is not created: the Son is the wisdom begotten of the Father, neither made nor created; and the entire Trinity is one wisdom, which is neither made nor created, neither begotten nor proceeding.[3] And so that text is to be taken to apply to the life of angels, of which Scripture says when it was made, namely *first of all things*.[4]—But again, another text of Scripture says: *In the beginning, God created heaven and earth*;[5] and in the Prophet: *At the beginning, you, Lord, established the earth, and the heavens are the work of your hands*.[6] —Some contradiction seems to arise from these assertions. For if *wisdom was created first of all things*, all things appear to have been made after it; and so heaven and earth appear to have been made after it, and it seems to have been made before heaven and earth. Again, if *in the beginning, God created heaven and earth*, nothing was made before heaven and earth, and even wisdom itself was not made before heaven and earth. Therefore, since these passages appear to be contradictory, and since it is not proper to think that there is any contradiction in divine Scripture, let us seek an understanding of the truth.

3. HE TEACHES WHAT IS TO BE HELD AND DETERMINES THE AUTHORITIES CITED ABOVE. And so it seems that it must be held that the spiritual creature (that is, the angelic one) and the corporeal one were created together: in this sense we may take that text of Solomon: *The one who lives in eternity created all things together*,[7] that is, spiritual and corporeal nature. And so the angels were not created earlier in time than the corporeal matter of the four elements. And yet *wisdom was created first of all things* because, if not in time, it still has precedence in dignity.

4. HE CONFIRMS BY AUTHORITY THAT CORPOREAL AND SPIRITUAL CREATURES WERE CREATED TOGETHER. Augustine, *On Genesis*, manifestly shows that corporeal and spiritual creatures were created together, saying that by *heaven and earth* are to be understood the spiritual and corporeal creatures; and these were created *in the beginning*, namely of time; or *in the beginning*, because they were made first.[8]

[2]According to, e.g., Augustine, *Confessiones*, bk 12 c15 n20.
[3]Cf. above, Bk 1 dist. 32 cc2-6.
[4]Cf. ordinary gloss, on Gen. 1, 3, from Augustine, *De Genesi ad litteram*, bk 1 c17 n32.
[5]Gen. 1, 1.
[6]Ps. 101, 26.
[7]Eccl. 18, 1
[8]Augustine, *De Genesi ad litteram*, bk 1 c1 nn2-3, and c3 n7.

Chapter 2 (8)

THAT NOTHING WAS MADE BEFORE HEAVEN AND EARTH, NOT EVEN TIME: FOR THESE WERE CREATED WITH TIME, BUT NOT FROM TIME. For before them, nothing was made. Not even time was made before the spiritual nature, namely the angelic one, and before the corporeal one, namely that matter composed of the four elements. For they were created with time, not from time, or in time; just as time itself was not created in time, because time did not exist before heaven and earth.—Hence Augustine, *On the Trinity*, says that God was lord before time existed, and he did not begin to be lord in time, because he was lord of time when time began to be; and certainly time did not begin to be in time, because time did not exist before time began.[1]

Chapter 3 (9)

1. THAT CORPOREAL AND SPIRITUAL CREATURES BEGAN TOGETHER WITH TIME AND THE WORLD. And so corporeal and spiritual creatures were made together with time and together with the world; the angelic creature did not exist before the world because, as Augustine says, "no creature is before the ages, but from the ages,"[1] with which it began.

2. JEROME SEEMS TO CONTRADICT THIS, AS IF ANGELS WERE BEFORE TIME. And yet Jerome, in *On the Epistle to Titus*, seems to feel otherwise, saying: "Not even six thousand years of our time have passed; but how many eternities, how many ages, how many origins of ages shall we adjudge to have passed during which Angels, Thrones, Dominations, and the other orders served God without changes and measures of times, and perdured by God's command?"[2] Some who have agreed with these words have said that worldly time began with the world, but that there was an eternal and changeless time before the world. They say that it was in that other time that the angels, without change and time, existed and served God at his command.

3. But to the best of our power of comprehension, we approve more what was said earlier, yet preserving our reverence for the mysteries, about which nothing is to be said presumptuously; and we adjudge that, in that text, Jerome was not reporting his own view, but the opinion of others.

[1]Augustine, *De Trinitate*, bk 5 c16 n17; see Bk 1 dist. 30 c1 nn1-2.

[1]Augustine, *De Genesi ad litteram*, bk 5 c19 n38.
[2]Jerome, *In Titum* 1, 2.

Chapter 4 (10)

1. WHERE THE ANGELS WERE AFTER THEY WERE CREATED: NAMELY IN THE EMPYREAN WHICH, AS SOON AS IT WAS MADE, WAS FILLED WITH ANGELS. It has already been shown when the angelic nature was created; now we must turn our attention to where it was made.

2. By the testimonies of some authorities, it is clearly shown that, before their fall, angels were in heaven, and that some fell from there to ruin because of pride, but those who did not sin remained there. Hence the Lord says in the Gospel: *I watched as Satan fell from heaven like a lightning-bolt.*[1] *Heaven* here does not stand for the firmament, which was made on the second day,[2] but for that splendid heaven which is called empyrean, that is, fiery, from its splendour, not its heat, which was filled with angels as soon as it was made, and which is above the firmament.

3. Some expositors of sacred Scripture wish to understand the empyrean by the name 'heaven' where Scripture says: *In the beginning, God created heaven and earth.*[3]—STRABUS. Strabus says: "It does not here call heaven the visible firmament, but rather the empyrean, that is, the fiery or intellectual one, which is so called not from its heat, but from its splendour, and which was filled with angels as soon as it was made. Hence: *When the morning stars praised me,*"[4] etc.[5]—BEDE. Concerning this, Bede too speaks as follows: "This higher heaven, which is separate from the instability of the world, was filled with holy angels as soon as it was created: the Lord attests that these were established in the beginning, with heaven and earth, saying: *Where were you when the morning stars praised me, and all the children of God rejoiced?*[6] He calls those same angels morning stars and children of God. For the heaven in which those bodies that give us light were placed"[7] was not made in the beginning, but on the second day.—From these comments, it is clear that all the angels were in the empyrean before the fall of some of them, and that the angels were created simultaneously with the empyrean heaven and with the formless matter of all corporeal creatures.

[1]Lk. 10, 18.
[2]Cf. Gen. 1, 8.
[3]Gen. 1, 1.
[4]Job 38, 7.
[5]Ordinary gloss, on Gen. 1, 1.
[6]Job 38, 7.
[7]Ordinary gloss, on Gen. 1, 2; summarized from Bede, *Libri quatuor in principium Genesis* 1, 2.

Chapter 5 (11)

THAT THE MATTER OF VISIBLE THINGS AND THE NATURE OF INVISIBLE THINGS WERE CREATED TOGETHER, AND EACH OF THEM WAS FORMLESS IN REGARD TO SOMETHING, AND FORMED IN REGARD TO SOMETHING ELSE. And so the matter of visible things and the nature of invisible things were established together, and each of them was formless in regard to something, and formed in regard to something else. For the confused and indiscriminately mixed matter of corporeal things, which is called chaos in Greek, in that beginning of its original condition had the form of confusion, and did not have the form of differentiation and separation into parts until after it was formed and assumed different species. Similarly, the spiritual and angelic nature was formed in its condition according to a state of nature, and did not yet have that form which it would afterwards take through love and conversion toward its Creator, and was formless without it.—Hence Augustine, expounding the aforesaid words of Genesis in many different ways, says that by *heaven* is understood "the formless nature of the spiritual life, as it can exist in itself, before turning to the Creator in whom it is formed; and by *earth* corporeal matter without any quality that appears in formed matter."[1]

Chapter 6 (12)

IN WHAT SENSE LUCIFER, ACCORDING TO ISAIAS, SAYS: I WILL ASCEND INTO HEAVEN, ETC., SINCE HE WAS IN HEAVEN. It is usual to ask here, if the angels were in the empyrean heaven as soon as they were made, how Lucifer, as we read in Isaias, says: *I will ascend into heaven, I will exalt my throne, and I will be like the Most High.*[1]—HE RESOLVES IT. But there Lucifer calls *heaven* God's highness, to which he wanted to be equal; and so, in this instance, *I will ascend into heaven*, that is, to equality with God.

DISTINCTION III

Chapter 1 (13)

1. WHAT QUALITIES THE ANGELS [HAD WHEN THEY] WERE MADE: FOUR THINGS WERE ALLOTTED TO THEM AT THE VERY BEGINNING OF THEIR ESTABLISHMENT. See, it has been shown where the angels were as soon as they were created; now it follows that we investigate what qualities they [had when they] were made at the very beginning of their establishment.

[1]Augustine, *De Genesi ad litteram*, bk 1 c1 n2.

[1]Is. 14, 13-14.

2. And four things seem certainly to have been their attributes at the beginning of their existence, namely a simple essence, that is, an indivisible and immaterial one; a distinct personal identity; and, through a naturally innate reason, intelligence, memory, and will or love; also free choice, that is, the free faculty of turning the will either to good or to evil, for through free choice, without violence and compulsion, they were able to turn toward either by their own will.

Chapter 2 (14)

1. WHETHER ALL THE ANGELS WERE EQUAL IN THREE THINGS, NAMELY IN ESSENCE, WISDOM, AND FREEDOM OF CHOICE. Here it is to be considered whether all [the angels] were equal in spiritual substance, and rational wisdom, and freedom of will, which were present in all of them, so the first consideration will be of substance, the second of form, the third of power. For person is a substance, wisdom is a form, and freedom of choice is a power; and to substance surely pertains fineness of nature, but to form perspicacity of the intelligence, and to power the aptitude of the rational will.

2. HERE HE SAYS THAT THEY DIFFERED IN THESE THINGS. And so those rational essences who were persons and spirits, simple by nature and immortal in their life, are rightly understood to have had a different fineness of essence, and a different perspicacity of wisdom, and a different aptitude for choice.

3. HE SHOWS THAT IT IS SO BY ANALOGY TO BODIES. In bodies, there is some difference according to essence and form and weight: for some have a better and worthier essence and form than others, and some are lighter and more agile than others. Therefore, it is to be believed that, in the same way, those spiritual natures at the beginning of their establishment received differences suitable to their purity and excellence in their essence, form, and power. As a result of these differences, some were made superior and some inferior to others by the wisdom of God, who confers greater gifts on some and lesser ones on others, so that those who at that time excelled the rest through their natural goods should afterwards also be preeminent over them through the gifts of grace. For those who were created finer in their nature and more far-seeing in their wisdom, also were endowed with greater gifts of grace and were established as more excellent than the others in dignity. But those who were established as less fine in nature and less far-seeing in wisdom, received lesser gifts of grace and were established as less excellent by the wisdom of God, who orders all things with equitable rule.

4. IN RESPECT TO WHAT IS THE DIFFERENCE IN THE POWER OF CHOICE TO BE CONSIDERED. The difference in the power of choice itself is to be per-

ceived according to the different power of nature, and the different force of knowledge and intelligence.

5. THAT A LESSER REFINEMENT OF ESSENCE, A LESSER COMPREHENSION OF WISDOM, AND A LESSER FREEDOM DO NOT, RESPECTIVELY, INDUCE WEAKNESS, IGNORANCE, OR NECESSITY. And just as a different vigour and refinement of nature does not lead to weakness, and a lesser comprehension of wisdom does not engender ignorance, so a lesser freedom does not impose as necessary any exercise of the will upon the faculty of choice.

Chapter 3 (15)

WHAT THINGS THE ANGELS HAD AS COMMON AND EQUAL. And just as the angels differed in the foregoing, so they also had some things as common and equal. That they were spirits, and that they were indestructible and immortal, this was equal and common to all. But in refinement of essence, and understanding of wisdom, and freedom of will, they were different. As for these intelligible differences of these invisible natures, he alone was able to understand and weigh them who made all things *in weight, number, and measure*.[1]

Chapter 4 (16)

1. WHETHER THE ANGELS WERE CREATED GOOD OR EVIL, JUST OR UNJUST, AND WHETHER THERE WAS ANY DELAY BETWEEN THEIR CREATION AND FALL. That too seems worthy of investigation, which is usual for many to ask: whether the angels were created good or evil, just or unjust, and whether there was any delay between their creation and fall, or whether they fell without delay at the very beginning of creation.

2. THE OPINION OF SOME WHO SAY THAT THE ANGELS WERE CREATED IN [A STATE OF] WICKEDNESS AND THAT THEY FELL TO RUIN WITHOUT ANY DELAY. For some have held that the angels who fell were created evil; and that they did not turn to wickedness by their free will, but that they were made by God in their [state of] wickedness, and that there was no delay between their creation and fall, but that they committed apostasy from the beginning; others, however, were created fully blessed.

3. They strengthen their opinion by the authority of Augustine, in *On Genesis*, speaking as follows: "It is not pointless to hold that the devil fell from the beginning of time, and that he did not live at any time with the holy angels as peaceful and blessed, but committed apostasy immediately. Hence the Lord says: *He was a murderer from the beginning, and did not*

[1] Wis. 11, 20.

stand in the truth,[1] so we may understand that he did not stand in the truth from the moment of his creation, who could have stood in it, if he had wished to do so."[2]—The same [Augustine] in the same place says: "Not without cause may it be held that the devil fell from the very beginning of time or of his existence, and never stood in the truth. From this, some think that the devil was not disposed to wickedness by his free choice, but that he was created in [a state of] wickedness, albeit by God, according to that text of blessed Job, who says: *He is the beginning of God's work, which God made so that he might be mocked by his angels*.[3] And the Prophet says: *This dragon, which you have shaped in order to mock it*,[4] as if he was immediately made evil, envious, and a devil, and not depraved by his own will."[5]

4. Those who say that the angels who fell were created evil and went to their ruin without delay use these and other testimonies.—As for those who remained steadfast, they maintain that they were created perfect and blessed, and they support this with the authority of Augustine, in *On Genesis*, who says that by *heaven* is signified "the spiritual creature, which is always perfect and blessed from the moment that it is made."[6]

5. THE PLAUSIBLE OPINION OF OTHERS, WHO SAY THAT ALL ANGELS WERE CREATED GOOD AND THAT THERE WAS SOME LITTLE DELAY BETWEEN CREATION AND FALL. But it seems to others that all angels were created good and that they were good, in the sense of without vice, at the first moment of creation; and they were just, in the sense of innocent, but not just in the sense of having practice in the virtues. For they were not yet endowed with the virtues which were added in confirmation through grace to those who remained steadfast. But the others became proud through their free choice, and so they fell.—They also say that there was some small delay between their creation and fall or confirmation. And in that brief space of time, they were all good, not indeed through the use of free choice, but by the benefit of creation. And they were such as to be able to stand, that is, not to fall, through the goods of creation, and to fall through their free choice. For they were able to sin and not to sin, but they were not able to make progress toward merit of life, except through the superaddition of grace, which was added to some in confirmation.

6. BY AUTHORITY, THEY AFFIRM THIS TO BE THE CASE.—AUGUSTINE. And to confirm this, they make use of the testimony of Augustine who, in *On Genesis*, says that the angelic nature was first created unformed and

[1]Jn. 8, 44.
[2]Augustine, *De Genesi ad litteram*, bk 11 c16 n21.
[3]Job 40, 14, according to Augustine's more ancient version.
[4]Ps. 103, 26.
[5]Augustine, *De Genesi ad litteram*, bk 11 cc19-20 nn26-27.
[6]Ibid., bk 1 c1 n3.

was called *heaven*; afterwards, when it had turned to the Creator and adhered to him in perfect love, it was formed and was called *light*. Hence it is first said: *In the beginning, God created heaven and earth*;[7] and afterwards, it was added: *God said: Let there be light, and the light was made*,[8] because what is first at issue is the creation of the unformed spiritual creature, and afterwards its formation.[9]

7. THEY REACH THE SAME CONCLUSION BY REASON. Reason is also an obstacle to those who say that the angels were created evil. For the Creator, who is most highly good, could not be the author of evil. And so all that came to them from him was good, and it was all good because it was all from him. In this manner, it is proved that all angels were good when they were first made, but by that goodness which their nature had received at its beginning.

8. HE ADDUCES A PROOF OF AUGUSTINE AGAINST THOSE WHO SAY THAT THE ANGELS WERE EVIL WHEN THEY WERE MADE; HE DETERMINES THE WORDS OF JOB, WHICH THEY HAD ADDUCED ON THEIR SIDE. Therefore, Augustine, rejecting the opinion of those who hold that the angels were created evil, proves by authority and reason that they were created good; he also reveals how we are to understand the words of blessed Job cited above, which they adduced on their side. In *On Genesis*, he speaks as follows: "God made all things *very good*";[10] and so he made the nature of the angels good. And "because it is unjust that, without any demerit, God damn in anyone that which he has himself created, we must believe that it was not nature which required punishment, but an evil will. It is not the devil's nature which is signified in the words: *He is the beginning of God's works*, etc.,[11] but some aerial body which God fashioned in a manner suitable to such a will; or God's very plan, by which he created him to be useful, although unwillingly so, to the good; or the fashioning of that angel himself because, although God foreknew that he would become evil by his own will, yet he made him, foreseeing how many great things he would draw from him by his own goodness. And so he is called God's work because, although God knew that he would become evil in his will to harm the good, yet he created him in order to aid the good through him. God, however, did this *so that he might be mocked*. For the devil is mocked when his temptation of the saints is turned to their advantage. In the same way, evil men (whom God foresaw would become evil, and yet he created them for the utility of the saints) are mocked when progress is granted to the saints by their temptation. But he is *the beginning* because

[7]Gen. 1, 1.
[8]Gen. 1, 3.
[9]Augustine, *De Genesi ad litteram*, bk 1 c3 n7.
[10]Gen. 1, 31.
[11]Job, 40, 14, according to Augustine's more ancient version.

he goes first in ancientness and as the prince of malice. However, this mockery of evil angels and men is done by the holy angels, because God makes subject to them those evil angels and men by permitting to the latter not as much power as they would like, but as much as they are allowed."[12] —See, he has shown plainly how the aforesaid words of Job are to be understood, and he has asserted that the angelic nature was created good.

9. HE DISCUSSES HOW THE AFOREMENTIONED WORDS OF THE LORD ARE TO BE UNDERSTOOD, CLEARLY TEACHING THAT THE ANGELS WERE CREATED GOOD AND THAT THEY FELL AFTER THEIR CREATION. Augustine next reveals how the words of the Lord, which he set out above,[13] are to be taken. He also determines how his own earlier words are to be taken, plainly teaching that the angels were created good and that they fell after some small delay from their creation. He speaks as follows: "The opinion that the devil never stood in the truth and never led a life of blessedness, but that he fell from the beginning, must not be understood in the sense that he be held to have been created evil by God, who is good. Otherwise, he would not be said to have fallen from the beginning: for if he had been made such, that is, evil, then he did not fall. For from what would he have fallen? And so, as soon as he was made, he turned away from the truth because of his delight in his own power, and he did not taste the sweetness of the life of blessedness, which he did not disdain after receiving it, but which he lost because he did not wish to receive it. Thus he was not able to foresee his own fall because wisdom is the fruit of piety.[14] But as soon as he was made, he fell, not from that which he had received, but from what he could have received, if he had been willing to be subject to God."[15] See, he declares plainly that the angels were created good and fell after their creation.

10. And there was small little delay there, if a very brief one. Origen confirms this; in *On Ezechiel*, he says: "The enemy serpent is opposed to truth, but he was not so from the beginning; neither did he, from the first, walk upon his breast and belly.[16] Just as Adam and Eve did not immediately sin, so also the serpent was for a while not a serpent, when he remained in the paradise of delights. For God did not make wickedness."[17] See, he plainly says that the devil fell after creation and the passage of some small delay.

[12]Augustine, *De Genesi ad litteram*, bk 11 cc21-22 nn28-29.
[13]Above, at the beginning of n3, namely Jn. 8, 44.
[14]Cf. Eccli. 43, 37.
[15]Augustine, *De Genesi ad litteram*, bk 11 c23 n30.
[16]Cf. Gen. 3, 14.
[17]Origen, *In Ezechielem*, hom. 1 n3.

11. And so it appears that those words[18] are to be taken in the following manner: *He was a murderer,* or *a liar*, *from the beginning*, that is, from immediately after the beginning, when he promised equality with God to himself[19] and killed his own self, which is called *man* in the Gospel.[20] And he did not *stand in the truth* because he was never in it, but he committed apostasy *from the beginning* of time, that is, immediately after the beginning of time.—That text can also be taken in the following way: *He was a murderer,* or *a liar*, *from the beginning*, that is, from the moment of the making of man, whom through envy he cast into death and seduced by deceit.[21]—And so, from the foregoing, it is clear that all angels were created good, and that, after their creation, some fell away from the good which they would have had, if they had remained steadfast.

Chapter 5 (17)

THAT THERE WAS A THREE-FOLD WISDOM IN THE ANGELS BEFORE THEIR FALL OR CONFIRMATION. Here it is usual to ask what wisdom they had before their fall or confirmation.—There was in them a three-fold natural knowledge, by which they knew that they had been made, and by whom they were made, and with whom they had been made. And they had some knowledge of good and evil, understanding what it was proper for them to desire and what to reject.

Chapter 6 (18)

WHETHER THEY HAD ANY LOVE OF GOD OR OF EACH OTHER. It is also usual to ask whether they had any love of God or of each other.—To this it can be said that they had natural love, as also memory, intellect, and ingenuity; by this, they loved God and themselves somewhat, and yet they did not gain merit by it.

DISTINCTION IV

Chapter 1 (19)

1. WHETHER GOD CREATED THE ANGELS PERFECT AND BLESSED, OR MISERABLE AND IMPERFECT. After these matters, it is to be seen whether God created the angels perfect and blessed, or miserable and imperfect.—To

[18]Jn. 8, 44.
[19]Cf. Is. 14, 13-14.
[20]Cf. Mt. 13, 28.
[21]Cf. Gen. 3, 1-6; Wis. 2, 24. For this and the above, cf. Augustine, *De Genesi ad litteram*, bk 11 c16 n21; *In Ioannem*, tr. 42 n11; *De civitate Dei*, bk 11 c13.

this it can be said that they were created neither in [a state of] blessedness, nor in misery. For they could not be miserable before sin, because misery is from sin;[1] indeed, if there had been no sin, there would be no misery. But those who fell were never blessed because they were unaware of what would happen to them, that is, of their future sin and punishment. For if they foreknew their fall, either they wished to avoid it but could not, and so they were miserable; or they could have but did not wish to, and so they were foolish and malign.[2]

2. THAT THE EVIL ANGELS DID NOT FOREKNOW THEIR FALL, BUT PERHAPS THE GOOD ONES FOREKNEW THEIR FUTURE GOOD. And so we say that they did not foreknow what would happen to them, and that knowledge was not granted to them of the things that would befall them in the future. But perhaps the good ones who remained steadfast had foreknowledge of their blessedness.—Hence Augustine, in *On Genesis*, says: "How could the devil, who did not foreknow his future sin and punishment, have been blessed among the angels? It is asked why he did not foreknow them. Perhaps God did not wish to reveal to the devil what the latter would do and suffer; but God was willing to reveal to the others that they would remain in the truth."[3]—By these words, Augustine appears to signify that the angels who fell to ruin did not foreknow their fall, and so they were not blessed. But the angels who remained steadfast foreknew their future blessedness and remained certain of it in hope: and so they were in some fashion already blessed. And indeed, if it was so, it could be said that they were in some fashion blessed; but not the others, who did not know what would happen to them.

3. THAT HE SAID THIS BY WAY OF OPINION, NOT OF ASSERTION, NAMELY THAT THE ANGELS WHO REMAINED STEADFAST FOREKNEW THEIR GOOD. But Augustine says these things more by way of opining and searching, than asserting. So it is that, in opposition to this opinion, he next adds: "But why were they separated from the others, so that God would not reveal to them what pertained to them, while revealing it to the others, since God does not punish before someone has sinned? For God does not condemn the innocent."[4] Here he seems to indicate that God did not reveal their future evil to those who would sin, nor their future good to those who would remain.—And so those who fell were never blessed, and those who remained steadfast were not blessed until the consummation [of their choice]; because they could not be blessed if they were not certain of their blessedness, or if they were uncertain of their damnation. Hence Augustine says in the same place: "But it is exceedingly presumptuous to say of

[1]Cf. Prov. 14, 34.
[2]Cf. Augustine, *De Genesi ad litteram*, bk 11 c18 n23.
[3]Ibid., bk 11 c17 n22.
[4]Ibid.

the angels that they can be blessed in their own kind, while they are uncertain regarding their damnation or salvation, and have no hope of their being changed for the better."[5] "For how can they be blessed, whose blessedness is uncertain?"[6]

4. HE MAKES A SUMMARY OF THE FOREGOING, CONFIRMING THAT ALL THE ANGELS WERE NOT BLESSED BEFORE THEIR CONFIRMATION OR FALL, UNLESS BY BLESSEDNESS BE UNDERSTOOD THAT STATE OF INNOCENCE IN WHICH THEY WERE BEFORE THE FALL. From the above, it follows that the angels who fell to ruin were never blessed, unless one take for blessedness that state of innocence in which they were before their sin. As for those who remained steadfast, however, either they foreknew their future blessedness by God's revelation, and so they were in some fashion blessed in the certainty of hope; or they were uncertain of their blessedness, and so they were no more blessed than those who fell. This latter view is the one that seems more probable to me.

5. RESPONSE TO THAT EARLIER QUESTION AS TO WHETHER THE ANGELS WERE CREATED PERFECT OR IMPERFECT; AND HE ANSWERS THAT THEY WERE PERFECT IN SOME RESPECT AND IMPERFECT RESPECT TO SOMETHING ELSE. In regard to that earlier question as to whether they were created perfect or imperfect, it can be said that they were perfect in some way and imperfect in another. For something is not said to be perfect in one way only, but in several.

6. THAT PERFECT IS SAID IN THREE WAYS: ACCORDING TO TIME, ACCORDING TO NATURE, AND UNIVERSALLY PERFECT. Indeed, 'perfect' is said in three ways: for something is perfect according to time, or perfect according to nature, or universally perfect. That is perfect according to time which has whatever the time requires and is suitable to be had according to time; and in this way, the angels were perfect before their confirmation or fall. That is perfect according to nature which has whatever is due or useful to its nature for glorification; and in this way, the angels were perfect after their confirmation, and the saints will be perfect after the resurrection. That is completely and universally perfect to which nothing is ever lacking and from which all good things come, which pertains only to God. And so the first perfection pertains to an established nature, the second pertains to a glorified nature, the third to an uncreated nature.

7. HE TOUCHES BRIEFLY ON THE AFORESAID, ADDING WHAT THE ANGELS WERE LIKE IN THEIR CONVERSION OR TURNING AWAY. It has been shown what the angels were at their creation, namely [they were] good, and not evil, and just, that is, innocent, and in some way perfect, but in another way imperfect. But they were not blessed until their confirmation, unless

[5] Augustine, *De Genesi ad litteram.*, bk 11 c19 n25.
[6] Ibid.

blessedness be taken, as has already been said,[7] as that state of innocence and goodness in which they were established.

DISTINCTION V

Chapter 1 (20)

ON THE CONVERSION AND CONFIRMATION OF THOSE WHO REMAINED STEADFAST, AND ON THE TURNING AWAY AND FALL OF THOSE WHO FELL. After these matters, reflection requires that we enquire what they were like after being separated by their defection and conversion. Indeed, immediately after their creation, some turned toward their Creator, some turned away. To turn toward God meant to adhere to him in love; to turn away meant to hold God in hate or to envy him; and indeed, the mother of envy is pride,[1] by which they wanted to make themselves equal to God.[2] In those who converted, God's wisdom, by which they were given light, began to shine as in a mirror; but those who turned away were made blind. And the former converted and were enlightened by God's grace which was bestowed upon them; but the latter were blinded not by an infusion of malice, but by the desertion of grace; they were not deserted by grace in the sense that it was taken away after having been previously given to them, but in the sense that it was never given to them so that they might convert. And so this is the conversion or defection by which they who were good by nature were separated: so that some are good over and above that [initial] good through justice, others are evil when that good was corrupted through fault. Conversion made some just, and defection made some unjust. Each act proceeded from the will, and the will of each was free.

Chapter 2 (21)

HE TOUCHES BRIEFLY ON FREE CHOICE, TEACHING WHAT IT IS. For all had free choice, which is a free power and aptitude of the rational will. For they were able to choose willingly what they pleased, and to make rational judgements, that is, to be discerning, and free choice consists in these things. And they were not created already willing to turn toward [God] or to turn away, but they were able to will the one or the other; and after their creation, by their spontaneous will, some chose evil and others good. And so *God* separated *light from darkness*, as Scripture says, that is, the good

[7]Above, n5.

[1]Cf. Augustine, *De Genesi ad litteram*, bk 11 c14.
[2]See above, dist. 2 c6.

angels from the evil ones; and *he called the light day*, but *the darkness night*, because he enlightened the good angels by his grace, but he blinded the evil ones.

Chapter 3 (22)

AFTER THEIR CREATION, SOMETHING, NAMELY COOPERATING GRACE, WAS GIVEN WITHOUT ANY MERIT OF THEIR OWN TO THOSE WHO REMAINED STEADFAST BY WHICH THEY MIGHT CONVERT. But if it is asked whether, after their creation, something was conferred on those who converted by which they might convert, that is, love God, we say that cooperating grace was conferred on them. Without such grace, the rational creature cannot make progress toward meriting life. For it can fall by itself, but it cannot make progress without the assistance of grace.

Chapter 4 (23)

WHAT GRACE THE ANGEL NEEDED AND WHAT HE DID NOT. The angel did not need the grace by which he might be justified, because he was not evil, but the one by which he might be helped to love and obey God perfectly.—WHICH GRACE IS 'OPERATING' AND WHICH 'COOPERATING.' That grace is called operating by which an impious person is justified, that is, from being impious he is made pious, from evil good; but cooperating grace is that by which he is assisted to will the good with efficacy, to love God before all things, to do good works, to persevere in the good, and suchlike; we will treat this more fully below.[1] And so cooperating grace was given to the angels who remained steadfast, by which they converted so that they might love God perfectly. Thus they converted from a good which they had and had not lost to a greater good which they did not have; and this conversion was done through grace cooperating with their free choice; this grace was not given to the others who fell.

Chapter 5 (24)

1. WHETHER THEY ARE TO BE BLAMED FOR HAVING TURNED AWAY. And so it is customary for some to object that those who defected rather than converted are not to be blamed because they could not convert without grace. Grace was not given to them, however; and it was not their fault that grace was not given, because there was not yet any fault in them.

[1]Dist. 26 and 27.

2. To this it can be said that this grace was not given to those who received it by reason of their merits: otherwise, it would not be grace, if it were given because of a merit which preceded grace.[1]

3. BY WHAT FAULT GRACE WAS NOT GIVEN TO THOSE WHO FELL. But that it was not given to the others was their own fault because, although they were able to do so, they did not will to stand firm until grace should be given to them; so the others remained steadfast until grace was given to them, while the former fell through pride. And so the fault of those who fell may be clearly taken to be this: that although they could not make progress without grace, which they had not received, yet they were able not to fall, that is, to stand firm, by that which had been granted to them at their creation, because there was nothing which compelled them to fall. They fell by their own spontaneous will. If they had not done this, what was given to the others would surely also have been given to them.

Chapter 6 (25)

1. THAT THE ANGELS BECAME BLESSED AT THEIR CONFIRMATION, BUT WHETHER THEY DESERVED IT THROUGH THE GRACE THEN GIVEN TO THEM IS AMBIGUOUS, FOR DIFFERENT PEOPLE HAVE FELT DIFFERENTLY CONCERNING THIS. Here it is usual to ask whether the angels became blessed at their confirmation, and whether in some way they deserved their blessedness.—Many authorities assert that they became blessed at their confirmation, and so it is to be held as certain.

2. But whether they deserved that blessedness through the grace then given to them is ambiguous. For some prefer the view that they deserved it through the grace which they received at their confirmation; they say that merit and reward were in them simultaneously, and that merit did not precede reward in time, but in cause.—But it seems to others that they did not merit the blessedness which they received at their confirmation through the grace that was then given to them. These say that grace was not conferred on them then so that they might gain merit, but so that they might live blessedly; the good which was then given to them was not that by which they might gain merit, but one which they might happily enjoy. They say that the angels merit what they received at that time as a reward for the services which they render to us in obedience and reverence to God; and so the reward preceded the merits. And I confess that this latter view is more pleasing to me.

[1]Cf. Rom. 11, 6. See also Bk 1 dist. 41 c2 n2.

DISTINCTION VI

Chapter 1 (26)

1. THAT SOME FELL FROM AMONG BOTH THE GREATER AND THE LESSER ONES, AND ONE OF THEM WAS AMONG THE HIGHEST, NAMELY LUCIFER. Moreover, it is fitting to know that, just as some remained constant from among both the greater and the lesser [angels], so some fell to their ruin from both. Among the latter, one was higher than all the others who fell, and there was none worthier than him among those who stood firm, as is shown by the testimonies of the authorities.

2. For Job says: *He is the beginning of God's ways.*[1] And we read in Ezechiel: *You were the seal of [God's] likeness, full of wisdom and beautiful in perfection in the delights of God's paradise.*[2] Expounding this, Gregory says: "The more refined his nature is, the more it is indicated that the image and likeness of God is impressed in him."[3]—Also, we read in Ezechiel: *Every precious stone was his covering,*[4] that is, every angel was, as it were, his covering because, as Gregory says, "by comparison with the others, he was the most illustrious."[5] That is why he was called Lucifer [i.e. morning star], as Isaias attests, saying: *How you have fallen, Lucifer, who used to rise in the morning*, etc.[6]

3. Lucifer is not to be taken as an order [of angels], but as one spirit. Isidore shows that this spirit, after being created, carefully assessed the eminence of his nature and the depth of his knowledge, and rose up in pride against his Creator to the point that he wanted to make himself God's equal, as is said in Isaias: *I will ascend into heaven, I will exalt my throne above the stars of heaven, and I will be like the Most High.*[7] In fact, he wanted to be like God not through imitation, but through equality of power.

Chapter 2 (27)

1. FROM WHAT AND TO WHAT HE WAS CAST DOWN BY REASON OF HIS PRIDE. And because of such great pride, he was cast down *from heaven*, that is, from the empyrean, where he had been with the others, into this cloudy atmosphere, together with all those who shared in his depravity. Indeed,

[1]Job 40, 19.
[2]Ezec. 28, 12-13.
[3]Gregory, *In Evangelia*, hom. 34 n7; *Moralia*, bk 32 c23 n47.
[4]Ezec. 28, 13.
[5]Gregory, *Moralia*, bk 32 c23 n48.
[6]Is. 14, 12.
[7]Is. 14, 13-14.

as John says in the Apocalypse, *a dragon*, falling from heaven, *dragged down with him a third part of the stars.*[1] For that Lucifer, who was greater than the rest, did not fall alone, but many others fell with him who agreed with him in wickedness. This cloudy atmosphere became the abode of all those who fell.

2. And this was done to test us, that it should be for us a source of training. Hence the Apostle: *Our struggle is against the princes and powers of this world, and against the rulers of darkness and the spiritual powers of evil in our heavens.*[2] For the demons, who are spiritual powers and evil, reside in the turbulent atmosphere next to us, which is called *heaven*; hence the devil is also called *prince of the air.*[3]

Chapter 3 (28)

THAT IT IS NOT GRANTED TO THEM TO LIVE IN HEAVEN OR ON EARTH. For it is not granted to them to live in heaven, because it is a bright and pleasant place, nor on earth with us, lest they be exceedingly troublesome to men. According to the teaching of the apostle Peter handed down in the canonical Epistle, they must dwell in this cloudy atmosphere, which has been assigned to them almost as a prison until the time of judgement.[1] Then they shall be cast into the depths of hell, according to the text: *Go, you accursed ones, into the eternal fire which has been prepared for the devil and his angels.*[2]

Chapter 4 (29)

THAT SOME OF THE DEMONS RULE OVER OTHERS OF THEM AND ALSO HAVE OTHER FORMS OF PRECEDENCE. And just as among the good angels some rule over others, so also among the evil ones some have been given precedence over others and some are subject to others. Indeed, for as long as the world lasts, angels rule over angels, men over men, and demons over demons; but in the future, every form of preferment will be done away with, as the Apostle teaches.[1]—Also, in accordance with their greater or lesser knowledge, some have a rule of greater scope, others of lesser. For some rule over one province,[2] others over one man, yet others over one

[1]Apoc. 12, 3-4.
[2]Eph. 6, 12.
[3]Cf. Eph. 2, 2.

[1]2 Pt. 2, 4.
[2]Mt. 25, 41.

[1]Cf. 1 Cor. 15, 24.
[2]Cf. Dan. 10, 13.

vice.[3] And so we say the spirit of pride, the spirit of lust, and suchlike, because he can tempt man most of all with regard to that vice for which he is named. That is why riches are called by the name of a demon, namely mammon.[4] For Mammon is the name of a demon, and riches are also called by this name in the Syriac language. And this is not so because the devil has the power to give to or take riches away from whomever he wills, but because he uses them to tempt and deceive men.

Chapter 5 (30)

WHETHER ALL DEMONS ARE IN THIS CLOUDY ATMOSPHERE, OR WHETHER SOME OF THEM ARE IN HELL. But it is usual to ask whether they are all in this cloudy atmosphere, or whether some of them are already in hell.—It is probable that some of the demons descend into hell each day as they lead souls to their sufferings there. And it is not far from the truth that there are always some of them there, perhaps taking turns, to hold prisoner and torment souls there. And that the souls of evil people descend to hell and are punished there follows from the fact that Christ descended into hell in order to lead out of it the just ones who were held there: for if the just descended there, much more did the unjust; and as authority has it,[1] when he led out the just, he left the unjust there. For he bit hell, but did not swallow it.

Chapter 6 (31)

1. SOME HOLD THAT LUCIFER, WHOM THEY SAY TEMPTED AND OVERCAME THE FIRST MAN, WAS BOUND IN HELL FROM THE TIME WHEN HE TEMPTED CHRIST AND WAS OVERCOME. But as to Lucifer, some hold the view that he is bound there and is not now free to tempt us, because we read in the Apocalypse: *When a thousand years will be completed, Satan will be freed from his prison and will go out to lead the nations astray.*[1] That will be in the final time of Antichrist, when there shall be such great tribulation that, if it were possible, even the elect would be troubled.[2] They say that he has been bound there since that time when he tempted Christ in the desert,[3] or at the passion, and was overcome by him. They believe that he tempted and overcame the first man;[4] secondly, [he tempted] God, but was over-

[3]Cf. Origen, *In Iosue* 11, 20, hom. 15 n5.
[4]Cf. Mt. 6, 24; Lk. 16, 9.

[1]Interlinear gloss, on Os. 13, 14.

[1]Apoc. 20, 7.
[2]Cf. Mt. 24, 21-24; Mk. 13, 19-22.
[3]Mt. 4, 1-11.
[4]Cf. Gen. 3, 1-6.

come by him and so is bound in hell.—OTHERS HOLD THAT HE HAS BEEN BURIED THERE SINCE HIS FALL. But others hold that, since the fall, he has been buried in hell because of the magnitude of his sin.

2. THAT LUCIFER DOES NOT HAVE THE POWER WHICH HE WILL HAVE IN THE TIME OF ANTICHRIST. But whether he is buried in hell or not, it is plausible that he does not have the power of gaining access to us which he will have in the time of Antichrist, when he will work with fraud and violence. And perhaps that is why it is said that he will be freed at that time, because then God will give him a power to tempt men which he does not have now.[5]

Chapter 7 (32)

THAT THOSE DEMONS WHO HAVE ONCE BEEN OVERCOME BY THE SAINTS DO NOT AFTERWARDS HAVE FURTHER ACCESS TO OTHER MEN. It seems too that the power to tempt other men is taken away from those demons who are overcome by the saints who live justly and decently. Hence Origen says: "It seems certain to me that the saints who fight against these tempters and defeat them diminish the army of demons, as they destroy many of them, and that it is no longer lawful for that spirit which has been overcome by some saint who lives chastely and decently to attack some other man again."[1]—But some believe that this is to be understood only of that vice in which he was overcome: so that if he tempts some holy man with pride, and he is overcome, it is no longer lawful for him to tempt that man or another with pride.

DISTINCTION VII

Chapter 1 (33)

THAT THE GOOD ANGELS HAVE BEEN SO CONFIRMED THROUGH GRACE THAT THEY CANNOT SIN, AND THE EVIL ONES ARE SO OBDURATE IN EVIL THAT THEY CANNOT LIVE WELL. It was said above[1] that the angels who remained steadfast were confirmed through grace, and those who fell were abandoned by God's grace. And certainly the good ones have been so confirmed through grace that they cannot sin; but the evil ones are so obstinate in wickedness that they cannot have a good will and are unable to will well, although what they sometimes will is good. For they sometimes

[5]Cf. Apoc. 20, 3 and 7.

[1]Origen, *In Iosue* 11, 17-18, hom. 15 n6.

[1]Dist. 5 c1.

will something to be done which God wills to be done; and it is entirely good and just that such a thing be done, and yet they do not will it by a good will, nor will it well.

Chapter 2 (34)

1. THAT BOTH HAVE FREE CHOICE, AND YET THEY CANNOT TURN TO BOTH. But since the good ones are not able to sin, and the evil ones are not able to will well or to work well, it seems that they no longer have free choice, because they cannot turn to both [good and evil], and free choice can bend itself to either of these.—Hence Jerome says, in the treatise *On the Prodigal Son*: "It is in God alone that sin cannot happen; as for the rest, since they have free choice, they can direct their will to either side."[1] Here he appears to say that every creature which has been established in free choice can turn to good and to evil. If it is so, then both good and evil angels can turn to either of these; and so the good ones can become evil and the evil ones good.

2. To this we say that the good angels have been confirmed by such grace that they cannot become evil, and the evil ones are so obdurate in their wickedness that they cannot become good. And yet both have free choice because the good angels choose the good and reject evil without any compelling necessity, but by their own spontaneous will assisted by grace. Similarly, the evil ones, by their own free will abandoned by grace, avoid the good and pursue evil. And the evil ones have free choice, but it is so base and corrupted that they are not able to rise to the good.

Chapter 3 (35)

1. THAT THE GOOD ANGELS AFTER THEIR CONFIRMATION HAVE A FREER CHOICE THAN BEFORE. But the good angels have a much freer choice after their confirmation than before. For as Augustine says in the *Enchiridion*, "they do not lack free choice by reason of being unable to will evil things. For the faculty of choice which cannot serve sin is much freer.[1] Nor is their will to be blamed, or is not a will, or is said not to be free, by which they so will to be blessed that not only do they not will to be miserable, but are entirely unable to will it."[2]

2. And so the good angels are not able to will evil, or to will to be miserable; and they have this not from a benefit of nature, but from one of grace. Indeed, before the confirmation of grace, angels were able to sin, and some of them did sin and became demons. Hence Augustine, in the

[1]Jerome, *Epistola 25* (*ad Damasum*), n40.

[1]Cf. Jn. 8, 34.
[2]Augustine, *Enchiridion*, c105.

book *Against Maximinus*: "The nature of celestial creatures was able to die because it was able to sin. Indeed, even angels sinned, and they became demons, whose prince is the devil. Even those who did not sin were able to sin. Any rational creature to whom the inability to sin has been granted owes it to God's grace and not to its own nature. And so the only one who was not, is not, will not be able to sin by his own nature and not by anyone's grace is God."[3] See, it is implied here that angels were able to sin before their confirmation, but are not able to do so after it. That they were able to sin was theirs from free choice, which is natural to them. That they are now unable to sin, however, is theirs not from their nature, that is, from their free choice, but from grace. It is also from this same grace that their free choice itself is no longer able to serve sin.[4]

Chapter 4 (36)

1. THAT AFTER THEIR CONFIRMATION, ANGELS ARE NOT ABLE TO SIN FROM NATURE AS BEFORE; NOT BECAUSE THEIR CHOICE WAS WEAKENED, BUT BECAUSE IT WAS CONFIRMED. And so after their confirmation, angels were not able to sin from nature as before: not that their free choice was weakened through grace, but rather that it was so confirmed that the good angel is no longer able to sin through it. And this is not at all from free choice itself, but from God's grace.

2. HE REVEALS HOW THE WORDS OF JEROME CITED ABOVE ARE TO BE UNDERSTOOD. And so what Jerome says: "As for the rest, since they have free choice, they can be direct their will to either side,"[1] ought to be taken in reference to the state in which creatures were created. For both man and angel were so created that they could turn to either [good or evil]. But afterwards the good angels are so confirmed through grace that they are unable to sin, and the evil ones are so obdurate in vice that they cannot live well.

3. ANOTHER TEXT IS TO BE UNDERSTOOD IN THE SAME WAY. In a similar way is also to be understood that statement of Isidore: "Angels are changeable by nature, immutable by grace."[2] By nature, at the beginning of their existence, they could be changed to good or evil; but afterwards, through grace, they became so devoted to the good that they cannot be changed from it: for it is grace that resists this change, not nature.

[3]Augustine, *Contra Maximinum*, bk 2 c12 n2.
[4]Cf. Jn. 8, 34.

[1]Above, c2 n1.
[2]Isidore, *Sententiae*, bk 1 c10 n2.

Chapter 5 (37)

THAT THE EVIL ANGELS DID NOT LOSE THEIR ACUITY OF PERCEPTION, AND IN WHAT WAYS THEY KNOW. And although the evil angels are so obstinate through wickedness, nevertheless they are not wholly deprived of their acuity of perception. Indeed, as Isidore teaches, "demons are powerful by a threefold acuteness of knowledge, namely by the fineness of their nature, their age-old experience, and the revelation of the higher spirits."[1]—Concerning this, Augustine too says: "Evil spirits are allowed to know certain things about temporal matters, in part by the refinement of their sense, in part because they are made shrewder by their experience over the ages, which is due to such great length of life, in part because the holy angels at God's command reveal to them what they have learned from God. At times too, these same evil spirits foretell what they themselves are about to do, as though pretending to divine it."[2]

Chapter 6 (38)

THAT THE MAGICAL ARTS ARE EFFECTIVE BY THE POWER AND KNOWLEDGE OF THE DEVIL. THIS POWER AND THIS KNOWLEDGE HAVE BEEN GRANTED TO HIM BY GOD EITHER TO LEAD EVIL MEN ASTRAY, OR TO ADMONISH OR TRAIN THE GOOD ONES. It is also by the knowledge and power of these evil spirits that the magical arts are practised. And yet, both the knowledge and the power have been given to them by God,[1] either to deceive the deceitful, or to admonish the faithful, or to train and test the patience of the just.—Hence Augustine says, in *On the Trinity*, book 3: "I see what may occur to a weak intelligence, namely why are miracles done also by the magical arts: for even the magicians of Pharaoh made serpents and other things.[2] But what is still more wonderful is how the power of the magicians, which was able to make serpents, failed entirely when it came to making very small flies, namely gnats, which were the third plague to afflict Egypt. At that point, the magicians certainly failed, saying: *The finger of God is here*.[3] From this, it is given to be understood that not even the transgressing angels and the powers of the air (who have been cast down from their dwelling in the sublime purity of the aether into this lowest darkness as if into a prison for their kind), through whom the magical arts are able to do whatever they can do, would be able to do anything, if power had not been given to them from above. And this power is at times given to deceive the deceitful, as when it was conferred on the

[1] Isidore, *Sententiae*, bk 1 c10 n17.
[2] Augustine, *De Genesi ad litteram*, bk 2 c17 n37.

[1] Cf. Eccli. 1, 1; Rom. 13, 1.
[2] Cf. Exod. 7-8.
[3] Exod. 8, 19.

Egyptians and those very magicians, so that they should seem admirable by the operation of the very spirits by whom they were made damnable; at times it is given to warn the faithful against the desire to do any such thing, as if it were a great thing to do them (it is for this same reason that they have been reported to us in Scripture); or to train, test, and reveal the patience of the just."[4]

Chapter 7 (39)

THE MATTER OF VISIBLE THINGS DOES NOT SERVE THE TRANSGRESSING ANGELS AT THEIR BIDDING. "And it is not to be thought that the matter of visible things serves the transgressing angels at their bidding; rather, it serves God, by whom this power is given to the extent that the unchangeable one determines."[1]

Chapter 8 (40)

1. THAT THEY ARE NOT CREATORS, EVEN THOUGH THE MAGICIANS MADE FROGS AND OTHER THINGS THROUGH THEM; GOD ALONE CREATES. "And those evil angels are by no means to be called creators because the magicians made frogs and serpents through them: for they did not create these things."[1]

2. ON THE SEEDS OF ALL BODIES, WHOSE CREATOR IS HE WHO ALONE IS CREATOR. "In truth, some hidden seeds of all things that are born corporeally and visibly are concealed in the corporeal elements of this world; God originally placed these seeds in them. And so he who is the creator of the invisible seeds is the creator of all things. For all things that come forth to our sight by being born receive the beginnings of their growth from these invisible seeds; and by virtue of the rules of their origin, so to speak, they take their proper increase in size and their distinctive forms."[2]

3. JUST AS PARENTS ARE NOT CALLED THE CREATORS OF THEIR CHILDREN, NOR FARMERS OF THEIR WHEAT, SO NEITHER ARE THE GOOD NOR THE EVIL ANGELS, EVEN IF CREATURES ARE MADE BY THEIR SERVICE. "And just as we do not call parents the creators of men, nor farmers the creators of wheat, although it is by the external application of their movements that God's power operates internally to create these things, so also it is not right to hold that not only the evil angels, but even the good ones, are creators. (NOTE: HERE HE INDICATES THAT THEY HAVE A BODY.) But by the refinement of their sense and body, they know the seeds of things

[4]Augustine, *De Trinitate*, bk 3 c7 n12.

[1]Augustine, *De Trinitate*, bk 3 c8 n13.

[1]Augustine, *De Trinitate*, bk 3 c8 n13.
[2]Ibid.

which are more hidden from us, and they sow them secretly through suitable combinations of the elements, and so furnish occasions for the birth of things and for speeding their increase. But the good angels do not do these things, except insofar as God commands, nor do the evil ones unjustly do them, except insofar as he justly allows."[3]

4. THE EVIL ONE HAS AN EVIL WILL FROM HIMSELF, BUT HE RECEIVES THE POWER [TO WILL] FROM GOD JUSTLY. "For the wickedness of the evil one makes his own will unjust, yet he does not receive the power [to will] other than justly, either for his own punishment or, in the case of others, for the punishment of the wicked or the praise of the good."[4]

Chapter 9 (41)

JUST AS GOD ALONE WORKS THE JUSTIFICATION OF OUR MIND, SO ALSO HE WORKS THE CREATION OF THINGS, ALTHOUGH THE CREATURE SERVES AS A MORE EXTERNAL CAUSE. "None but God can form our mind by justifying it, but men too are able to preach the Gospel as an external cause, and not only the good ones *in truth*, but also the bad ones *in pretence*.[1] In the same way, it is God who interiorly works the creation of visible things; but the exterior operations"[2] and mixtures or occasions are furnished by good and evil angels, and even by men.—"But these things are applied by men with so much more difficulty insofar as their senses are less refined and their earthy and sluggish bodies are less quick in their movements. And so for both kinds of angels, the easier it is to gather the proximate causes from the elements, the more wonderful is their greater speed in works of this kind. But there is no other creator than the one who originally forms these things; nor can anyone do this other than the one creator God."[3]—"For it is one thing to create and administer the creature from the deepest and highest turning-point of causation, which the creator God alone does; but it is another thing to conduct some operation by an external means in accordance with the forces and powers that come from him so that what is created may come forth at this or that time, and in this or that manner. For all these things originally and primordially have already been created in some framework of the elements, but come forth when given the opportunity."[4]

[3]Augustine, *De Trinitate*, bk 3 c8 n14.
[4]Ibid.

[1]Cf. Phil. 1, 18.
[2]Augustine, *De Trinitate*, bk 3 c8 n14.
[3]Ibid., bk 3 c9 nn17-18.
[4]Ibid., bk 3 c9 n16.

Chapter 10 (42)

1. THAT THE EVIL ANGELS HAVE THE POTENTIAL TO DO MANY THINGS BY THE STRENGTH OF THEIR NATURE WHICH THEY CANNOT DO BECAUSE OF THE PROHIBITION OF GOD OR OF THE GOOD ANGELS, THAT IS, BECAUSE THEY ARE NOT ALLOWED. It is also to be known that the evil angels have the potential to do some things by the fineness of their nature, which they nevertheless cannot do because of the prohibition of God or of the good angels, that is, because they are not allowed to do these things by God or by the good angels: they, who made frogs and serpents, were entirely capable of having made the gnats. But some things they are unable to do, even if they are allowed by the higher angels, because God does not allow it.

2. WHY THEY WHO MADE FROGS AND SERPENTS WERE NOT ABLE TO PRODUCE GNATS. Hence Augustine, in *On the Trinity*, book 3: "It happens from the ineffable power of God that what the evil angels could do if they were allowed, they are not able to do because they are not allowed. For no other reason explains why they who had made frogs and serpents were not able to make gnats, unless the greater power of God was there forbidding them through the Holy Spirit; even the magicians themselves acknowledged this, saying: *The finger of God is here.*[1] But what they can do by nature, what they cannot do because of prohibition, and what they are not allowed to do by the condition of their nature, it is difficult, indeed impossible, for a man to ascertain. (HE SHOWS IT BY ANALOGY.) We know that a man can walk, and that he cannot do even this if he were not allowed; but he cannot fly, even if he were allowed. In the same way, those angels can do some things, if they were allowed by the more powerful angels at God's command; but some things they cannot do, even if they were allowed by those angels, because he does not allow it from whom they have the kind of nature which is theirs, and often, through his angels, he does not allow even those things [to be done] which he has granted that they be able to do."[2]

DISTINCTION VIII

Chapter 1 (43)

1. WHETHER ALL ANGELS ARE CORPOREAL: THIS SEEMED TO BE THE CASE TO SOME, AND AUGUSTINE APPEARS TO AGREE WITH THEM, SAYING THAT ALL ANGELS BEFORE THE FALL HAD FINE AND SPIRITUAL BODIES, BUT THE

[1]Exod. 8, 19.
[2]Augustine, *De Trinitate*, bk 3 c9 n18.

BODIES OF THE EVIL ONES WERE CHANGED FOR THE WORSE IN THEIR FALL SO THAT THEY MIGHT SUFFER IN THEM. It is also usual among the learned to discuss the question of whether all angels, both good and evil, are corporeal, that is, have bodies united to them.—Some hold this to be the case, and they rely on the words of Augustine, who seems to say that all angels before their confirmation or fall had aerial bodies, formed from the purer and higher part of the air and suitable for acting, but not for suffering. And such bodies were preserved for the good angels who remained steadfast, so that they can act in such bodies, but not suffer. These bodies are of such fineness that they cannot be seen by mortals, unless they are clothed by some grosser form. They are seen when they take on such form, and are no longer seen when they set it aside. But the bodies of the evil angels in their fall were changed into an inferior quality of thicker air. For just as they were cast down from a worthier place to a lower one, that is, into this cloudy atmosphere, so their refined bodies were transformed into inferior and thicker ones, in which they can suffer from a superior element, that is, from fire.

2. And this seems to have been Augustine's thought, as he says, in *On Genesis*: "The demons are called aerial animate beings because they are endowed with bodies of an aerial nature; and they are not dissolved by death, because there prevails in them an element which is more prone to being active than passive. Water and earth tend to be passive; air and fire tend to be active. But it is not surprising if the transgressing angels and their prince (now a devil, then an archangel) were cast into this darkness after their sin. And neither is it surprising if, as a punishment, they were changed into an aerial nature in which they can suffer from fire. But they are allowed to keep only to the darkness of the air, which is like a prison for them, until the time of judgement."[1] See, with these words Augustine appears to convey the opinion that some hold regarding the bodies of angels.

3. IT SEEMS TO SOME THAT AUGUSTINE DID NOT SAY THIS AS HIS OWN VIEW, BUT AS REPORTING AN OPINION. But some say that he did not say this as his own view, but as reporting the opinion of others. They wish to conclude this from Augustine's own words, in which he says: 'The demons *are called* aerial animals,' and does not say *are*; for there were some people who said this.[2] But as to their dwelling in the cloudy atmosphere into which they were cast, they say that Augustine did not say this by way of opinion, but asserting the truth of the matter, as is shown by the linguistic distinction which he makes. They also say that many Catholic writers

[1]Cf. Augustine, *De Genesi ad litteram*, bk 3 c10 nn14-15.

[2]Cf. Apuleius, *De deo Socratis*, as to which, see Augustine, *De civitate Dei*, bk 8 cc15-16.

have agreed on this and have taught unanimously that the angels are incorporeal and do not have bodies united to them. At God's disposition, at times they take on bodies in order to perform a service commanded to them by God, and they set them aside when their service is completed. It was in such bodies that they appeared and spoke to men, and at times they spoke in the character of God, without any distinction of person, and at other times in the person of the Father or of the Son or of the Holy Spirit.

Chapter 2 (44)

1. THAT GOD APPEARED IN THOSE ANCIENT BODILY FORMS. Nor is it to be doubted that God appeared in bodily forms to men, as Augustine shows in *On the Trinity*, book 2, reporting various testimonies of Scripture, from which he proves that God appeared to men in bodily shapes; and sometimes God's speech was addressed to men in the character of God without distinction, and at other times with a distinction of persons.[1]

2. ON THE PERPLEXING QUESTION POSED BY AUGUSTINE, WHO ASKS WHETHER A NEW CREATURE WAS FORMED TO SHOW THESE BODILY APPARITIONS, OR WHETHER ANGELS WHO ALREADY EXISTED WERE SENT. AND IF SUCH ANGELS WERE SENT, DID THEY TAKE ON SOME CORPOREAL SHAPE FROM MORE FLESHLY MATTER WHILE PRESERVING THE QUALITY OF THEIR SPIRITUAL BODY, OR DID THEY CHANGE THEIR OWN BODY INTO A SHAPE SUITABLE FOR THEIR ACTION. But in asserting that God appeared to men in bodily likenesses, he poses a perplexing question which he does not resolve. He asks "whether in those bodily apparitions some creature was created for the sole end that God appear to men in it; or whether angels who already existed were so sent that, while remaining in their spiritual bodies, they assumed from the fleshly matter of the lower elements a bodily form which, as in the manner of a garment, they can change into whatever bodily forms they please; or did they change their own body into forms suitable to their actions, through the power given to them by God."[2]

3. For Augustine speaks as follows, in *On the Trinity*, book 3: It is to be asked, "regarding those ancient bodily forms and visions," "whether a creature was formed to the sole end that God, as he then judged it fitting, might be shown to human sight; or were pre-existent angels so sent that they might speak in the character of God, taking on a bodily form from a corporeal creature to use in their ministry; or did they, in accordance withthe power given to them by the Creator, change and transform their ownbody, to which they are not subject, but which they rule over subject to

[1]Augustine, *De Trinitate*, bk 2 cc7-18.
[2]Ibid., bk 2 c7 n13.

themselves, into the forms they chose which were fitting and suitable for their actions."[3]

4. HE GRANTS THAT ANGELS ARE SENT, BUT HE IS NOT ABLE TO RESOLVE THE REST. "But I confess that it exceeds the strength of my insight whether the angels, preserving the spiritual quality of their body and working through it in a hidden manner, take from the inferior and more fleshly elements something which they adapt, convert, and change, as in the manner of a garment, into any bodily form whatsoever, even their true ones, as true water was changed into true wine by the Lord;[4] or do they transform their own bodies into that which they wish, suitable for what they do. Since I am but a man, I cannot comprehend which of these is true by my own experience, as the angels can who do these things."[5]

5. Note, reader, that he does not resolve the question which he posed. He leaves unsettled whether the angels who were sent, while keeping their own spiritual bodies, were clothed with some more fleshly form in which they could be seen, or whether they changed and transformed their own body into whatever form they chose in which they could be seen. In these words, Augustine seems to attest that angels are corporeal and have their own spiritual bodies.[6]

Chapter 3 (45)

THAT GOD HAS NEVER APPEARED TO MORTALS IN THE FORM BY WHICH HE IS GOD. Leaving aside these matters as too deep and obscure, let us hold this without doubt: that God never appeared to mortals in the form of his essence. As he says to his servant Moses: *No man shall see me and live.*[1] And we read in the Gospel of John: *No one has ever seen God*.[2] "For there is nothing visible which is not changeable." And so "the substance or essence of God, because it is in no way changeable, can in no way be visible in its very self. Accordingly, it is manifest that all those appearances to the Fathers were done by means of a creature, although God was present in them. And although we do not know how God did these things through the ministry of the angels, yet we say that they were done through angels."[3] "Therefore, with confidence, I dare to say that neither God the Father, nor his Word, nor his Spirit, who is one God, is in any

[3]Augustine, *De Trinitate*, bk 3 prol. nn3-4.
[4]Cf. Jn. 2, 9.
[5]Augustine, *De Trinitate*, bk 3 prol. n5.
[6]Cf. especially *De civitate Dei*, bk 21 c10.

[1]Exod. 33, 20.
[2]Jn. 1, 18.
[3]Augustine, *De Trinitate*, bk 3 cc10-11, n21-22.

way changeable through that which he is and by which he is, and so much less is he visible."[4]

Chapter 4 (46)

1. WHETHER DEMONS ENTER THE BODIES OF MEN SUBSTANTIALLY AND INSINUATE THEMSELVES INTO THEIR MINDS. It also seems worthy of consideration whether demons, be they corporeal or incorporeal, enter the bodies of men substantially and insinuate themselves into their souls. Or are they said to enter souls because they exercise the effect of their wickedness there, oppressing and vexing them with God's permission, or drawing them into sin as they please.—The Gospel plainly declares that they enter into men and are expelled from them; it relates that demons had entered some people and were cast out by Christ.[1] But it is not at all clear whether they had entered according to substance, or whether they are said to have entered because of their evil effect.

2. THAT DEMONS DO NOT INSINUATE THEMSELVES INTO THE SOULS OF MEN SUBSTANTIALLY, BUT THEY ARE SAID TO ENTER BECAUSE OF THE EFFECT OF WICKEDNESS. Concerning this, Gennadius says, in the *Definitions of Ecclesiastical Dogmas*: "We do not believe that demons insinuate themselves substantially into the soul by energy (operation), but that they unite themselves to it by attaching themselves and overpowering it. To become insinuated into the mind, however, is possible for him alone who created it and who, subsisting incorporeally by nature, is capable [of being received] by his creature."[2] See, he appears to indicate here that demons do not insinuate themselves or enter into the hearts of men substantially.

3. Bede too, on that passage in the Acts of the Apostles where Peter says to Ananias: *Why did Satan tempt* or *fill your heart*,[3] says: "It is to be noted that nothing other than the creating Trinity can fill the mind of man according to substance because the soul is filled with created things only according to the operation and instigation of the will. Satan fills the heart of someone not by entering into him and his consciousness, nor by going into the inner sanctum of his heart, for this power belongs to God alone. Instead, he enters by shrewd and fraudulent deception, drawing the soul to a disposition for wickedness through the preoccupation with and the incentive of the vices, with which he is filled. And so Satan filled the heart of Ananias not by entering it, but by inserting in it the poison of his own wickedness."[4]—The same: "The unclean spirit, expelled from the hearts

[4]Augustine, *De Trinitate*, bk 3 c10 n21.

[1]Cf. Mt. 8, 16; Mk. 1, 23-26; Lk. 4, 41, etc.
[2]Gennadius, *Liber seu diffinitio ecclesiasticorum dogmatum*, c83.
[3]Acts 5, 3.
[4]Bede, *In Acta* 5, 3.

of the faithful by the flame of the virtues, hurls the poison of persecution against the teachers of truth."[5]

4. By these authorities, it is shown that demons do not enter into the hearts of men substantially, but do so through the effect of their wickedness; and they are said to be expelled from them when they are not allowed to do harm.

DISTINCTION IX

Chapter 1 (47)

ON THE DISTINCTION OF ORDERS [OF ANGELS], AND HOW MANY THERE ARE. After the above matters, it remains to know what Scripture teaches concerning the orders of angels; in several places,[1] it proclaims that there are nine orders of angels, namely Angels, Archangels, Principalities, Powers, Virtues, Dominations, Thrones, Cherubim, and Seraphim.—And three groups of three are found to be in these orders, and three orders in each of the threes, so that the likeness of the Trinity is shown to be impressed on them. Hence Dionysius teaches that there are three orders of angels, and he posits a three-fold distinction in each.[2] For there are three higher, three lower, and three middle; the higher: Seraphim, Cherubim, Thrones; the middle: Dominations, Principalities, Powers; the lower: Virtues, Archangels, Angels.

Chapter 2 (48)

1. WHAT AN ORDER IS, AND WHAT THE REASON IS FOR THE NAME OF EACH. Here it is to be considered what an order is; and then[1] whether the distinction of those orders existed from creation itself.

2. An order of angels is a multitude of celestial spirits who resemble each other by some gift of grace, just as they also agree in the gift of natural endowments. For example, those who burn with charity more than the others are called *Seraphim*: seraphim is interpreted as ardent or ablaze; *Cherubim* are those who are pre-eminent in knowledge, for cherubim is interpreted as fullness of knowledge. A throne is a seat; as blessed Gregory says, they who are filled with the grace of divinity are called *Thrones*, so that God may sit on them and decree and form his judgements through

[5]Bede, *In Acta* 28, 3.

[1]Cf. Is. 6, 6 and 37, 16; Ps. 17, 11 and 79, 2; Dan. 3, 55 and 10, 21; Tob. 3, 25; Eph. 1, 21; Col. 1, 16.

[2]Pseudo-Dionysius, *De caelesti hierarchia*, c6 § 2.

[1]Below, c4.

them.[2] *Dominations* are those who surpass Principalities and Powers. *Principalities* are so called because they dispose what is to be done by those subject to them, and lead them to fulfil the divine mysteries. *Powers* are those who have received more power in their order than the others, so that by this power they may restrain the evil powers subject to them lest these be able to tempt men as much as they desire. *Virtues* are those through whom signs and miracles are frequently done; *Archangels* are those who announce the greater things and *Angels* announce the lesser ones.

Chapter 3 (49)

1. THAT THESE NAMES WERE NOT GIVEN TO THEM FOR THEIR OWN SAKE, BUT FOR OURS, AND THEY ARE TAKEN FROM GIFTS OF GRACE WHICH THEY DO NOT HAVE SINGLY, BUT EXCELLENTLY, AND THEY ARE NAMED AFTER WHAT EACH POSSESSES PRE-EMINENTLY. These names were not given to them for their own sake, but for ours. For they are known to each other through contemplation, but they become known to us by their names. And the several orders are named after the gifts of grace which have been given to them to share, not singly, but pre-eminently. For in that heavenly fatherland, where the fullness of good is, although some things are given [more] excellently, yet nothing is possessed singly. For all things are in all, but not equally, because some possess those things—which they nevertheless all have—in a more sublime way. And although the superior orders received all the gifts of grace more sublimely and perfectly, yet they have taken their names from those that are pre-eminent, leaving the rest for the naming of the lower orders. And so the Seraphim, which is held to be the most excellent order, received both love and knowledge of the divinity, as well as the other gifts of the virtues, in a more sublime manner than all the rest. And yet that superior order took its name from the more excellent gift, namely from charity, for charity is a greater gift than knowledge.[1] Also, to know is greater than to judge, for knowledge informs judgement; and so the second order, namely the Cherubim, is named after the second gift, that is, the knowledge of truth. The same is to be understood of the other orders.

2. And so the excellence of the orders is designated in accordance with the excellence of the gifts; and yet, as Gregory says, all the gifts are common to all.[2] For all burn with charity and all are filled with knowledge, and so also with the other gifts. But the higher orders, as was already said, have received more excellently than the rest those gifts after which they

[2]Gregory, *In Evangelia*, hom. 34 n10.

[1]Cf. 1 Cor. 8, 1 and 13, 8-13.
[2]Gregory, *In Evangelia*, hom. 34 n14.

are named. Hence Gregory: "In that most high city, each order is known by the name of that thing which it has received most fully in gift."[3]

3. QUESTION ARISING FROM THE WORDS OF GREGORY. But here the following question arises: If each order is named after that gift which it possesses more fully, then the order of Cherubim excels all others in knowledge because it is named after knowledge. But he who loves more knows more; for as authority has it, there each knows as much as he loves;[4] and so the Seraphim are pre-eminent not only in charity, but also in knowledge.

4. EXPLANATION OF THAT AUTHORITY. And so it seems that that authority[5] is to be understood in such a way that the comparison is not related to all the orders, but only to some, namely the lower ones. For that order [of Cherubim] does not receive knowledge as a gift more fully than the Seraphim, but more fully than the other orders which are lower. Nor is each order named for all that it received more fully than the others, but from some one of the things which it so received.

5. ANOTHER DETERMINATION OF THE SAME QUESTION. Or the comparison can be referred not to the orders themselves, but to the other gifts; and not to all the other gifts, but to some. For just as men, when they have several gifts, possess some of them more excellently than others, so too perhaps the angels are more powerful in some gifts and less in others.

Chapter 4 (50)

1. WHETHER THE ORDERS WERE SO DISTINGUISHED FROM THE BEGINNING OF CREATION. It now remains to enquire whether these orders were distinguished in this way from the beginning of creation.—That they were so distinguished from the beginning of their existence appears to be indicated by the testimony of authority[1] which teaches that some fell from each order. And indeed, Lucifer, than whom none worthier[2] was established, was from a higher order. The Apostle too speaks about *Principalities* and *Powers of Darkness*,[3] showing that they fell from those orders and, although they exercise their ministry over the evil ones, yet they have not been entirely deprived of the names of their orders.

2. But it does not seem that this can stand. For they did not then [i.e. as soon as they were created] burn with charity, nor were they powerful in wisdom, nor did God use them as his throne; for if they had had these

[3]Gregory, *In Evangelia*, hom. 34 n10.
[4]These words are not found in Gregory's text.
[5]Gregory, *In Evangelia*, hom. 34 n14.

[1]That is, the text of Scripture adduced here and above, dist. 6 c1.
[2]Cf. Ez. 28, 12-19, and above dist. 6 c1 n2.
[3]Eph. 6, 12.

things, they would not have fallen. It follows that there were not Seraphim, or Cherubim, or Thrones at that time.

3. THAT THESE ORDERS DID NOT EXIST BEFORE THE FALL, BECAUSE THEY DID NOT HAVE AT THAT TIME THE GIFTS OF GRACE WHICH, AFTER THE FALL OF SOME, WERE GIVEN TO THE OTHERS. To this we say that these orders did not exist before the fall of some because they did not yet have the gifts in which they share by participation; after the fall of some of them, these gifts were given to the others, and these same gifts would have been conferred on those who fell, if they had remained steadfast. And so Scripture says that some fell from each order, not because they had been in those orders and later fell to ruin, but because, if they had remained steadfast, some of them would have been in each of the orders since they, like the ones who remained steadfast, had different degrees of fineness of nature and discernment of form.—For as we said earlier,[4] some were established as superior, others as inferior. The superior ones were those who were made more refined in nature and more penetrating in wisdom; the lower ones were less refined in nature and less penetrating in intelligence. But he alone could weigh these invisible differences of invisible things who *disposed all things in number, measure, and weight*[5] (AUGUSTINE, *ON GENESIS*): "that is, in himself, who is the measure that gives its boundary to each thing, and the number that gives each thing its form, and the weight that draws each thing to stability, that is, bounding and forming and ordering all things."[6]

Chapter 5 (51)

1. WHETHER ALL ANGELS OF THE SAME ORDER ARE EQUAL. Moreover, it is suitable to consider whether all angels of the same order are equal.—It pleased some that this should be the case; but this is neither probable, nor worthy of assertion, because Lucifer, who was of the fellowship of the higher ones, was even worthier than those who had been created more excellent than the rest. From this it is perceived that, if he had remained steadfast, he would have been in the superior order, and he would have been worthier than the others of the same order.

2. BY ANALOGY, HE SHOWS THAT NOT ALL OF THE SAME ORDER ARE EQUAL. For just as the order of Apostles is one thing and that of Martyrs another, and yet some of the Apostles are more worthy, and similarly some of the Martyrs are superior to others, it is rightly believed that the case is similar in the orders of angels.

[4]Dist. 3 cc2-3.
[5]Wis. 11, 21.
[6]Augustine, *De Genesi ad litteram*, bk 4 c3 n7.

Chapter 6 (52)

1. IN WHAT WAY SCRIPTURE SAYS THAT A TENTH ORDER IS COMPLETED FROM MEN, SINCE THERE ARE NO MORE THAN NINE ORDERS. It is also to be noted that we read that a tenth order is to be restored from men. But since there are no more than nine orders, and there would not have been more if those who fell had remained steadfast, readers are troubled by Scripture's statement that a tenth order is to be completed from men.[7]

2. Indeed, Gregory says that men are to be taken up in the order of angels:[8] some of them are to be taken up in the order of the higher ones, namely those who burn with greater charity; others in the order of the lower ones, namely those who are less perfect. From this it appears that a tenth order is not to be formed from men, as if there were nine orders of angels and a tenth of men, but men are to be assigned to the orders of angels according to the quality of their merits.

3. And so, when we read that a tenth order is to be completed from men, perhaps we can take it in this sense: that what fell in the case of the angels will be restored from men, and that so many fell from among the angels that a tenth order could be made. Because of this, the Apostle says that *all things* will be restored *in Christ, both those which are in heaven and those which are on earth*.[9] Because humankind was redeemed through Christ, it is from men that reparation is made for the fall of angels. And yet man would not be less saved, even if the angel had not fallen.

Chapter 7 (53)

1. THAT MEN ARE TAKEN UP IN PROPORTION TO THE NUMBER OF THE ANGELS WHO STOOD FIRM, NOT OF THOSE WHO FELL. For it is not in proportion to the number of those who fell, but of those who remained, that men are allowed into blessedness. Hence Gregory: "That supernal city is made up of angels and men; and we believe that so much of humankind is to ascend to it as were the angels who remained there, as it was written in the Canticle of Deuteronomy: *He established the boundaries of the people according to the number of the angels of God*."[1,2]

2. SOME SAY THAT MEN ARE TO BE RESTORED IN PROPORTION TO THE NUMBER OF THE ANGELS WHO FELL. And yet, it is held by some that men shall be restored in proportion to the number of the angels who fell, so that the heavenly city may neither be deprived of the number of its citi-

[7]That is, ordinary gloss, on Lk. 15, 8; from Gregory, *In Evangelia,* hom. 34 n6.
[8]Gregory, *In Evangelia*, hom. 34 n1.
[9]Eph. 1, 10.

[1]Deut. 32, 8.
[2]Gregory, *In Evangelia*, hom. 34 n11.

zens, nor rule over a greater abundance of them.[3]—This appears to be the view of Augustine in the *Enchiridion*, who does not assert that more men will be saved than angels were ruined, but that they will not be fewer. He says: "The heavenly Jerusalem, *our mother*,[4] the city of God, will not be defrauded in the number of her citizens, and perhaps shall even reign over a greater abundance. For we do not know the number either of saintly men, or of unclean demons. In the latter's place shall succeed the children of the Catholic mother, who seemed sterile on earth,[5] and they will remain without end of time in that peace from which the others fell. But the number of these citizens, as it now is, or as it was, or as it will be, is in the contemplation of that artificer *who calls [into existence] the things which are not as much as those which are*."[6,7] See, he plainly says that no fewer men will be saved than angels were ruined, but he does not assert that more will be.

DISTINCTION X

Chapter 1 (54)

1. WHETHER ALL CELESTIAL SPIRITS ARE SENT, AND HE SETS OUT TWO OPINIONS AND THE AUTHORITIES BY WHICH THEY ARE SUPPORTED. It is also to be investigated whether all those celestial spirits are sent to announce external things.—Some believe that there are some angels in that multitude who go out to serve and others who always take up their position within, as is written in Daniel: *Thousands of thousands ministered to him, and ten thousand times a hundred thousand stood beside him.*[1] Also, Dionysius, in the *Hierarchy*, which means the sacred principate, speaks of the order of precedence among spirits: "Those superior ranks never depart from the inmost depths because the higher orders do not fulfil any exterior service."[2] Those who deny that angels, other than the lower ones, are sent find support in these authorities.

2. OBJECTION TO THEM. To these is objected what Isaias says: *One of the Seraphim flew to me*,[3] which is a higher and more excellent order. Therefore, if they are sent from that order, it is not to be doubted that they are sent also from the others. The Apostle too says: *All are ministering*

[3]Cf. Hugh of St. Victor, *De sacramentis*, bk 1 c5 n31.
[4]Cf. Gal. 4, 26.
[5]Cf. Gal. 4, 27; Is. 54, 1.
[6]Rom. 4, 17.
[7]Augustine, *Enchiridion*, c29.

[1]Dan. 7, 10.
[2]Pseudo-Dionysius, *De caelesti hierarchia*, cc6-7.
[3]Is. 6, 6.

spirits, sent to serve.[4] On these authorities, some say that all angels are sent. And it ought not to be thought unworthy if even the higher ones are sent, since even he who is creator of all descended to these depths.

3. QUESTION: IF ALL ARE SENT, WHY DOES ONLY ONE ORDER GO BY THE NAME OF ANGELS. Here the question arises: if all are sent and are messengers of God, why does only one of the nine orders go by the name of angels?—Some say to this that all are indeed sent, but some more often and, as it were, from a duty imposed on them, and these are properly called Angels or Archangels.[5] But others are sent more rarely, namely the greater ones; these are sent when some cause beyond the ordinary dispensation has arisen and, just as they take up the ministry of Angels, they also take their name. Hence in the Psalm: *Who makes the spirits his angels*,[6] because those who are spirits by nature are sometimes made angels, that is, messengers.

Chapter 2 (55)

1. SOME HOLD THAT MICHAEL, GABRIEL, RAPHAEL WERE FROM A SUPERIOR ORDER, AND THESE ARE NAMES OF SPIRITS, NOT OF ORDERS. And they hold that Michael, Gabriel, Raphael were from a superior order. "Michael means 'who is like God'; Gabriel, the fortitude of God; Raphael, the medicine of God."[1] And these are not the names of orders, but of spirits.—And some say that every single one of these names is properly and singly the name of a spirit; but others hold that each of these is not the name singly and specifically of one spirit, but that it is the name now of this, now of that spirit, according to the quality of the things which they are sent to announce or do. Similarly, there are some names of demons which some hold to be proper to one of them, but others hold them to be common to several. Thus 'devil,' which is so called from the Greek, is interpreted as accuser, or as the one who flows downwards, and in Hebrew he is called Satan, that is, adversary. He is also called Belial, that is, apostate and without yoke. He is also called Leviathan, that is, something added to them.[2] And you will find many other names which are either proper to one spirit, or common to many.

2. HOW THEY WHO SAY THAT ALL ANGELS ARE SENT DETERMINE THE ABOVE AUTHORITIES, WHICH SEEM TO BE CONTRADICTORY. But those who

[4]Hebr. 1, 14.
[5]Cf. Gregory, *In Evangelia*, hom. 34 n12.
[6]Ps. 103, 4.

[1]Gregory, *In Evangelia*, hom. 34 n9.
[2]Devil: Apoc. 12, 9 and 20, 2; Satan: Zach. 3, 1; Belial: 2 Cor. 6, 15; Leviathan: Job 40, 20 and Is. 27, 1. For the interpretation of the names, see Isidore, *Etymologiae*, bk 8 c11 nn18-19.

assert that all angels are sent determine the above authorities, namely of Daniel and Dionysius,[3] in the following way: the superior ranks are said to stand beside God and never to depart from the inmost depths, not because they are not sometimes sent, but because they most rarely proceed to external service; and even then they do not withdraw from the inmost depths, because they always stand in God's presence and gaze; this is also the case with those who are sent frequently.[4]

3. WHICH ONES OTHERS SAY ARE SENT AND WHICH ONES ARE NOT SENT, WITH A DETERMINATION OF THE AUTHORITIES THAT APPEAR TO CONTRADICT EACH OTHER. But some say that the three highest orders, namely Seraphim, Cherubim, and Thrones, stand beside the Creator in such a way that they never go out to external service; the three lower orders are sent to external service. The three middle orders, however, stand between the other two groups, not only in dignity and place, but also in function, because they receive the divine command from the higher ones and transmit it to the lower ones. And so, since the highest angels announce God's command to the middle ones, the middle ones to the lowest ones, and these to men, they say that they are all deservedly called angels. And it was perhaps for this reason that the Apostle said that *all* are *ministering spirits* of the Son and are *sent to serve*;[5] or by *all*, he did not include individual orders, but only individual angels from the lower orders. As for that which Isaias says,[6] they determine it by the words of Dionysius, who says: "Those spirits who are sent take the name of those whose office they fulfill."[7] Hence they say that the angel who was sent to Isaias to cleanse and burn the Prophet's lips was from a lower order; but he was said to be from the Seraphim because he came to burn and consume Isaias's sins.

DISTINCTION XI

Chapter 1 (56)

1. THAT EACH SOUL HAS A GOOD ANGEL TO WATCH OVER IT AND AN EVIL ONE TO TRAIN IT. It is also to be known that the good angels are assigned to watch over men so that each of the elect has an angel especially delegated for his advancement and guardianship.—Hence in the Gospel, Truth, forbidding anyone to cause scandal to the little ones, says: *Their*

[3]Above, c1 n1.
[4]Cf. Gregory, *Moralia*, bk 17 c13 n18; *In Evangelia*, hom. 34 nn12-13.
[5]Cf. Hebr. 1, 14.
[6]Is. 6, 6; above, c1 n2.
[7]Pseudo-Dionysius, *De caelesti hierarchia*, c13 § 2; but the text is Gregory's, *In Evangelia*, hom. 34 n12.

angels always behold the face of the Father.[1] He says that they are *their* angels, to whose guardianship they are assigned. Commenting on this, Jerome teaches that each soul has an angel assigned to guard it from the moment of birth. He says as follows: "Great is the dignity of souls, so that each of them, from the moment of birth, has an angel delegated to guard it."[2]

2. Gregory too says that each soul has a good angel assigned to watch over it, and an evil one to train it.[3] For although all good angels will our good and jointly seek the salvation of all, nevertheless the one who is assigned to watch over someone especially encourages that person to the good, as we read of the angel of Tobias,[4] and the angel of Peter in the Acts of the Apostles.[5] Similarly, although all the evil angels desire evil for men, yet the one who is assigned to test someone incites that person more persistently to evil and encourages him more strongly to do harm.

3. WHETHER SINGLE ANGELS ARE ASSIGNED TO SINGLE HUMANS, OR ONE TO MANY. But it is usual to ask whether single angels are assigned to watch over or test single humans, or one to many. But since there are as many elect as good angels, it is clear that there are more men, good and evil together, than there are good angels. And since there are as many elect as there are good angels, and there are more good angels than evil ones, and there are more evil men than good ones, there is no doubt that there are more good men than evil angels and more evil men than there are evil or good angels.

4. HE CONFIRMS THAT ONE ANGEL IS ASSIGNED TO MANY HUMAN BEINGS, WHETHER CONCURRENTLY OR AT DIFFERENT TIMES. And so it is fitting to say that one and the same angel, good or evil, is assigned to watch over or test many human beings, whether at the same time or at different ones. And we say 'at the same time or at different ones' because it seems to some that all humans who exist simultaneously at one time may each have an angel, good or evil.[6] This is so because, although the number of humans is greater than that of angels, if we add together all men who were, who are, and who will be, nevertheless it is possible that all men, while they are in this life, may each have an angel, good or evil, assigned to watch over or train him, since men succeed to men who have died, and so they are not all simultaneously in this life, but the angels never die and so all exist simultaneously. Moreover, whether in this manner or not, it is not to be doubted that each person has an angel assigned to himself, either

[1]Mt. 18, 10.
[2]Jerome, *In Matthaeum* 18, 10.
[3]Gregory of Nyssa, *De vita Moysi*, following Origen, *In Lucam*, hom. 12.
[4]Cf. Tob. 5-12.
[5]Acts 12, 15.
[6]Cf. Hugh of St. Victor, *De sacramentis*, bk 1 c5 n31.

designated for several simultaneously, or for one singly. And it is not to be wondered at that one angel is assigned to watch over many men since the guardianship of many men is assigned to one man, in such a way that each of them is said to have his own lord or bishop or abbot.

Chapter 2 (57)

1. WHETHER ANGELS MAKE PROGRESS IN MERIT OR IN REWARD UNTIL JUDGEMENT. Moreover, it is fitting to consider whether the good angels make progress in merit or in reward until judgement.

2. IT SEEMS TO SOME THAT THEY MAKE PROGRESS IN EACH OF THESE. It seems to some that they progress in merits and are more and more worthy each day because each day they serve men's utility and devote themselves to men's progress. It seems to the same that angels also progress in reward, namely in the knowledge and love of God. For although, as they say, angels in their confirmation received eternal and perfect blessedness, yet their blessedness is increased each day as they love and know God more and more.—CHARITY IS NOW THEIR MERIT AND THEIR REWARD. And their charity, by which they love God and ourselves, is both their merit and their reward: merit, because through it and the services which they render to us by it, they acquire merit and make progress in blessedness, and it is also their reward because they are blessed by it.

3. THEY CONFIRM WHAT THEY SAY WITH AUTHORITIES. And they confirm with the testimonies of the Saints that the angels make progress in knowledge and, through this, in blessedness. For Isaias, speaking in the person of the angels admiring the magnificence of Christ in his ascension, says: *Who is this who comes from Edom, with dyed garments from Bosra?*[1] And in the Psalm: *Who is this king of glory?*[2] From these words, it appears that the angels knew the mystery of the Word made flesh more fully after its completion than before. And just as they made progress in their knowledge of this mystery, they say that the angels also make progress in their knowledge of the divinity.—And that they made progress in their knowledge of this mystery, the Apostle teaches clearly, saying: *This is the dispensation of the mystery hidden in God from the beginning: that the manifold wisdom of God should become known through the Church to the Princes and Powers in the heavens.*[3] Commenting on this, Jerome says that "the angelic dignities did not understand the above-said mystery in its purity until the passion of Christ was complete, and the preaching of the Apostles had spread among the nations."[4]

[1]Is. 63, 1.
[2]Ps. 23, 8.
[3]Eph. 3, 9-10.
[4]Jerome, on Eph. 3, 9-10.

4. THAT AUGUSTINE SEEMS TO BE OPPOSED TO WHAT JEROME SAYS IN THIS SENTENCE. But Augustine appears to contradict this; on the same text of the Epistle, he says: "That mystery of the kingdom of heaven, which was revealed at an opportune time for our salvation, was not hidden from the angels. The above-mentioned mystery was known to them *from the beginning*, because no creature is from before the beginning, but [only] from the beginning."[5]

5. DETERMINATION OF THE ABOVE AUTHORITIES.—HAYMO. Note well, reader, that illustrious doctors seem to disagree as to this sentence. And so, in order that all contradiction may be removed from our midst, let us determine the above by following Haymo in saying that "[those mysteries] were known in part *from the beginning* to those angels of greater dignity by whose ministry they were announced, and as to household servants and messengers; but they remained unknown to angels of lesser dignity"[6] until they were fulfilled and preached *through the Church*; then they were known perfectly by all the angels.

6. And so it is certain that all angels made progress in the knowledge of divine mysteries with the passage of time. Thus, not incongruously, these same people say that the knowledge and blessedness of the angels are increased until the consummation which is to come, when they shall be most perfect in knowledge and blessedness, with no further increase or diminution.

7. THE OPINION OF OTHERS, WHO SAY THAT THE ANGELS DID NOT MAKE PROGRESS IN SOME OF THE AFORESAID. But others say that the angels, in their confirmation, were endowed with such love and knowledge of the divinity that they have not made and will not make any further progress in these. And yet they did make progress in their knowledge of external things, as in their knowledge of the mystery of the incarnation, and suchlike; but they did not make progress in their contemplation of the divinity, because they do not and will not understand more fully the trinity in unity and the unity in trinity that they perceived from their confirmation. In the same way, they also say that the angels did not make progress in charity after their confirmation, because their charity was not afterwards increased. And so they say that they did not make progress in merits, namely with respect to the capacity for deserving, but they did make progress with respect to the number of merits. For they did many good things afterwards which they had not then done; but their charity, from which those goods proceeded, was not increased: from this charity, they deserved as much before these goods were added as after their addition.

[5]Augustine, *De Genesi ad litteram*, bk 5 c19 n38.
[6]Haimo of Auxerre, on Eph. 3, 10.

8. WHAT IS MORE PROBABLE. But what those others said above seems more probable, namely that angels make progress in knowledge and in other things until judgement.

9. SOME AUTHORITIES APPEAR TO CONTRADICT THE MORE PROBABLE SENTENCE. But the words of some authorities appear to contradict what was said. For Isidore, in the book *On the Highest Good*, says: "In the Word of God, angels know all things before they are made."[7]—DETERMINATION. But he did not say that all angels know all things perfectly; and so he did not dispose of [the question of] whether they make progress in knowledge.

10. Also, Gregory, in the book of *Dialogues*, says: "What is there which they do not know, since they know the one who knows all things?"[8] He appears to say that the angels know all things, and that there is nothing which they do not know.—ALSO, ANOTHER DETERMINATION. But this is to be taken of those things whose knowledge makes their knower blessed, such as those things which pertain to the mystery of Trinity and unity.

DISTINCTION XII

Chapter 1 (58)

1. AFTER THE ACQUISITION OF SOME KNOWLEDGE OF THE ANGELS, THE CREATION OF OTHER THINGS IS DISCUSSED, AND PARTICULARLY THE DISTINCTION OF THE WORKS OF THE SIX DAYS. Let what we have said of the condition of the angelic nature suffice. Now it remains to set forth something on the creation of other things, and particularly on the distinction of the works of the six days.

2. When God in his wisdom established the angelic spirits, he also created other things, as the above-mentioned Scripture of Genesis shows.[1] It says that *in the beginning* God created *heaven*, that is, the angels, *and earth*, namely the matter of the four elements, which was still confused and formless, which is called chaos by the Greeks; and this happened before any day. Afterwards, he distinguished the elements and gave their proper and distinct forms to individual things according to their kind. And he did not form them simultaneously, as it pleased some of the Fathers [to hold], but at intervals of time and in the course of six days, as it has seemed to others.[2]

[7]Isidore, *Sententiae*, bk 1 c10 n17.
[8]Gregory, *Dialogi*, bk 4 c33.

[1]Cf. Gen. 1, 1; cf. above, dist. 2 cc1, 2, 5.
[2]Cf. Augustine, *De Genesi contra Manichaeos*, bk 1 c5 n9.

Chapter 2 (59)

THAT THE SAINTS WHO HAVE TREATED THIS APPEAR TO HAVE TAUGHT ALMOST OPPOSITE VIEWS, SOME SAYING THAT ALL THINGS WERE MADE SIMULTANEOUSLY IN MATTER AND FORM, OTHERS [THAT IT WAS DONE] AT INTERVALS OF TIME. Indeed, some of the holy Fathers, who have excellently examined the words and secret things of God, appear to have written almost opposite things regarding this.—For some taught that all things were created simultaneously in matter and form; this appears to have been Augustine's opinion.[1]—But others have deemed the latter view more acceptable and asserted that a rough and formless matter, containing a mixture and confusion of the four elements, was created first; but afterwards, at intervals over six days, the kinds of different corporeal things were formed from that matter according to their proper classes. This is the view which is commended and preferred by Gregory, Jerome, Bede, and many others;[2] it is also the view which seems more congruent with the Scripture of Genesis, from which the first knowledge of this topic came down to us.

Chapter 3 (60)

1. HOW CORPOREAL THINGS WERE ESTABLISHED AT INTERVALS OF TIME. And so let us examine the order and mode of creation and of the formation of things according to this latter tradition. As was recounted above,[1] *in the beginning, God created heaven*, that is, the angelic nature, but still formless, as some prefer to hold;[2] *and earth*, that is, that confused matter of the four elements.

2. WHY THAT CONFUSED MATTER IS CALLED EARTH, THE ABYSS, OR WATER. As Augustine says, in *Against the Manichees*, Moses called this matter earth, "because the earth is the least beautiful of all the elements"; and it was *waste and disordered*[3] "because of the mixture of all the elements."[4]—He also calls the same matter *the abyss*, saying: *And darkness came over the face of the abyss*,[5] because it was confused and mixed, lacking distinct form.—"And the same formless matter is also called *water*, over which *the spirit of the Lord hovered*,[6] as the will of the arti-

[1]Augustine, *De Genesi ad litteram*, bk 1 c15 n29; bk 7 c28 nn41-42.
[2]Gregory, *Moralia*, bk 32 c12 n16; Jerome, *Hebraicae quaestiones in libro Genesis* 1, 1; Bede, *Libri quatuor in principium Genesis* 1.

[1]Above, c1 n2.
[2]Cf. above, dist. 2 c5.
[3]Cf. Gen. 1, 2. The Vulgate has 'empty' instead of 'disordered.'
[4]Augustine, *De Genesi contra Manichaeos*, bk 1 c7 n12.
[5]Gen. 1, 2.
[6]Ibid.

ficer hovers over the things which are to be made";[7] "because what he had begun to form and perfect was subject to the good will of the Creator,"[8] who "as lord and maker presided over the flowing and confused matter, so that he might distinguish it through different forms when he willed"[9] and as he willed. "And this matter was called *water* because all things which are born on the earth, whether animals or vegetation or similar things, begin to be formed and nourished by moisture."[10] That formless matter is called by all these terms "so that an unknown thing might be indicated to those less knowledgeable by known terms; and not by one term alone because, if it had been signified by one term alone, it might be thought to be what people are accustomed to understand by that term. And so that unseen and formless matter which could not be seen or touched in any form is signified by these terms,"[11] that is, "by the names of those visible things which were going to be made from it, because of the weakness of the little ones, who are less capable of understanding invisible things."[12]

3. And then there was *darkness*, that is, the absence of light.—AUGUSTINE: "For darkness is not anything, but the very absence of light. As silence is not any thing, but we call it silence when there is no sound. And nudity is not any thing, but we call nudity the absence of covering over the body. As also emptiness is not any thing, but we call that place empty in which there is no body,"[13] and the absence of a body emptiness.

Chapter 4 (61)

IN WHAT SENSE DARKNESS IS SAID NOT TO BE ANYTHING, AND IN WHAT SENSE IT MAY BE SAID TO BE SOMETHING. Note that Augustine says here that darkness is not anything, but elsewhere darkness is placed among the creatures which bless the Lord; and so it is said: *Bless the Lord, light and darkness*.[1]—For that reason, it is to be known that darkness is taken in different ways: namely, either as the absence of light, as Augustine took it above, and according to this understanding, it is not anything; or as darkened air, or the dark quality of the air; and in this sense, it is some created thing. Hence he says that darkness then *was over the face of the abyss*,[2] "because there was not yet light; for if there had been, it would have been

[7]Augustine, *De Genesi contra Manichaeos*, bk 1 c7 n12.
[8]Augustine, *De Genesi ad litteram*, bk 1 c5 n11.
[9]Ordinary gloss, on Gen. 1, 2.
[10]Augustine, *De Genesi contra Manichaeos*, bk 1 c7 n12.
[11]Ibid.
[12]Ibid., bk 1 c5 n9.
[13]Ibid., bk 1 c4 n7.

[1]Dan. 3, 72; cf. also Is. 45, 7.
[2]Gen. 1, 2.

above and diffused over it";[3] but God had not yet adorned his work with the grace of light, which was formed afterwards, on the first day.

Chapter 5 (62)

1. TWO THINGS ARE TO BE CONSIDERED HERE: WHY THAT CONFUSED MATTER IS CALLED FORMLESS, AND WHERE IT CAME FORTH INTO BEING AND HOW HIGH UP IT ROSE. But before we treat that, two things seem to us to require discussion: first, why that confused matter is called formless, whether because it lacked all form or for some other reason; second, where it came forth into being and how high up it rose.

2. BRIEF RESPONSE TO THE FIRST. And so, briefly responding to what was posed first, we say that that primal matter is not said to have been formless because it had no form at all, since no corporeal thing can exist which has no form. But we say that it is not absurd to call it formless because, subsisting in some confusion and mixture, it had not yet received any beautiful, clear, and distinct form such as we now see. Therefore, that matter was made in a form of confusion before the form of arrangement. All corporeal things first were created materially, simultaneously, and at once in a form of confusion; afterwards, they were set in order in six days in a form of arrangement.—See, what was first proposed for discussion has been resolved, namely why that matter is called formless.

3. HERE HE RESPONDS TO WHAT WAS ASKED IN THE SECOND PLACE. Now it remains to explain what was proposed in the second place, namely where that matter subsisted and how far up it extended.—Without making any rash assertions, we say to this that that first mass of all things, when it was created, appears to have come into being in the same place where it is now after being formed. And this earthly element was in the lowest place, sinking down to the same middle position [where it now is], while the rest [of the elements] were mixed in one confusion. These spread all around it in the manner of a cloud and covered it so much that what it was could not be seen. In fact those three elements, confused in one mixture and suspended all around, reached as far up as the highest point of corporeal creation does now.—And it seems to some that that mass extended beyond the firmament because it was thicker and grosser in its lower part, but thinner, lighter, and finer in the higher; some hold that the waters which are said to be above the firmament were made of this thinner substance.[1] —Such was the face of the world in the beginning, before it received form or spatial arrangement.

[3]Cf. Augustine, *De Genesi ad litteram*, bk 1 c1 n3.

[1]Cf. Augustine, *De Genesi ad litteram*, bk 2 c4.

4. AFTER SHOWING WHAT THE OUTWARD APPEARANCE OF THE WORLD WAS AT THE VERY BEGINNING, HE BEGINS TO PURSUE THE DISTINCTION OF THE WORKS OF THE SIX DAYS. Now it remains to pursue that spatial arrangement in order and how it was brought to completion. As the Scripture of Genesis teaches, in six days God distinguished and reduced to their proper forms all that he had made materially and simultaneously. He completed *his work on the sixth day*, and so afterwards, *on the seventh day, he rested from all work*,[2] that is, he ceased making new creatures.[3] For in the six days, he distinguished the six classes of things, and afterwards he made nothing which is not contained in one of these classes. Nevertheless he did work afterwards, as Truth says in the Gospel: *My Father works even now, and I, too, work.*[4]

Chapter 6 (63)

ON THE FOUR MANNERS OF DIVINE ACTIVITY. For as Alcuin says, in *On Genesis*, God works in four manners: "First, in the Word, by disposing all things; second, in the formless matter of the four elements, creating it from nothing, and so: *The one who lives in eternity created all things at the same time*,[1] namely he created all the elements and all bodies materially and simultaneously; third, he distinguished the various creatures through the works of the six days; fourth, unknown natures do not arise from the primordial seeds, but the known ones are formed again more frequently so that they do not perish."[2]

DISTINCTION XIII

Chapter 1 (64)

WHAT THE FIRST WORK OF DISTINCTION WAS. The first work of distinction was the making of light, as Scripture shows, which, after recalling the formlessness of things, began [the account of] their spatial arrangement with light, adding: *God said: Let there be light, and the light was made; and he divided light from darkness, and he called the light day and the darkness night. And it became evening, and morning, the first day.*[1]

[2]Cf. Gen. 2, 2.
[3]Cf. below, dist. 15 c7.
[4]Jn. 5, 17.

[1]Eccli. 18, 1.
[2]Alcuin, *Interrogationes et responsiones in Genesim*, inter. 19.

[1]Gen. 1, 3-5.

Fittingly, the beautiful arrangement of the world began with light, by which all other things that were to be created might be seen.

Chapter 2 (65)

1. WHAT THAT LIGHT WAS, WHETHER CORPOREAL OR SPIRITUAL. If it is asked what that light was, namely whether corporeal or spiritual, we respond with what we have read that the Saints have handed down. For Augustine says that that light can be understood as either corporeal or spiritual.[1]

2. ON THE SPIRITUAL LIGHT. If it is taken as spiritual, the angelic nature is understood, which at first was formless, but afterwards was formed, when it turned toward the Creator and adhered to him in charity. Its formless creation was signified above, when it was said: *In the beginning, God created heaven and earth.*[2] Here, however, its formation is shown, when it says: *Let there be light, and the light was made.*[3] And so this angelic nature was first darkness, and afterwards light, because first it had formlessness and imperfection, but afterwards the perfection of formation; and thus God divided light from darkness. For as Augustine says, in *On Genesis*, the formlessness and imperfection of this creature existed before it was formed in the love of the Creator; it was formed, however, when it turned to the unchangeable light of the Word.[4]

3. HERE ON CORPOREAL LIGHT. But if that light was corporeal, which is entirely probable, it is understood to have been a luminous body, as, for example, a luminous cloud; this was made not formally from nothing, but from pre-existing matter, so that it should be light and have the power of lighting. With it, the first day arose because, before light, there was no day or night, although there was time.

Chapter 3 (66)

1. THAT THAT LIGHT WAS MADE WHERE THE SUN NOW SHINES, AND THAT IT COULD SHINE THROUGH THE WATERS.—AUGUSTINE, IN *ON GENESIS*: "But if it is asked where that light was made, since the abyss covered all the heights of the earth, it can be said that it was made in those parts over which now shines the daily light of the sun. And it is not strange that the light can shine through the waters, since these are often lit even by sailors; diving in the deep, they make light for themselves in the water by spouting oil from their mouths. And the waters were much less deep in the

[1]Augustine, *De Genesi ad litteram*, bk 1 cc3-5 and c17.
[2]Gen. 1, 1.
[3]Gen. 1, 3.
[4]Augustine, *De Genesi ad litteram*, bk 1 cc4-5 nn9-10.

beginning than they are now because they had not yet been gathered in one place."[1]

2. And so this light that was made had the function and place of the sun; propelled in a circular course by its own motion, it distinguished night from day. Therefore, it seems probable that this light first appeared where the sun appears after completing its daily course so that, travelling around in the same path and descending for the first time to the west, it might make the evening; then, called back to the east, it might make the dawn, that is, illumine the morning.—And so God *divided light* and darkness, and *he called the light day and the darkness night.*[2]

Chapter 4 (67)

1. THAT DAY IS TAKEN IN DIFFERENT WAYS. Here it is to be noted that day is taken in different ways in Scripture. For that light which lit the darkness on the first three days is called day. The very illumination of the air is also called day. Day is also called the space of twenty-four hours, which is how it is taken when Scripture says: *And it became evening and morning, the first day.*[1]

2. HOW THAT PHRASE OUGHT TO BE DISTINGUISHED: AND IT BECAME EVENING AND MORNING, THE FIRST DAY. This is to be distinguished as follows: evening was made first, and afterwards the morning, and so was completed one day of twenty-four hours, namely a natural day, which had an evening, but not a morning. For the end of the preceding day and the beginning of the following one is called morning because it is dawn, which has neither full light nor total darkness.—And so the first day did not have a morning because no day preceded it that might end at the beginning of the next day; and also especially because, with the appearance of light, there was immediately a full and most clear day over the earth. This day began not from dawn, but from a full light, and was completed on the morning of the next day.—BEDE. Hence Bede, in *On Genesis*: "It was fitting that day begin from light and extend to the morning of the following day, so that the works of God be signified to have started with the light and to be completed in the light."[2]—But the other days had a morning and evening, and each of them began on its morning and extended until the morning of the following day.

[1]More correctly, Bede, *Libri quatuor in principium Genesis* 1, 3.
[2]Gen. 1, 4-5.

[1]Gen. 1, 5.
[2]Bede, *Libri quatuor in principium Genesis* 1, 5.

Chapter 5 (68)

1. ON THE NATURAL ORDER OF COMPUTATION OF DAYS AND ON THE ONE WHICH WAS INTRODUCED FOR THE SAKE OF THE MYSTERY. This is the natural order of distinction of days, that days be distinguished and computed from morning to morning. But afterwards, as matter for allegory, it was done that days be computed from evening to evening and that the day be added to the preceding night in the computation, even though, according to the natural order, the preceding day is to be added to the night that follows it. (HERE IS THE ALLEGORY.) This was done because man, through sin, fell from light into the darkness of ignorance and sins; then, through Christ, he returned from darkness to light. Hence the Apostle: *We were for a time darkness, but now we are light in the Lord.*[1]

2. And so the first day began not at dawn, but from full light; after a while, when the light had set little by little, it became evening, and it was completed by the morning of the following day. Hence Bede: "With the light setting little by little and, after the space of a day's duration, going under the lower regions, it was evening, as also happens now with the usual course of the sun. And then, with the light returning over the earth and the beginning of another day, it was morning, and one day of twenty-four hours was complete. And on those [first] three days, the night was entirely dark, which would be illuminated with some light after the creation of the heavenly bodies."[2]

3. WHY WAS THE SUN MADE, IF THAT LIGHT WAS SUFFICIENT.— AUGUSTINE. But it is usual to ask, "why was the sun made, if that light was sufficient to make the day."[3]—To this it may be said that perhaps that light illuminated the higher regions, and it was necessary for the sun to be made to illuminate the lower ones; or perhaps it is rather because "with the making of the sun, the brightness of the day was increased: for the day shone with much greater brightness afterwards than before."[4]

4. But if it is asked what has become of that light, since it does not appear now, it can be said either that the body of the sun was formed from it, or that "it is in that part of the sky where the sun is: not that it is itself the sun, but that it is so united to the sun that it cannot be distinguished from it."[5]

[1]Eph. 5, 8.
[2]Bede, *Libri quatuor in principium Genesis* 1, 5.
[3]Augustine, *De Genesi ad litteram*, bk 1 c11 n23.
[4]Ibid.
[5]Ibid., bk 1 c10 n22.

Chapter 6 (69)

HOW THAT STATEMENT, 'GOD SAID,' IS TO BE TAKEN: WHETHER GOD SAID IT BY THE SOUND OF HIS VOICE OR IN ANOTHER WAY. Moreover, one must inquire how that statement should be taken: *God said*,[1] whether he said it in time, or by the sound of his voice, or in some other way.—Augustine, in *On Genesis*, teaches that God spoke neither in time, nor by the sound of a voice.[2] For if God spoke in time, then he spoke changeably; and if the voice of God be said to have resounded in a bodily way, there was no language by which he could speak, nor was there anyone who could suitably hear and understand. And so it is well to refer the voice of God to the nature of the Word, through whom all things were made. And so God said: *Let there be*, etc., not in time, not by the sound of a voice, but in the Word coeternal with himself, that is, he generated the Word outside time, in whom it was, and he disposed from eternity that what was made in time should be so made.

Chapter 7 (70)

1. HOW THIS STATEMENT SHOULD BE TAKEN: THE FATHER WORKS IN THE SON, OR THROUGH THE SON, OR IN THE HOLY SPIRIT. Here it is usual to ask how this statement should be taken: the Father works in the Son, or through the Son, or in the Holy Spirit. For Scripture frequently sets such things before us as: *Lord, you made all things in wisdom*,[1] that is, in the Son; and: *In the beginning*, that is, in the Son, *God created heaven and earth*;[2] and also: *Through whom he made the world of time*.[3] Also, on that passage of the Psalm: *The heavens were made firm by the word of the Lord*,[4] Augustine says that "the Father works through his Word and the Holy Spirit."[5] And so how should this be taken?

2. Taking from the above words an occasion to err, some heretics held that the Father, as author and artificer, used the Son and the Holy Spirit almost like an instrument in the making of things. Pious faith rejects such a notion as blasphemous and contrary to sound doctrine.

3. HERE HE REVEALS IN WHAT SENSE THE FATHER IS SAID TO WORK IN THE SON OR THROUGH THE SON. We are not to understand Scripture's frequent recalling of the Father working in the Son, or through the Son, as if the Son could not do anything without the Father stretching out his right

[1]Gen. 1, 3.
[2]Augustine, *De Genesi ad litteram*, bk 1 c2 nn4-6.

[1]Ps. 103, 24.
[2]Gen. 1, 1.
[3]Hebr. 1, 2.
[4]Ps. 32, 6.
[5]Augustine, *Enarrationes in Psalmos*, exp. 2 on Ps. 32, sermon 2 n5.

hand to him, or as if he were some instrument of the Father at work. Instead, by these words, Scripture wanted it to be understood that the Father works with the Son and the Holy Spirit, and does nothing without them.

4. THE HERETIC RISES UP AGAINST THIS EXPLANATION. But the heretic says: By this reasoning, it might have said that the Son works through the Father or in the Father, and the Holy Spirit with both or through both, because the Son works with the Father and the Holy Spirit with both.—RESPONSE. The brief answer to this is that the one expression was used, and not the other, to show that authority is in the Father.[6] For it is not the Father who works from the Son, but the Son from the Father, and the Holy Spirit from both. And so we have also read that the Son works through the Holy Spirit because he works with the Holy Spirit, who has it from the Son that he work.

5. ANOTHER EXPOSITION OF THE ABOVE. It may also be taken in another way, so that the Father is said to work in the Son or through the Son because he begot him as the artificer of all things; in the same way, he is said to judge through him because he begot him as judge.[7] So also the Father or the Son is said to work through the Holy Spirit because the Holy Spirit proceeds from both as maker of all things.—Hence John Chrysostom, in his *Exposition of the Epistle to the Hebrews*, says as follows: "It is not the case, as the heretic inanely suspects, that the Son was, as it were, some instrument of the Father. Nor is the Father said to have created through him as if he himself could not create. But just as the Father is said to judge through the Son because he begot him as judge, so also he is said to work through the Son because it is clear that he begot him as artificer. (NOTE: HERE, THE FATHER IS CALLED CAUSE OF THE SON.) For if the Father, according to his being Father, is the cause of the Son, much more is he the cause of those things which were made through the Son."[8]—These are the things said of the work of the first day.

DISTINCTION XIV

Chapter 1 (71)

ON THE WORK OF THE SECOND DAY, ON WHICH THE FIRMAMENT WAS MADE. Then God said: Let there be a firmament in the middle of the waters, and let it divide waters from waters. And he divided the waters which were below the firmament from those which were above the firmament.[1]

[6]Cf. above, Bk 1 dist. 12 c2 n5; also dist. 20.
[7]Cf. Jn. 5, 22.
[8]John Chrysostom, *Expositio epistolae ad Hebraeos*, hom. 2 n2.

[1]Gen. 1, 6-7.

Chapter 2 (72)

THAT HEAVEN IS HERE SAID TO BE CREATED.—BEDE. It is to be known that, as Bede says of that passage, in *On Genesis*, "here is described the creation of the heaven, in which the stars are fixed. Below it were placed the waters which are in the air and on the earth, and above it were placed other waters, of which it is said: *You cover his heights with waters.*[1] And so in the middle is the firmament, that is, the starry heaven."[2]

Chapter 3 (73)

OF WHAT MATTER THAT HEAVEN IS MADE. "This can be believed to be made of waters. For crystalline stone,[1] which has great strength and clarity, is made from water."[2]

Chapter 4 (74)

1. HOW THERE CAN BE WATERS ABOVE HEAVEN, AND WHAT THOSE WATERS ARE LIKE. "But if anyone is troubled as to how waters, which are by nature fluid and tend downwards, can be above heaven, let him remember that it is written of God: *Who binds up waters in his clouds.*[1] For he who binds the waters under heaven, which are retained for a time in the vapours of the clouds, can also suspend the waters above the sphere of heaven, and not by the thinness of vapours, but with the hardness of ice, so that they should not fall down.[2] As to how and to what end they were so established, he knows it who established them."[3]—See, with these words, it is shown which heaven was made, namely that in which the stars are fixed, that is, which is beyond the earth's atmosphere; and from what matter, namely from water; and what these waters which are above that heaven are like, namely as solid as ice.

2. OTHERS HOLD THAT THAT HEAVEN IS OF A FIERY NATURE, AND AUGUSTINE AGREES WITH THEM. But some say that the heaven which is beyond the expanse of the earth's atmosphere is of a fiery nature; they maintain that "above the air is pure fire, which is said to be heaven; and they conjecture that the stars and heavenly bodies were made from this fire."[4] Augustine appears to agree with them.—But whether by the name

[1]Ps. 103, 3.
[2]Bede, *Libri quatuor in principium Genesis* 1, 6-8.

[1]Cf. Eccli. 43, 22.
[2]Bede, *Libri quatuor in principium Genesis* 1, 6-8.

[1]Job 26, 8.
[2]Cf. Augustine, *De Genesi ad litteram*, bk 2 c5 n9.
[3]Bede, *Libri quatuor in principium Genesis* 1, 6-8.
[4]Cf. Augustine, *De Genesi ad litteram*, bk 2 cc3-4.

of firmament "is here understood the heaven which is beyond the earth's atmosphere, or the atmosphere itself," is a question which Augustine himself raises, but does not resolve.[5] And yet he seems to approve more the view that heaven is to be understood here as that which is beyond the expanse of the earth's atmosphere.

3. WHAT THE WATERS WHICH ARE ABOVE HEAVEN ARE LIKE AND HOW THEY CAME TO BE THERE ACCORDING TO AUGUSTINE. But he says that the waters which are above that heaven "are drawn up in the form of vapour and are suspended as very light drops; just as that cloudy air, by exhalation of the earth, draws up waters in the form of vapour, suspends them in very small particles, and, after they come together in larger masses, pours them back again as rain. And so if, as we see, water is able to reach such a small size that it is borne up as vapour above the air, which is naturally lighter than water, why may we not believe that it can also rise above that lighter heaven and rest there in the form of very small drops and very light vapours? But however they come to be there, we do not doubt that they are there."[6]

Chapter 5 (75)

1. WHAT THE SHAPE OF THE FIRMAMENT IS.—AUGUSTINE, IN *ON GENESIS*. "It is also usual to ask what the shape of heaven is. But although our [sacred] authors knew it, the Holy Spirit did not wish to say more through them than is profitable for our salvation."[1]

2. WHETHER HEAVEN IS FIXED OR MOVES, AND WHY IT IS CALLED THE FIRMAMENT. "It is also asked whether heaven is fixed or moves. If it moves, they say, how is it the firmament? If it stands still, how do the stars fixed in it move in a circle? It can be called the firmament not because it is at rest, but because it is a firm and intransgressible boundary of the waters. But if it is at rest, nothing impedes the stars from moving and circling."[2]

Chapter 6 (76)

WHY SCRIPTURE DID NOT SAY ABOUT THE WORK OF THE SECOND DAY WHAT IT SAID OF THE OTHERS. After these matters, it is usual to ask why it is not said here, as it was for the works of the other days: *God saw that it*

[5] Augustine, *De Genesi ad litteram*, bk 2 c1 n1.
[6] Ibid., bk 2 cc4-5 nn7-9.

[1] Augustine, *De Genesi ad litteram*, bk 2 c9 n20.
[2] Ibid., bk 2 c10 n23.

was good.[1] Some sign is here set forth: and perhaps it was not said here,[2] as it was done with regard to the others, because the number two is the principle of otherness and a sign of division.[3]

Chapter 7 (77)

ON THE WORK OF THE THIRD DAY, WHEN THE WATERS WERE GATHERED IN ONE PLACE. Next: *God said: Let the waters be gathered in one place and the dry land appear.*[1] The work of the third day is the gathering of the waters in one place.—BEDE: "For all the waters that were below heaven were gathered in one" source, "so that the light, which on the previous two days had illumined the waters with a clear light, might shine more fully in the pure air, and that the earth, which had lain hidden, might appear. And so the earth, which was muddy with water, might become dry and suitable for seedlings."[2] Indeed, on the same day, *the earth brought forth seed-bearing grasses and trees that bear fruit.*[3]

Chapter 8 (78)

BUT WHERE WERE THE WATERS GATHERED?—BEDE: "But if it is asked where the waters, which had covered space up to heaven, were gathered, it could be that the earth subsided and provided concave parts in which to receive the flowing waters. It can also be believed that these primal waters, which covered the earth like a cloud, were light, but were then condensed by being gathered together"[1] and so they could easily be gathered in one place.

2. HOW ALL THE WATERS WERE GATHERED IN ONE PLACE, SINCE THERE ARE MANY SEAS AND RIVERS. "And although it is clear that there are many seas and rivers, nevertheless it says that the waters were gathered in one place due to the interconnectedness of all the waters which are on the earth, since all rivers and seas are joined to the great sea. That explains why, after having said that all the waters were gathered in one place, it

[1]Gen. 1, 4; 1, 10; 1, 12, etc.
[2]According to the version of Genesis which Augustine followed, it was said here too: cf. *De Genesi ad litteram*, bk 2 c1 n1.
[3]Jerome, *Adversus Jovinianum*, bk 1 n16.

[1]Gen. 1, 9.
[2]Bede, *Libri quatuor in principium Genesis* 1, 9.
[3]Gen. 1, 12.

[1]Bede, *Libri quatuor in principium Genesis* 1, 9.

then adds in the plural: *And the gatherings of the waters*,[2] because of their many-branched channels; but the origin of all of them is the great sea."[3]

Chapter 9 (79)

1. ON THE WORK OF THE FOURTH DAY, WHEN THE LIGHT-GIVING BODIES WERE MADE. Next: *God said: Let there be lights in the firmament of heaven, and let them separate day from night.*[1]

2. THAT ON THE PRECEDING THREE DAYS, THE DISPOSITION AND SPATIAL ARRANGEMENT OF THE FOUR ELEMENTS HAD BEEN ACHIEVED; ON THE NEXT THREE DAYS, THE WORLD WAS ADORNED. On the preceding three days, the whole fabric of this world was disposed and arranged in its parts. For after the formation of light on the first day, so that it might illumine all things, the next two days were given to the highest and the lowest part of the world, namely to the firmament, the air, earth, and water. Indeed, on the second day, the firmament was spread out above; on the third day, with the gathering of the masses of water in their receptacles, the earth was revealed and the air was made clear. And so, on these days, the four elements of the world were differentiated and ordered in their places. But on the next three days, these four elements were adorned. For on the fourth day, the firmament was adorned with sun, moon, and stars. On the fifth, the air received the adornment of flying creatures and the waters of fishes. On the sixth, the earth received beasts of burden and reptiles and wild animals. After all these things, man was made, from earth and on earth; and yet not for earth or for earth's sake, but for heaven and for the sake of heaven.

3. THE ADORNMENT OF HEAVEN IS TREATED BEFORE THE OTHERS BECAUSE IT WAS DONE FIRST. And because heaven excels the other elements in its beauty and was made before the others, so it was also adorned before the others, on the fourth day, when the heavenly bodies were made.

Chapter 10 (80)

FOR WHAT USE THE LIGHT-GIVING BODIES WERE MADE.—AUGUSTINE, *ON GENESIS*. And they were made so that through them, "the lower part should be illumined so as not to be dark to its inhabitants. And provision was made for the weakness of men, so that, by the circling of the sun, they should have the succession of day and night on account of the need for sleep and wakefulness. And also so that the night should not remain

[2]Cf. Gen. 1, 10.
[3]Bede, *Libri quatuor in principium Genesis* 1, 9.

[1]Gen. 1, 14.

devoid of beauty, and that those men who find it needful to work at night should be consoled by the moon and stars; moreover, there are some animals which cannot bear the light."[1]

Chapter 11 (81)

HOW THAT STATEMENT IS TO BE TAKEN: TO BE AS SIGNS AND FOR THE FIXING OF TIMES.—AUGUSTINE, IN THE SAME PLACE. But it is usual to ask how the phrase that follows is to be taken: *to be as signs and for the fixing of times and days and years.*[1] For this appears to be said as if time began on the fourth day, as if the previous three days had been without time. And so we must take the times marked by the stars not as units of time marked by duration, but as climatic changes, because these occur by the movement of the heavenly bodies, as do the days and the years to which we are accustomed. For they are *as signs* of calm weather and of storms; and *for the fixing of times* because through them we distinguish the four seasons of the year, namely spring, summer, fall, and winter.[2]—BEDE: Or they are *as signs and for the fixing of the times*, that is, to keep distinct the hours of time, "because, before they were made, the order of time was not marked by any indicators, whether of the noon hour or of any other."[3]—These were made on the fourth day.

DISTINCTION XV

Chapter 1 (82)

ON THE WORK OF THE FIFTH DAY, WHEN FROM THE WATERS GOD MADE FLYING AND SWIMMING CREATURES. *And God said: Let the waters bring forth the crawling creature of living spirit and the one to fly over the earth*, etc.[4] The work of the fifth day is the formation of fishes and birds, by which two elements are adorned. And he created fishes and birds from the same matter, that is, from the waters, raising the flying creatures into the air and sending the swimming ones back into the deep.

Chapter 2 (83)

ON THE WORK OF THE SIXTH DAY, WHEN THE ANIMALS AND THE CRAWLING CREATURES OF THE EARTH WERE CREATED. Next: *God said: Let the earth*

[1]Augustine, *De Genesi ad litteram*, bk 2 c13 n27.

[1]Gen. 1, 14.
[2]Augustine, *De Genesi ad litteram*, bk 2 c14 nn28-29.
[3]Bede, *Libri quatuor in principium Genesis* 1, 14.
[4]Gen. 1, 20.

bring forth living creatures, beasts of burden and crawling creatures and the wild animals of the earth, according to their kinds, etc.[5] The work of the sixth day is described when the earth is said to be adorned with its animals.

Chapter 3 (84)

WHETHER HARMFUL POISONOUS ANIMALS WERE MADE AFTER SIN, OR WHETHER THEY WERE MADE HARMLESS FIRST AND THEN BEGAN TO DO HARM AFTER SIN.—AUGUSTINE, *ON GENESIS*. It is usual to ask, concerning poisonous and dangerous animals, whether they were created after man's sin as punishment, or whether creatures which had first been harmless began to be harmful to those who had sinned.—SOLUTION. It can unequivocally be said that created things would have done no harm to man, if he had not sinned. For they began to be harmful in order to punish vices and scare their practitioners, or to test and perfect virtue. And so they were created harmless, but were made harmful because of sin.[1]

Chapter 4 (85)

WHETHER SOME VERY SMALL ANIMALS WERE CREATED AT THAT TIME.—AUGUSTINE. There is also the question of whether some very small animals were created in these original conditions, or whether they came into existence afterwards from corrupted things. For many such are generated from the defects or exhalations of humid bodies, or from corpses; some also from the rotting of woods, grasses, and fruits; and God is the author of all.[1]—SOLUTION.—AUGUSTINE. But it may be said that those which are born from the bodies of animals, particularly of dead ones, were not created with the animals, except potentially and materially; however, those which are born from the earth or from waters, or from those things which come from the germinating earth, may not incongruously be said to have been created at that time.[2]

Chapter 5 (86)

1. WHY MAN WAS MADE AFTER ALL THINGS. When all things had been created and properly ordered, man was made last of all as their lord and

[5]Gen. 1, 24.

[1]Augustine, *De Genesi ad litteram*, bk 3 c15 n24.

[1]Augustine, *De Genesi ad litteram*, bk 3 c14 n22.
[2]Ibid., bk 3 c14 n23.

possessor who was to be set over all of them. Hence it follows: *God saw that it was good, and said: Let us make man*, etc.[1]

2. BEFORE HE TREATS THE MAKING OF MAN, HE DISCUSSES MORE FULLY THE MANNER OF THE FIRST CONDITION OF THINGS, WHICH HE HAS BRIEFLY TOUCHED UPON EARLIER: AS TO THIS, CATHOLICS SEEM TO DISAGREE. SOME SAY THAT THE WORLD WAS CREATED ALL AT ONCE AS IT IS IN MATTER AND FORM, BUT OTHERS THAT IT WAS MADE AT INTERVALS OF TIMES AND DAYS; THE EXPOSITION ABOVE HAS THUS FAR FOLLOWED THIS LATTER VIEW. But before we treat the creation of man, let us make clearer, by a fuller examination, what we briefly touched upon earlier.[2] For as we said above, Catholic writers are seen to disagree as to this distinction of things. Some say that things were created and distinguished according to their kinds at intervals in the course of six days. Because their view seems to be better supported by the literal meaning of Genesis, and the Church favours it, we have thus far studiously taught that common and formless matter was made first, and afterwards the various classes of corporeal things were formed distinctly from it over the course of six days.

Chapter 6 (87)

1. HERE HE PURSUES THE OPINION OF THOSE WHO CONTEND THAT ALL THINGS WERE CREATED SIMULTANEOUSLY. But it seems to others that things were not made at intervals of time, but came forth into being already formed and all at once. Augustine, in *On Genesis*, strives to prove this in several ways.[1] He says that the four elements existed from the beginning in the forms in which they now appear, and heaven was adorned with its stars; some things, however, were then made materially, not formally, and afterwards, with the passage of time, they were distinguished in their forms, like plants, trees, and perhaps animals. And so these say that all things were made at the very beginning of time, but some formally and according to the forms which we see they have, like the larger parts of the world; some, however, were only made materially.

2. But Moses, they say, speaking to a rough and carnal people, tempered his manner of speech, speaking of God by analogy with man, who completes his works over periods of time, even though he had done his works all at once. Hence Augustine says: "And so Moses reports that God did those works separately because what could be done by God simultaneously could not be said by man simultaneously."[2] Also: "Scripture

[1]Gen. 1, 25-26.
[2]Above, dist. 12 c2.

[1]Augustine, *De Genesi ad litteram*, bk 1 cc14-15 nn28-29; bk 4 cc33-34, nn51-55; bk 7 c28 n42.
[2]Cf. Augustine, *De Genesi ad litteram*, bk 1 c15 n29.

was able to split up in time, in the telling of it, what God had not split up in the doing."[3] Those who agree with these and similar authorities say that the four elements and heaven's light-giving bodies came into being at once already formed. They term those six days which Scripture recalls the six classes of things, or distinctions, which were made simultaneously, in part formally, in part causally.

Chapter 7 (88)

HOW IT IS TO BE UNDERSTOOD THAT GOD RESTED FROM ALL HIS WORK. It is now suitable that we say something about resting on the seventh day. It is written that *on the seventh day, God completed his work, and he rested on the seventh day from all the work which he had done.*[1]—BEDE: God is said to have rested on the seventh day, "not as if he were tired from his work, but he rested from *all the work* because he ceased to make any new creature. For to rest means to cease; hence in the Apocalypse: *They had no rest, saying: Holy, holy, holy,*[2] that is, they did not cease to say this."[3] —AUGUSTINE: And so God is said to have rested, because "he ceased from making kinds of creatures, because he did not make any further new ones. And yet even to this very day, as Truth says in the Gospel, the Father works with the Son,[4] namely in governing all those kinds which were then established at that time. For the power of the Creator is the cause of every creature's existence. And so the phrase: *My Father works even now, and I, too, work*[5] shows his continuing governance of every creature. And on the seventh day, he rested, so that he made no more new creatures whose matter or form had not already existed; but he works even now so as not to cease holding together and governing what he established."[6]

Chapter 8 (89)

1. HOW IS IT TO BE TAKEN THAT GOD IS SAID TO HAVE COMPLETED HIS WORK ON THE SEVENTH DAY, WHEN HE THEN RESTED FROM ALL HIS WORK. But it is asked how God is said to have completed his work on the seventh day, when on that day he rested from all his work, and he did he not make any new kind of thing.

[3]Augustine, *De Genesi ad litteram*, bk 1 c15 nn29.

[1]Gen. 2, 2.
[2]Apoc. 4, 8.
[3]Bede, *Libri quatuor in principium Genesis* 2, 2.
[4]Cf. Jn. 5, 17.
[5]Jn. 5, 17.
[6]Augustine, *De Genesi ad litteram*, bk 4 c12 nn22-23.

2. ACCORDING TO ANOTHER VERSION, WHICH AUGUSTINE FOLLOWS, NO QUESTION ARISES HERE. Another translation has: *God completed his work on the sixth day,*[1] which leaves no cause for question, because things that were made on that day were manifest, and the completion of all things was brought to perfection on that day, as Scripture shows by saying: *God saw all the things that he had made, and they were very good.*[2]

Chapter 9 (90)

1. HOW ALL THE THINGS WHICH GOD MADE ARE SAID TO BE VERY GOOD.—AUGUSTINE, IN THE *ENCHIRIDION*. For all these things were naturally good and they had nothing of vice in their nature. And the things which God established are good "even singly, but in their totality they are *very good*, because the wonderful beauty of the universe is composed of all of them. In this universe, even that which is called evil is well ordered and has its place; it makes the good things more eminently attractive, so that they should please more and be more worthy of praise when they are compared to evil things."[1] And so on the sixth day, the completion of all things was achieved.

2. HERE HE RETURNS TO THE QUESTION WHICH HE HAD POSED, NAMELY HOW IT IS TRUE THAT GOD COMPLETED HIS WORK ON THE SEVENTH DAY.—BEDE. And so the question posed earlier arises, "how is God said to have completed his work on the seventh day, as the Hebrew text has it, on which day he, nevertheless, is said not to have created anything new. (SOLUTION.) Perhaps, he is said to have completed his work on the seventh day because he blessed and sanctified it, as Scripture immediately adds: *He blessed the seventh day and sanctified it.*[2] For blessing and sanctification is work, as Solomon did some work when he dedicated the temple."[3,4]

Chapter 10 (91)

1. WHAT THE SANCTIFICATION AND BLESSING OF THE SEVENTH DAY IS. But he is said to have sanctified and blessed that day because he endowed it with a mystical blessing and sanctification above and beyond the other days. And so the Law says: *Remember to sanctify the Sabbath day.*[1]

[1]Cf. Augustine, *De Genesi ad litteram*, bk 4 c1.
[2]Gen. 1, 31.

[1]Augustine, *Enchiridion*, cc10-11.
[2]Gen. 2, 3.
[3]Cf. 3 Kings 8.
[4]Bede, *Libri quatuor in principium Genesis*, 1.

[1]Exod. 20, 8.

2. WHY WE STOP AT SEVEN IN OUR NUMBERING OF THE DAYS. And so it is that, in numbering the days, we stop at seven and say that there are seven days, by the repetition of which all time is marked. It is not that there is not an eighth day, and a ninth, and so on, but that the various kinds of things were distinguished in six days, and on the seventh, although no new kind of thing was established, yet there was in it a new state, as it were, of sanctification of works and rest for the worker.

3. ANOTHER SOLUTION, BY WHICH THE LETTER IS EXPOUNDED. That text may also be expounded as follows: *On the seventh day, God completed his work*,[2] that is, he saw that it was complete and brought to perfection.

DISTINCTION XVI

Chapter 1 (92)

ON THE CREATION OF MAN, IN WHICH IS TO BE CONSIDERED WHY MAN WAS CREATED AND HOW HE WAS ESTABLISHED: THESE TWO WERE TREATED ABOVE; ALSO, WHAT HE WAS LIKE WHEN HE WAS MADE AND HOW HE FELL, AND FINALLY HOW HE WAS RESTORED: THESE ARE TO BE DISCUSSED. After having gone over these things, we now take up what we promised above to fulfil and explain in order concerning the creation of man.[3] In this, the following seem worthy of consideration: namely why man was created and how he was established, and with what qualities and in what manner he was made; then, how he fell; finally, how and by what means he was restored. But the first and second of these, namely the cause of human creation and the manner of establishment, we have treated above to the best of our small ability.[4] And so it remains for us to discuss with what qualities and in what manner he was made.

Chapter 2 (93)

HOW 'LET US MAKE MAN IN OUR IMAGE AND LIKENESS' IS TO BE UNDERSTOOD. In Genesis, we read: *Let us make man in our image and likeness*.[1] —BEDE: "In saying *let us make*, the one operation of the three persons is shown; but in saying *in our image and likeness*, the one and equal substance"[2] of the three persons is demonstrated. For this is said in the person of the Father to the Son and the Holy Spirit, and not, as some hold, to the

[2]Gen. 2, 2.
[3]See above, dist. 15 c5.
[4]Above, dist. 1 cc4-6.

[1]Gen. 1, 26.
[2]Bede, *Libri quatuor in principium Genesis* 1, 26.

angels, because the image or likeness of God and the angels is not one and the same.

Chapter 3 (94)

1. THAT 'IMAGE' AND 'LIKENESS' HERE IS TAKEN DIFFERENTLY BY DIFFERENT PEOPLE: BY SOME AS UNCREATED, BY OTHERS AS CREATED; AND THE UNCREATED ONE EITHER AS THE ESSENCE OF THE TRINITY, OR AS THE SON AND HOLY SPIRIT. But image and likeness in this passage is understood either as uncreated, that is, the essence of the Trinity, after which man was made; or created, in which man was made and which was given shape in man. Bede appears to have understood the image which is God to be uncreated, when he says that it is not the image of God and the angels that is one and the same, but that of the three persons;[1] and so speech there is addressed to the persons and not to the angels.—But image is improperly said, because an image is so called relative to something whose likeness it bears and which it was made to represent. So it was with the image of Caesar, which bore his likeness and in some way represented him. But it is improper to call that in whose likeness something is made an image, just as it is proper to call that which is taken from something else a copy, and that from which something is taken an exemplar. And yet, in violation of proper usage, sometimes the one is posited for the other; and so it is less than properly that image is taken as 'essence of the Trinity,' if indeed that is what is meant by the term 'image' in this passage.

2. THE OPINION OF THOSE WHO HELD THAT THE SON IS TO BE TAKEN HERE BY THE TERMS IMAGE AND LIKENESS. The Son, however, is properly called the image of the Father, as we said above, in the treatise on the Trinity.[2]—AUGUSTINE, IN *ON THE TRINITY*, BOOK 7. Hence, there were a few "who made a distinction, in such a way that they understood the Son to be the image in this passage; man, however, they said was not the image, but was made after the image. The Apostle refutes them, saying: *For a man is the image and glory of God*.[3] Indeed, this image, that is, man, when he is said to be made in the image, is not said to be made as if after the Son; otherwise, the Father would not say *in our image*. For how could he say *our*, since the Son is the image of the Father alone?"[4]

3. THE OPINION OF OTHERS WHO SAID THAT IMAGE [REFERS TO] THE SON AND LIKENESS TO THE HOLY SPIRIT. But there were also others treating these matters with greater acuity who by *image* understood the Son and by *likeness* the Holy Spirit, who is the likeness of Father and Son. And so

[1] Above, at the end of c2.
[2] Above, Bk 1 dist. 27 c3 nn4-6.
[3] 1 Cor. 11, 7.
[4] Augustine, *De Trinitate*, bk 7 c6 n12.

they held that *our* was said in the plural by reference to *likeness* alone; but *image* was to be understood as if preceded by *my*. Man, however, they taught, is also an image, made in the image and likeness [of God], and that he is an image of the image and likeness.

4. HE DOES NOT APPROVE THE VIEW OF THESE LATTER, BUT HE TEACHES THAT THE IMAGE AND LIKENESS OF GOD IS TO BE SOUGHT AND CONSIDERED IN MAN, AND THAT IMAGE AND LIKENESS IS UNDERSTOOD TO BE CREATED. But although this distinction does not seem entirely worthy of rejection, nevertheless, because it does not emanate from *the middle* of the mountain,[5] that is, from the authorities of the Saints, the image and likeness of God is more fittingly to be sought and considered in man himself.

5. IN WHAT THINGS IS THE IMAGE AND LIKENESS CONSIDERED. And so man was made in the image and likeness of God in respect to his mind, by which he excels irrational creatures;[6] in his image, however, according to memory, intelligence, and love;[7] in his likeness according to innocence and justice, which are naturally in the rational mind.—Or image is considered in the knowledge of truth, his likeness in the love of virtue; or image in all other things, likeness in the essence, because it is immortal and indivisible.—Hence Augustine, in the book *On the Quantity of the Soul*: "The soul was made like God, because God made it immortal and indestructible."[8] And so image pertains to form, likeness to nature. Hence man was made, in respect to his soul, in the image and likeness, not of Father or Son or Holy Spirit, but of the whole Trinity.

6. THAT BOTH THE IMAGE ITSELF AND THAT IN WHOM IT IS IS CALLED THE IMAGE OF GOD.—AUGUSTINE, IN *ON THE TRINITY*, BOOK 15. And so, in respect to his soul, man is said to be the image of God because the image of God is in him, "just as both the canvas and the picture which is on it are called images. But it is because of the picture which is on it that the canvas too is called an image; similarly, because of the image of the Trinity, even that which contains this image is called by the name of image."[9]

Chapter 4 (95)

1. WHY IS MAN SAID TO BE IMAGE AND IN THE IMAGE, BUT THE SON IS SAID TO BE IMAGE, BUT NOT IN THE IMAGE. And so man is said to be both image and in the image; the Son, however, is image, but not in the image, because he was born, not created, equal and in no way unlike. Man was created by God, not begotten; he is not equal by parity, but approaches

[5]Cf. Ps. 103, 10.
[6]Augustine, *De Genesi ad litteram*, bk 3 c20 n30.
[7]See above, Bk 1 dist. 3 c2.
[8]Augustine, *De quantitate animae*, c2 n3.
[9]Augustine, *De Trinitate*, bk 15 c23 n43.

God by some likeness. Hence Augustine, in *On the Trinity*, book 7: "We read in Genesis: *Let us make man in our image and likeness.*[1] It said *let us make* and *our* in the plural, and it is not fitting for this to be taken other than of relations, so that Father, Son, and Holy Spirit be understood to make man in the image of Father, Son, and Holy Spirit that man might subsist as image of God. But because that image was not made entirely equal, as not being born from him, but created by him, so man is an image in such a way that he is in the image because he is not made equal by parity, but approaches by some likeness. The Son, however, is image, but not in the image, because he is equal to the Father. Therefore, man is said to be *in the image* because of the unequal likeness; and *our*, so that man be understood to be the image of the Trinity, and not equal to the Trinity, as the Son is equal to the Father."[2] See, it has been shown in what respect man is like God, namely in respect to the soul.

2. THAT HE MAY BE SAID TO HAVE BEEN MADE IN THE LIKENESS OF GOD IN RESPECT TO THE BODY.—BEDE. But also "in the body, he has some property which indicates this, because his stature is erect, so that the body suits the rational soul because it is erect toward heaven."[3]

DISTINCTION XVII

Chapter 1 (96)

1. ON THE CREATION OF THE SOUL, WHETHER IT WAS MADE FROM SOMETHING OR NOT, AND WHEN IT WAS MADE, AND WHAT GRACE IT RECEIVED AT ITS CREATION. Here it is usual to ask many things concerning the origin of the soul, namely from what it was created, and when, and what grace it received in creation.

2. The formation of man in respect to the body is described in the statement: *God formed man from the mud of the ground*;[1] similarly, his making in respect to the soul is described by what comes next: *And breathed in his face the breath of life*. For God formed the body from the mud of the earth and *breathed* the soul in it, or, according to another version, *blew* or *blew forth* the soul.[2] It is not that he blew with his cheeks or formed the body with corporeal hands: for God is spirit and not composed of the features of limbs.

[1]Gen. 1, 26.
[2]Augustine, *De Trinitate*, bk 7 c6 n13.
[3]Bede, *Libri quatuor in principium Genesis* 1, 26.

[1]Gen. 2, 7.
[2]According to the Septuagint.

3. THAT GOD IS NOT TO BE UNDERSTOOD TO HAVE FORMED OR BLOWN BY CORPOREAL MEANS.—BEDE: "Therefore, let us not carnally hold that God formed the body with corporeal hands or breathed the soul with his cheeks," but rather that it was "by commanding and willing" that he *formed man from the mud of the ground* in respect to the body, that is, he willed it and "by his word commanded that it be so; and he *breathed in his face the breath of life*,[3] that is, he created the substance of the soul in which he might live,"[4] and not from any corporeal or spiritual matter, but from nothing.

4. THE OPINION OF SOME HERETICS WHO HELD THAT THE SOUL IS FROM THE SUBSTANCE OF GOD. For some heretics held that God created the soul from his own substance.[5] Adhering stubbornly to the words of Scripture, where it says: *he breathed*, or *he blew forth*, etc., they say that, when a man breathes or blows forth, he sends out his breath from himself; so also, when God is said to have blown forth or breathed his breath in the face of man, he is understood to have sent out the spirit of man from himself, that is, from his own substance.

5. RESPONSE OF AUGUSTINE. Those who say this do not understand that *breathed* or *blew,* was said metaphorically, that is, God made the breath of man, namely the soul. For to blow is to make a breath; to make a breath is to make a soul, hence the Lord says through Isaias: *I made every breath.*[6] —"Do not listen to those who hold that the soul is part of God. For if this were so, it could not be deceived by itself or another, nor could it be compelled to do or suffer evil, nor could it be changed for better or worse. And so the breath by which he animated man was made by God, not from God; nor from any matter, but from nothing."[7]

Chapter 2 (97)

1. HERE [HE CONSIDERS] WHEN THE SOUL WAS MADE, WHETHER BEFORE THE BODY OR IN THE BODY. But whether [it was made] in the body or outside the body is also a tangled question among the learned.

2. OPINION OF AUGUSTINE, WHO SAYS THAT IT WAS CREATED WITH THE ANGELS AND CAME INTO THE BODY BY ITS OWN WILL. For Augustine, in *On Genesis*, teaches that the soul was created with the angels and without a body; it came into the body afterwards.[1] And it was not compelled to come into the body, but "it willed this naturally, that is, it was created so

[3]Gen. 2, 7.
[4]Bede, *Libri quatuor in principium Genesis* 2, 7.
[5]Cf. Augustine, *De Genesi ad litteram*, bk 7 cc2-3.
[6]Is. 57, 16, according to the Septuagint.
[7]Bede, *Libri quatuor in principium Genesis* 2, 7.

[1]Augustine, *De Genesi ad litteram*, bk 7 c24 n35.

as to will it, just as it is natural for us to will to live. But to will to live evilly does not pertain to nature, but to a perverse will."[2]

3. THE VIEW OF OTHERS WHO SAY THAT THE SOUL WAS CREATED IN THE BODY. But others say that the soul of the first man was created in the body, and they expound those words: *And breathed in his face the breath of life*,[3] as follows, that is, he created the soul in the body so that it might animate the whole body. It especially mentioned the *face* because this part is adorned with the senses for pondering higher things.[4]

4. But whatever may be thought about the soul of the first man, it is most certainly to be held about the others that their souls are created in the body: for in creating them God infuses them, and creates by infusing them.[5]

5. THAT THAT SOUL HAD NO FOREKNOWLEDGE OF FUTURE DEEDS.—AUGUSTINE. It is to be said "too that that soul was not created so as to have foreknowledge of future deeds, just or unjust."[6]

Chapter 3 (98)

1. AT WHAT AGE OF LIFE WAS MAN WHEN GOD MADE HIM. It is also usual to ask whether God made man immediately of a fully mature age, or whether as progressing and growing in age, as now he forms [us] in [our] mother's womb.

2. MAN WAS MADE OF A FULLY MATURE AGE, AND THIS IN ACCORDANCE WITH HIGHER CAUSES, NOT LOWER ONES. Augustine, in *On Genesis*, says that Adam was made immediately of a fully mature age;[1] and this in accordance with higher causes, not lower ones, that is, according to God's will and power, which he did not bind to the kinds of nature [which he had created], just as the staff of Moses was turned into a snake.[2] "Such things are not done against nature, except for us, for whom the course of nature has been known [in the past] to be otherwise; for God, however, nature is what he does."[3] "And so God did not do this against his own disposition. For it was in the first condition of causes that man could be so made, but it was not necessary that he should be so made there. For this was not in the condition of the creature, but in the good pleasure of the Creator, whose will is necessity."[4] "For that necessarily will be which

[2]Augustine, *De Genesi ad litteram*, bk 7 c27 n38.
[3]Gen. 2, 7.
[4]Cf. Bede, *Libri quatuor in principium Genesis* 2, 7.
[5]See below, dist. 18 c7.
[6]Augustine, *De Genesi ad litteram*, bk 7 c26.

[1]Augustine, *De Genesi ad litteram*, bk 6 c13.
[2]Exod. 7, 10-11.
[3]Augustine, *De Genesi ad litteram*, bk 6 c13 n24.
[4]Ibid., bk 6 c15.

he wills and foreknows. Many things, however, would be according to lower causes which are not going to be in God's foreknowledge. But if they are going to be otherwise in his foreknowledge, then they are going to be as they are there, where he who cannot be deceived foreknows them."[5]—And so Adam was so made not according to lower causes, for it was not in the seminal causes of things that he should be so made, but according to higher causes, which do not work against nature, because it was in the natural causes of things that he could be so made.

Chapter 4 (99)

THAT MAN WAS CREATED OUTSIDE PARADISE AND WAS PLACED IN PARADISE, AND WHY IT WAS SO DONE. As Scripture teaches, *God took man*,[1] who had been so formed, *and placed him in the paradise of delights*,[2] which *he had planted from the beginning*.[3] With these words, Moses plainly indicates that man, who was created outside paradise, was afterwards placed in paradise. This is said to have been done because he was not going to remain in it; or so that this might be ascribed not to nature, but to grace.

Chapter 5 (100)

1. THAT THAT PARADISE WAS EARTHLY AND LOCAL. But the paradise in which man was placed is understood to be local and earthly.

2. THERE ARE THREE VIEWS OF PARADISE, AND WHAT THEY ARE. For there are three general views of paradise: one is that of those who wish it to be understood exclusively in a corporeal sense; second, that of those who wish it to be understood only spiritually; third, that of those who take paradise in both senses. I profess that the third one pleases me, that man is placed in a corporeal paradise.

3. FROM WHAT BEGINNING WAS PARADISE PLANTED.—BEDE. It can be taken to have been planted from that *beginning* at which God, after the removal of the waters, commanded the whole earth to produce plants and trees.[1]

4. WHAT KIND OF PLACE PARADISE IS AND WHERE IT IS. He holds that, although paradise is, as it were, the type of the present or future Church, yet it is literally to be understood to be a large and most pleasant place with fruitful trees, kept fertile by a great spring. And where we read *from*

[5]Augustine, *De Genesi ad litteram*, bk 6 c17.

[1]Gen. 2, 15.
[2]Ibid.
[3]Gen. 2, 8.

[1]Bede, *Libri quatuor in principium Genesis* 2, 8. See Gen. 1, 11.

the beginning, an ancient translation says *toward the Orient.*[2] And so some want paradise to be in the Eastern parts, hidden from the regions inhabited by men by a long intervening stretch of sea or land; and it is placed on high, extending up to the moon's orbit. So it was that the waters of the Flood did not reach there.

Chapter 6 (101)

1. ON THE TREES OF PARADISE, AMONG WHICH WAS THE TREE OF LIFE, AND THE TREE OF THE KNOWLEDGE OF GOOD AND EVIL. And in this paradise, there were trees of different kinds, among which there was one that was called *the tree of life,* and another *the tree of the knowledge of good and evil.*[1]

2. WHY IT WAS CALLED THE TREE OF LIFE. As Bede and Strabus teach,[2] it was called the tree *of life* because it was divinely given the power that, if one ate of its fruit, one's body would be strengthened in constant health and perpetual firmness, and it would not fall, by any illness or infirmity of age, into debility or death.

Chapter 7 (102)

1. WHY IT WAS CALLED THE TREE OF THE KNOWLEDGE OF GOOD AND EVIL. But the tree of the knowledge of good and evil did not take its name from nature, but by reason of what happened afterwards.—Augustine, in *On Genesis*: "For that tree was not evil, but it was called *of the knowledge of good and evil* because, after God's prohibition, a transgression would be done regarding it by which man would learn from his experience the difference between the good of obedience and the evil of disobedience. And so the name was not used in regard to the fruit which would issue from that tree, but in regard to the thing that would follow the transgression."[1] For man knew good and evil before he touched this tree; he knew the good, however, through both prudence and experience, but the evil only through prudence. He knew it also by experience, however, after his illicit use of the tree which had been forbidden to him, because by his experience of evil he learned the difference between the good of obedience and the evil of disobedience.

2. EVEN IF THE FIRST HUMANS HAD NOT SINNED, IT WOULD NONETHELESS BE CALLED THE TREE OF THE KNOWLEDGE OF GOOD AND EVIL. But if

[2]Septuagint.

[1]Cf. Gen. 1, 11.
[2]Cf. Bede, *Libri quatuor in principium Genesis* 2, 9, and ordinary gloss, on Gen. 2, 9.

[1]Augustine, *De Genesi ad litteram*, bk 8 c6 n12.

our first parents had been obedient and had not sinned against God's command, yet it would nonetheless be called *the tree of the knowledge of good and evil*, because the same would have happened from touching it, if it had been taken without right.— AUGUSTINE, IN *ON GENESIS*: "And so man was forbidden the tree which was not [in itself] evil, so that the very keeping of the command should be a good to him, its transgression an evil. There is no better way to consider how evil disobedience is than this, namely that man is perceived to have been made guilty by touching a thing after having been prohibited to do so, when, if he had touched it without having been so prohibited, he would neither have sinned, nor incurred punishment. For if you touch a poisonous plant after being forbidden to do so, a punishment follows; even if no one had forbidden it, the punishment would still follow. If a thing is forbidden to be touched whose touching would be harmful to the one who forbids, and not to the one who touches it, as in the case of a person's money, then the touching is a sin to the one forbidden because it is harmful to the one forbidding. But when something is touched which, if not forbidden, is not harmful to the toucher, nor to anyone else if it were touched, then it is prohibited so that the good of obedience and the evil of disobedience might be shown in themselves."[2] And so the first man, forbidden from a good thing, incurs punishment so that the penalty would be shown to be not from an evil thing, but from disobedience, just as the palm [of victory] is from obedience.[3]

DISTINCTION XVIII

Chapter 1 (103)

1. ON THE FORMATION OF WOMAN. And in the same paradise, God formed a woman from the substance of the man. After the planting of paradise and the placing of man in it, and after all the animals had been brought before him and had been designated by their names, Scripture adds: *God cast Adam into a deep sleep and, as he slept, took one of his ribs* and formed it *into a woman*.[4]

2. WHY HE FIRST CREATED MAN, AND AFTERWARDS THE WOMAN FROM THE MAN, AND NOT BOTH AT ONCE. Here we must attend to why he did not create man and woman at the same time, as with the angels, but first created the man, and afterwards the woman from the man. For this reason: namely that there should be one beginning of humankind, so that the devil's pride should be confounded in this and the lowliness of human

[2]Augustine, *De Genesi ad litteram*, bk 8 c13 nn28-29.
[3]Cf. Prov. 21, 28.
[4]Gen. 2, 21-22.

nature be raised by its likeness to God. For the devil had desired to be one beginning other than God; in order that the devil's pride might be blunted, man received in gift that which the devil had perversely wanted to steal, but was not able to obtain. And through this, the image of God appeared in the man because, as God was the beginning of creation for all things, so the man was the beginning of generation for all men.

3. ANOTHER REASON WHY ALL HUMAN BEINGS ARE FROM THE ONE MAN. God also willed all human beings to be from the one man so that, recognizing that they are all from one, they might love each other as if one.

Chapter 2 (104)

WHY WOMAN WAS FORMED FROM THE MAN'S SIDE AND NOT FROM SOME OTHER PART OF HIS BODY. But although woman was made from man for these reasons, nevertheless she was formed not from just any part of his body, but from his side, so that it should be shown that she was created for the partnership of love, lest, if perhaps she had been made from his head, she should be perceived as set over man in domination; or if from his feet, as if subject to him in servitude. Therefore, since she was made neither to dominate, nor to serve the man, but as his partner, she had to be produced neither from his head, nor from his feet, but from his side, so that he would know that she was to be placed beside himself whom he had learned had been taken from his side.

Chapter 3 (105)

1. WHY THE RIB WAS TAKEN FROM THE MAN WHILE ASLEEP AND NOT WHILE AWAKE. It was also not without cause that the rib was taken from the man while asleep rather than while awake from which the woman was made in order to be of help to man in generation. This was done so that it might be demonstrated that he was undergoing no punishment by this, and at the same time a wonderful work of divine power was shown, a power which opened the side of the sleeping man, and yet did not arouse him from the repose of sleep.

2. ON THE SACRAMENT OF THIS WORK. In this work, the sacrament of Christ and his Church is also prefigured. For just as the woman was formed from the side of the sleeping man, so the Church was formed from the sacraments which flowed from the side of Christ sleeping on the cross, namely blood and water, by which we are redeemed from punishments and washed clean of our faults.

Chapter 4 (106)

1. THAT BY GOD'S POWER, SHE WAS MADE FROM THAT RIB, WITHOUT THE ADDITION OF ANYTHING EXTRINSIC, JUST AS THE FIVE LOAVES OF BREAD WERE MULTIPLIED FROM THEMSELVES. It is also usual to ask whether the woman was made from that rib, without the addition of anything extrinsic. This did not please some people. But if God added anything extrinsic in making the body of the woman, then the addition would be greater than the rib itself; and so the woman should rather be said to have been made from that from which she had received the greater part of her substance than from the rib. So it remains that the body of the woman be said to have been made by divine power from the substance of that rib alone, without any extrinsic addition, by that very same miracle by which Jesus would later multiply the five loaves of bread with a heavenly blessing, and five thousand men were filled.[5]

2. THAT ALTHOUGH THAT WORK WAS COMPLETED WITH THE SERVICE OF ANGELS, YET THE ANGELS WERE NOT CREATORS.—AUGUSTINE, IN *ON GENESIS*. It is also fitting to know that, although the formation of woman was done with the service of angels, yet the power of creation is not to be attributed to them. "For the angels cannot create any nature: and so they could neither form the rib into the woman, nor make up for the deficiency of flesh in the place of the rib. It is not that they do not act so that something is created, but not in such a way that they are creators, just as farmers are not the creators of crops and trees."[1] God alone, that is, the Trinity, is creator. "And so the woman was made by God, even if the rib was made ready by angels."[2]

Chapter 5 (107)

1. WHETHER WOMAN WAS SO MADE ACCORDING TO HIGHER OR LOWER CAUSES, THAT IS, WHETHER SEMINAL REASON ARRANGED IT THAT SHE BE SO MADE, OR ONLY THAT SHE BE ABLE TO BE SO MADE, BUT THAT THE CAUSE THAT SHE BE SO MADE WAS IN GOD ALONE.—AUGUSTINE, IN *ON GENESIS*: But it is asked whether the order which God created with the first works arranged it that, in accordance with itself, the woman must necessarily be made from the side of the man, or only that it was possible that she be so made.[1]

2. HE DISCUSSES THE CAUSES OF THINGS MORE BROADLY: THAT THE CAUSES WHICH ARE IN GOD ARE PROPERLY CALLED PRIMORDIAL, AND WHY

[5]Cf. Mt. 14, 15-21.

[1]Augustine, *De Genesi ad litteram*, bk 9 c15 n26.
[2]Ibid., bk 9 c16 n30.

[1]Augustine, *De Genesi ad litteram*, bk 9 c17 n31.

THEY ARE SPOKEN OF IN THE PLURAL. With regard to this, it is to be known that the causes of all things are in God from eternity: for it has been in God's power and disposition from eternity that man, or a horse and suchlike, should be so made. And these are called primordial causes, because they are not preceded by other causes, but they precede the others, and are the causes of causes. But although divine power, disposition, or will is one thing, and so the principal cause of all things is one, yet, because of its different effects, Augustine says in the plural that the primordial causes of all things are in God, using the metaphor of the artificer in whose disposition lies what kind of box is to be made.[2] So also the cause of each future thing preceded in God.

3. THAT NOT ALL THE THINGS WHICH ARE MADE HAVE THEIR CAUSES IN CREATURES. The causes of many things, but not of all of them, are in creatures because, as Augustine says, God placed seminal reasons in things. By these reasons, some things come from others, as such a grain from this seed, such a fruit from this tree, and suchlike.[3]

4. THAT EVEN THE CAUSES WHICH ARE IN CREATURES ARE NEVERTHELESS CALLED PRIMORDIAL, ALTHOUGH IMPROPERLY, AND WHY THEY ARE SO CALLED. And these are also called primordial causes, even though not properly so, since they have an eternal cause that precedes them, which properly and universally is the first cause. But they are called first in respect to certain things, namely the ones that come from them.—ANOTHER REASON WHY THEY ARE CALLED PRIMORDIAL. They are also called primordial because they were placed in things by God at the first creation of things. And just as creatures are changeable, so these causes can also be changed; but whatever is a cause in the unchangeable God cannot be changed.

Chapter 6 (108)

1. A MOST USEFUL DISTINCTION BETWEEN THE CAUSES OF THINGS, NAMELY THAT SOME ARE IN GOD AND IN CREATURES, SOME ONLY IN GOD. And so the causes of all things are in God; but the causes of some things are both in God and in creatures; the causes of others, however, are only in God. And the causes of these latter things are said to be hidden in God, because it is in the divine disposition that this or that thing should be made in such a way; this is not so in the seminal reason of the creature.

2. WHY THEY ARE SAID TO BE MADE NATURALLY OR NOT. And those things which are made according to seminal cause are said to be made

[2]Cf. Augustine, *De diversis quaestionibus 83*, q46; *In Ioannem*, tr. 1 n17; *De Trinitate*, bk 3 cc8-9, nn15-16; *Retractationes*, bk 1 c3 n2.

[3]Augustine, *De Genesi ad litteram*, bk 6 cc10 and 18; bk 9 c17 n32.

naturally, because the course of nature has become known to men to be such; but other things, whose causes are only in God, [are said to be made] apart from nature.—AUGUSTINE, IN *ON GENESIS*. Augustine says that these things are the ones which are made through grace, or are made miraculously, not naturally, in order to signify those things which are made through grace.[1] Among these, he places the making of woman from the man's rib, saying as follows: "That it would be necessary for woman to be made in this way was not established in things, but hidden in God. Each and every course of nature has its natural laws. Over this natural course, the Creator has at his disposal the power over all things to do something other than their natural order requires: namely, that a dry staff suddenly flower and bear fruit;[2] and that a woman who was sterile in her youth should give birth in her old age;[3] that a she-donkey speak,[4] and suchlike. But he granted to natures that even such things could be done from them, not that they should have these in their natural motion."[5]

3. ON THE TWO-FOLD WORK OF PROVIDENCE. "Therefore, God has, hidden in himself, the causes of some future things which he did not place in created things; and he does not fulfil them by the same work of providence by which natures exist so that they might be, but by that by which he governs as he willed the things which he has made as he has willed. Hence the causes of all things which were made miraculously, not by the natural motion of things, in order to signify grace, have been hidden in God; one of these was that woman was made from the side of the sleeping man. It was not part of the first condition of things that woman should be so made, but [only] that she could be made, lest God be held to do by a changeable will something against the causes which he had willingly established."[6]

Chapter 7 (109)

1. ON THE SOUL OF THE WOMAN: THAT IT IS NOT FROM THE MAN'S SOUL, AS SOME HELD, WHO SAY THAT SOULS DERIVE FROM ONE ANOTHER. As the body of the woman was derived from the body of the man, so some believed that her soul was propagated from the man's soul, and that all souls other than the first, like bodies, are derived from one another.—THE OPINION OF OTHERS WHO HELD THAT ALL SOULS WERE CREATED

[1]Augustine, *De Genesi ad litteram*, bk 9 cc17-18 nn31-34.
[2]Cf. Num. 17, 8.
[3]Cf. Gen. 18, 10-14; 21, 2; Lk. 1, 13-25.
[4]Cf. Num. 22, 28.
[5]Augustine, *De Genesi ad litteram*, bk 9 c17 n32.
[6]Ibid., bk 9 c18 nn33-34.

SIMULTANEOUSLY FROM THE BEGINNING. But others held that all souls were created simultaneously from the beginning.[1]

2. THE SENTENCE OF THE CATHOLIC CHURCH. But the Catholic Church teaches neither that souls were made simultaneously, nor from one another, but that they are infused into bodies which have been inseminated and formed through coition, and they are created at the moment of their infusion.

3. HERE ARE REJECTED TWO FALSE OPINIONS AND THE SENTENCE OF THE CHURCH IS CONFIRMED.—AUTHORITY OF GENNADIUS. Hence in *On Ecclesiastical Dogmas*: "We do not say that human souls existed from the beginning among the other intellectual natures, or that they were created all at once, as Origen falsely states. Neither are souls inseminated with the bodies through coition, as the Luciferians, and Cyril, and some presumptuous Latins affirm. We say that the body alone is inseminated by the conjugal union, but that the Creator alone knows the creation of the soul. It is by his judgement that the body is composed, brought together, and formed in the womb; once the body is formed, the soul is created and infused, so that in the womb lives a human being composed of body and soul, and a living person comes from the womb, filled with human substance."[2]

4. Jerome also condemns under the bond of anathema those who say that souls are derived from one another; he adduces the authority of the Prophet: *He who fashioned the hearts of each of them.*[3] Jerome says that the Prophet here sufficiently indicates that God does not make soul from soul, but he creates souls one by one from nothing.[4]

DISTINCTION XIX

Chapter 1 (110)

1. ON THE FIRST STATE OF MAN BEFORE SIN, NAMELY WHAT HE WAS LIKE IN RESPECT TO THE BODY AND IN RESPECT TO THE SOUL. It is usual to ask many things regarding the first state of man before sin, namely what man was like before he sinned, both in respect to the body and the soul, and whether mortal or immortal, and whether capable or incapable of suffering; regarding the end of the lower life and the transition to the higher one; regarding the manner of propagating children, and many other things, which it is not useless to know, although they are sometimes asked out of [mere] curiosity.

[1]Cf. Augustine, *De Genesi ad litteram*, bks. 7 and 10.
[2]Gennadius, *Liber seu diffinitio ecclesiasticorum dogmatum*, c14.
[3]Ps. 32, 15.
[4]Jerome, *Contra Ioannem Hierosolymitanum*, n22.

2. BEFORE TREATING THOSE THINGS PERTAINING TO THE SPIRIT, HE DISCUSSES WHAT MAN WAS LIKE WITH REGARD TO THE BODY BEFORE SINNING, AND SEVERAL OTHER THINGS. And before we pursue those things which pertain to the quality of the spirit, let us examine his quality with regard to the body, and the mode of propagating children, and several other things.

3. THAT MAN IN HIS FIRST STATE, NAMELY BEFORE SIN, WAS MORTAL AND IMMORTAL IN RESPECT TO THE BODY; IN HIS SECOND STATE, NAMELY AFTER SIN, HE WAS MORTAL AND DEAD; IN HIS THIRD STATE, HE SHALL BE ENTIRELY IMMORTAL, THAT IS, UNABLE TO DIE. And so the first man, with regard to the nature of his earthly body, was immortal in some respect, because he was able not to die; but also mortal in some way, because he was able to die. And so in that first state, he had the power to die and the power not to die; and this was the first immortality of the human body, namely the power not to die. But in his second state, after sin, he had the power to die and no power not to die, because in this state it is a necessity to die. In his third state, he shall have the power not to die and no power to die, because to that state pertains the impossibility of dying; this will be from grace, not from nature.

Chapter 2 (111)

1. HOW MAN IS SAID TO HAVE BEEN MADE INTO A LIVING SOUL. In the first state, the human body was animal, that is, it required the support of food; hence man is said to have been made into *a living soul*, not a spiritual one, that is, a soul endowing with sensation a body which was still animal, not spiritual, and which required food in order to live through the soul. And so *he was made into a living soul*,[1] that is, a soul which gave life to the body, yet through the sustenance of food. And at that time the body was both mortal and immortal, because it had the power to die and not to die. But after sin, it was rendered dead, as the Apostle says: *The body is dead because of sin*,[2] that is, it has in itself the necessity of dying.

2. But at the resurrection, it will be spiritual, that is, agile and not in need of food, and immortal: not only as it was in the first state, namely having the power not to die, but even not having the power to die. Hence Augustine, in *On Genesis*: "The Apostle says: *The body is dead because of sin*, etc.[3] First, from the mud of the earth, was formed an animal body, not the spiritual one with which we will rise again. For we shall be renewed from our ancient state not into the animal body as it was, but into a better one, that is, a spiritual one, *when this mortal one shall put on im-*

[1]Gen. 2, 7; 1 Cor. 15, 44-45.
[2]Rom. 8, 10.
[3]Ibid.

mortality,[4] into which Adam was to be changed, if he had not deserved the death of his animal body by sinning. The Apostle does not say: The body is *mortal* because of sin, but *dead*."[5]

Chapter 3 (112)

1. THE BODY OF MAN BEFORE SIN WAS MORTAL AND IMMORTAL. "For before sin, it was mortal and immortal, because it was able to die and not to die. But it is one thing not to have the power to die, and another to have the power not to die. And so through sin, it was made not mortal, which it already was, but dead, which it would not have become without sin. For our body is not animal in the same way as that of the first man, but it is now worse, since it is subject to the necessity of dying."[1] See, Augustine here clearly reveals that the body of man before sin was mortal and immortal, but not as it shall become at the resurrection.

2. IN WHAT SENSE THE BODY IS CALLED DEAD. On this same subject, Bede, in *On Genesis*, says: "It is not to be believed that, before sin, bodies were dead in the same way as they are now. For the Apostle says: *The body is dead because of sin*.[2] But although they were animal bodies, and not yet spiritual ones, nevertheless they were not dead, namely, subject to the necessity of dying."[3]

Chapter 4 (113)

1. WHETHER THE IMMORTALITY WHICH HE HAD BEFORE SIN WAS FROM THE CONDITION OF NATURE OR FROM A BENEFIT OF GRACE. It is usual to ask here, since the first man had a mortal and immortal body, whether he had both from the condition of the nature of the body itself, or whether the latter was a benefit of grace, namely immortality, that is, the power not to die.

2. RESPONSE, BY WHICH IT IS SAID THAT ONE WAS FROM CONDITION, NAMELY THE POWER TO DIE, THE OTHER FROM A GIFT OF GRACE, NAMELY THE POWER NOT TO DIE. To this it may be said that he had one from the nature of the body, namely the power to die; but the other, namely the power not to die, came to him from the tree of life, namely from the gift of grace. Hence Augustine, in *On Genesis*: "In some manner, man was created immortal, which came to him from the tree of life, not from the condition of nature. He was mortal by the condition of his animal body,

[4]1 Cor. 15, 54.
[5]Augustine, *De Genesi ad litteram*, bk 6 c19 n30; cc23-24, nn34-36.

[1]Augustine, *De Genesi ad litteram*, bk 6 cc25-26.
[2]Rom. 8, 10.
[3]Bede, *Libri quatuor in principium Genesis* 2, 18.

immortal by the benefaction of the Creator. For the body was not immortal so that it was entirely unable to die: this will not be, except when it will be a spiritual body."[1] He plainly says that it was not from nature, but from the tree of life, that the first man had the power not to die.

3. SOME SAY THAT IF ADAM DID NOT MAKE USE OF THE TREE OF LIFE, HE WOULD NOT HAVE LIVED FOREVER BECAUSE HE WOULD HAVE SINNED. Because of this, some say that, unless he made use of that tree, he would not live forever because he would have sinned. For he would have sinned if he did not made use of that tree, because he had been commanded to eat of every tree of paradise, except for the tree of knowledge of good and evil.[2] And so, just as he sinned by eating what was forbidden, he would also have sinned by not eating what had been commanded.

Chapter 5 (114)

1. IF IT HAD NOT BEEN COMMANDED THAT HE EAT OF THAT TREE, AND HE HAD MADE USE OF OTHER TREES AND NOT OF THAT ONE, WHETHER HE WOULD HAVE THE POWER NOT TO DIE. But at this point it is asked: if it had not been commanded that he eat of that tree, and he had fed on other trees and not on that one, would he have the power not to die? If he lived forever without making use of that tree, his power not to die did not come to him from that tree; but if he was not able to live forever, it came to him from that tree.

2. THE OPINION OF SOME WHO SAY THAT, THOUGH HE DID NOT EAT OF THAT TREE, HE HAD THE POWER NOT TO DIE, SO LONG AS HE MADE USE OF THE OTHERS. Some say that, if he had not been commanded to nourish himself from that tree, and he fed on the others and not on that one, he would live forever. It is in this way that they determine what Augustine said above, namely: "Which came to him from the tree of life, not from the condition of nature,"[1] that is, alone; as if to say: it did not come to him from the condition of nature alone, but also from that tree.

3. OTHERS ASSERT THAT THE POWER NOT TO DIE AND TO LIVE FOREVER CAME TO HIM FROM THAT TREE. But it seems to others that the power not to die came to him from the tree of life, not from nature: for that is why he is said to have had the power not to die, because he could have made use of that tree and, if he had eaten of it, he would not die.

[1]Augustine, *De Genesi ad litteram*, bk 6 c25.
[2]Cf. Gen. 2, 16-17.

[1]Above, c4 n2.

Chapter 6 (115)

1. QUESTION OF AUGUSTINE: HOW WAS MAN MADE IMMORTAL. But concerning this immortality of man and what it was like, Augustine, in *On Genesis*, raises a question in the following terms: "It is asked how, in contrast with the other animals, man was made immortal, and yet he shared their common sustenance."[1]

2. HE BEGINS TO RESOLVE IT. "But the immortality of the flesh which we received in Adam is one thing, the one for which we hope at our resurrection through Christ is another. The former was made an immortal man in the sense that he would be able not to die if he did not sin, but would die if he sinned; the children of the resurrection, however, will neither be able to sin any further, nor to die. Our flesh will not then need to be restored by food because it will be impossible for any deficiency to occur. Adam's flesh was created immortal before sin so that, helped by nourishment, it would be free of death and suffering. Therefore, man's flesh was made immortal and incorruptible so that it would keep its immortality and incorruptibility by observing of God's mandates. (NOTE THAT IN THE COMMANDS GIVEN BY GOD TO THE FIRST MAN IT WAS ALSO CONTAINED THAT HE EAT OF ALL THE TREES, OTHER THAN THE TREE OF THE KNOWLEDGE OF GOOD AND EVIL.) In these mandates, it was contained that he eat of the trees which were allowed to him and abstain from the one that was forbidden. By eating of these, he would have preserved the gifts of immortality until, by the processes of change proper to bodies, he would have reached the age which might have pleased the Creator, [and] after the generation of offspring, at God's command, he would then have eaten of the tree of life and, made perfectly immortal by it, he would no longer have required the nourishment of food."[2]

3. HE BRIEFLY SUMMARIZES THE MEANING OF THE ABOVE WORDS. See, by these words, Augustine appears to teach that the flesh of the first man had immortality in it which, by the nourishment of food, would have been preserved until the time of his transfer to a better condition, when he would have eaten of the tree of life and would have been made entirely immortal, so that he would not be able to die.

4. THAT FROM THE FOREGOING IT SEEMS TO FOLLOW THAT MAN WAS IN SOME WAY IMMORTAL FROM THE CONDITION OF HIS NATURE, BUT HE WOULD NOT HAVE BECOME ENTIRELY IMMORTAL EXCEPT BY PARTAKING OF THE TREE OF LIFE. And so some say that he had immortality from nature, by which he was able not to die, and he was able to preserve it by eating of the other trees; but it could not have been perfected, except by taking of the tree of life.—This appears to be Augustine's sense, who

[1]Rather, Bede, *Libri quatuor in principium Genesis* 1, 29-30.
[2]Ibid.

says, in *On Genesis*: "I also add this, that that tree furnished such a food by which the body of man would have been strengthened in unwavering good health: not as from other food, but by some hidden infusion of healthfulness."[3] Here he seems to indicate that the body could have been sustained with other foods, but with this food it would have been confirmed in unfailing good health.—From this it seems to follow that, just as he had some mortality in his nature, namely the capacity to die, so he had some immortality in his nature, that is, a capacity by which he was able not to die, helped by foods; but if he had stood firm, the perfection of immortality would have been given to him from the tree of life.

5. But let those who teach this inquire diligently how Augustine's words above,[4] by which he says that man was immortal from the tree of life, do not in contradict their view.

DISTINCTION XX

Chapter 1 (116)

1. ON THE MANNER OF PROCREATING CHILDREN, IF [OUR FIRST PARENTS] HAD NOT SINNED, AND WHAT KIND OF CHILDREN WOULD HAVE BEEN BORN. After these matters, it is to be seen how our first parents, if they had not sinned, would have procreated children, and what kind of children would have been born.

2. THE OPINION OF SOME WHO SAY THAT THE FIRST HUMANS IN PARADISE WOULD NOT HAVE BEEN ABLE TO JOIN SEXUALLY BEFORE SIN.— AUGUSTINE, *ON GENESIS*. Some hold that the first humans in paradise would not have been able to join sexually for the procreation of children, except after sin, since they say that sexual intercourse cannot occur without corruption or stain. But there could be neither corruption nor stain in humankind before sin because these things were the consequence of sin.[1]

3. RESPONSE AGAINST THEIR OPINION, WHERE IT IS SAID THAT, IF THEY HAD NOT SINNED, THEY WOULD HAVE COME TOGETHER WITHOUT SIN AND THE BURNING OF LUST, JUST AS NOW HAND IS JOINED TO HAND WITHOUT PRURIENCE. To this it is to be said that, if the first humans had not sinned, they would have come together in carnal coupling in paradise without any sin and stain, and there would be *a marriage bed without stain*[2] there, and a commingling without concupiscence; and they would exercise the same control over their genitals as over their other members, so that they would

[3]Augustine, *De Genesi ad litteram*, bk 8 c5 n11.
[4]Above, c4 n2.

[1]Cf. Augustine, *De Genesi ad litteram*, bk 9 cc8-9.
[2]Cf. Hebr. 13, 4.

feel no unlawful motion there. And as we move some members of the body toward some others, as the hand to the mouth, without the burning of lust, so they would use their genital members without any prurience of the flesh. For this "lethal illness"[3] inhered in human members from sin. And so they would have begotten children in paradise through a spotless joining, free of corruption.—Hence Augustine, in *On Genesis*: "Why may we not believe that the first humans before sin would have been able to command their genital members for procreation, just as they did their other members in any activity without the prurience of sensuality? For it is not incredible that God made those bodies such that, if they had not sinned, they would have commanded those members as they did their feet, and they would neither have sowed with ardor, nor given birth with pain. But after sin, they deserved that movement [of the flesh] which marriage regulates and continence suppresses."[4] "For the infirmity which tends toward a shameful ruin is relieved by the decency of marriage, and what would have been a proper function to the healthy has become a remedy to the sick."[5] "After being cast out of paradise, they came together and begot offspring; but it was possible for them to have honourable nuptials in paradise and *a marriage bed without stain*,[6] without the burning of lust, without the labour of childbirth."[7]

Chapter 2 (117)

WHY THEY DID NOT HAVE SEXUAL INTERCOURSE IN PARADISE.—HE RESOLVES IT IN TWO WAYS.—AUGUSTINE, IN *ON GENESIS*: "And so why did they not have sexual intercourse in paradise? Because their transgression occurred immediately after the creation of woman, and they were cast out of paradise. Or because God had not yet ordered them to have intercourse, and divine authorization might well have been awaited, where concupiscence did not yet cause anguish. But God had not yet commanded them, because he foreknew that those from whom the human race would be propagated would fall."[1] See, you have here expressly the manner of propagating children.

[3]Augustine, *De Genesi ad litteram*, bk 9 c10 n17.
[4]Ibid., bk 9 c10 n18.
[5]Ibid., bk 9 c7 n12.
[6]Cf. Hebr. 13, 4.
[7]Augustine, *De Genesi ad litteram*, bk 9 c3 n6.

[1]Augustine, *De Genesi ad litteram*, bk 9 c4 n8.

Chapter 3 (118)

1. ON THE END OF THAT INFERIOR LIFE, WHETHER THEY WOULD HAVE BEEN TRANSFERRED IN SUCCESSION AFTER THE BEGETTING OF CHILDREN, OR ALL AT ONCE. But as to the end of time at which they would have been transferred to a spiritual and celestial life, Scripture does not teach anything certain. And so it is uncertain whether parents, after the begetting of children and the fulfilment of the just requirements of their human office, would have been transferred to a better state, not by death, but by some change. Or would fathers remain in some state of life, making use of the tree of life, until their children reached the same state and, when the number was complete, all would have been transferred together to better things, in order to be *as the angels of God in the heaven.*[1]

2. Concerning this, Augustine, in *On Genesis*, provides an ambiguous discussion, stating as follows: "The first humans were able to beget children in paradise, not so that the children should succeed to their dying parents, but that while these remained in some state of maturity and received vigour from the tree of life, their children should also reach the same state until the number [of men] was fulfilled. Then, without death, their animal bodies would have passed into another quality, in which they would have been entirely subject to the spirit ruling them, and they would have been kept alive by the spirit alone and would have lived without bodily sustenance."[2] Or "the parents were able to give way to their children, so that their number should be filled by successions. After the begetting of children and the fulfilment of the just requirements of their human duty, they would have been transferred to a better state, not by death, but by some change."[3]—See, we have here a discussion of the transit of men to better things, but we are left uncertain as to whether they would all be transferred at once, or through successions.

Chapter 4 (119)

1. WHAT KIND OF CHILDREN THEY WOULD HAVE PROCREATED, WHETHER AS HAVING THEIR FULL HEIGHT AND THE USE OF THEIR MEMBERS, AS THE FIRST MAN WAS ESTABLISHED. But if it is asked what kind of children man would have begotten, if he had not sinned, namely whether, just as the first man himself, as soon as he was made, was fully grown with respect to his height and the use of members, so also his children would have been fully grown at the very moment of their birth, so as to be able to walk and speak and do all other things: it may be answered that it was

[1]Mt. 22, 30.
[2]Augustine, *De Genesi ad litteram*, bk 9 c3 n6.
[3]Ibid., bk 9 c6 n10.

required that the children be born small because of the needs of the maternal womb.

2. RESPONSE, IN WHICH, AFTER POSITING ONE THING WITHOUT AMBIGUITY, HE ADDS A THREEFOLD DISTINCTION. But we do not have a definitive answer from our authors as to whether they would have had fullness of growth and the use of their members as soon as they were born; or whether they would have been able to use the functions of their members even when small and at a younger age [than now]; or whether they would have received fullness of growth and use of their members over intervals of time, in the same way as happens now.

3. HE CITES THE AMBIGUOUS WORDS OF AUGUSTINE, WHERE THE LATTER NEVERTHELESS APPEARS TO SUGGEST THAT CHILDREN AND INFANTS WOULD HAVE BEEN ABLE TO USE THE FUNCTIONS OF THEIR MEMBERS. Augustine speaks ambiguously concerning this matter as well, saying: "We are troubled by the question of whether, if the first humans had not sinned, they would have had such children as would not have use of either tongue or hands. Indeed, because of the need of the womb, it was perhaps necessary that they be born small. But even though a rib is a very small part of a man's body, yet it did not follow from this that God made a small spouse for the man; and so the omnipotence of the Creator could also have made the man's children to grow up as soon as they were born. But setting this aside, he could surely grant to them what he has granted to many animals, whose young, although they are small, yet run and follow their mothers as soon as they are born. On the contrary, a newly-born human at birth has neither feet fit for walking, nor even hands able to scratch; and even if the mother's breast is placed near them, the newborn are more able to cry in their hunger than to suck. This infirmity of the flesh is properly congruent with the weakness of their mind."[4] By these words, it seems to be implied that children, even little ones, would have been able to make use of their members.

4. NOT ABSURDLY, IT HAS PLEASED SOME [TO THINK] THAT CHILDREN WOULD HAVE BEEN BORN SMALL AND MAKE PROGRESS, AS THEY DO NOW, IN STATURE AND OTHER THINGS WITH THE PASSAGE OF TIME, AND THAT THIS MUST NOT BE ACCOUNTED A DEFECT. But since Augustine does not firmly assert anything concerning these matters, it has not unreasonably pleased some that the children of the first parents would have been born small. Afterwards, at intervals of time, by the same law by which we discern human birth to be regulated even now, they would have received growth in stature and the use of their members, and would have to await the age at which they could walk and speak, as is now the case with us.

[4]Augustine, *De peccatorum meritis et remissione et de baptismo parvulorum*, bk 1 cc37-38.

This would not at all be attributed to a defect, but to the condition of nature; in the same way, they were not able to abstain entirely from food, and yet this was not from a defect, but from their natural condition.

5. THE OBJECTION OF SOME WHO WISH TO PROVE THAT THEY COULD LIVE WITHOUT SUSTENANCE. But the following objection is made to this: If they did not sin, they would not die; but they would not sin if they did not eat; and so they could live without sustenance.—RESPONSE. But, as we said above,[5] they would have sinned not only if they ate of the forbidden tree, but also if they did not make use of what had been allowed them; for just as they had been commanded not to feed on that tree, they had also been commanded to feed on the others.—THE REASON WHY THEY WOULD SIN, IF THEY DID NOT MAKE USE OF THE TREES THAT WERE ALLOWED. Moreover, they would be acting against natural reason, by which they understood that they were to eat of those trees; and they also desired this naturally.

6. ANOTHER OBJECTION CONCERNING THE SAME. An objection is also made as follows: Since hunger is a punishment of sin, if they were not to sin, they would not feel hunger; but without hunger it seems superfluous to eat; hence some hold that they would not have needed food before sin, because they could not be hungry if they had not sinned.—RESPONSE. To this it may be said that hunger truly is a defect and a punishment of sin: for it is an immoderate appetite for eating, to which man would not have been subject, if he had not sinned. But without a doubt he would sin, if he did not forestall this defect with food. For he had a natural and moderate appetite which he was to satisfy so as not to feel the defect of hunger.

7. JUST AS IT WAS NOT THE RESULT OF A DEFECT THAT HE NEEDED FOOD BEFORE SIN, SO IT WOULD NOT BE THE RESULT OF A DEFECT IF HIS CHILDREN WERE TO BE BORN NOT YET FULLY GROWN, AND WERE THEN TO MAKE PROGRESS IN THAT AND IN OTHER THINGS. And so, it was not the result of a defect, but from the condition of nature, that man needed food before sin. Similarly, it would not be from a defect, but from nature, if the condition of man, after having started out fully grown at its beginning, that is, in the first parent, should in subsequent propagation make progress from lesser to greater things, namely that it should receive increase of bodily stature and the use of members at intervals of time.

Chapter 5 (120)

1. WHETHER, AS IN BODILY STATURE, SO THEY WOULD BE BORN SMALL ALSO IN SENSE OF MIND AND WITH THE PASSAGE OF TIME WOULD PROGRESS IN SENSE AND KNOWLEDGE OF TRUTH, OR WOULD THEY BE FULLY

[5] Dist. 19 c4 n3.

DEVELOPED IN THESE THINGS AS SOON AS THEY WERE BORN. And since it is not absurd or unsuitable to hold this view concerning the human body, it is usual to ask whether the same is to be thought concerning the sense of the soul and the knowledge of truth. Namely, would those who would have been born without sin be imperfect in sense and intelligence of mind, and with the passage of time progress to perfection in these things; or would they receive perfection of sense and knowledge as soon as they were established.

2. RESPONSE, WHERE HE SAYS THAT IT SEEMS SO TO SOME, NAMELY THAT THEY WOULD PROGRESS IN THESE AS IN OTHER THINGS. Those who think that, after being born small in bodily stature and in the use of their members, they would progress with the passage of time, do not deny that they would also be imperfect in sense at the moment of their birth, and over time, they would make progress in sense and knowledge until they reached perfection.

3. SOME MAKE OBJECTION TO THEIR VIEW. Some make objection to this, saying: If they did not have perfection of sense and intelligence as soon as they were born, there would be ignorance in them; but ignorance is a punishment of sin.—But those who say this do not sufficiently consider that not everyone who does not know something, or who knows something less than perfectly, is immediately to be said to have ignorance or to be in ignorance.

4. HOW IGNORANCE IS SAID TO BE IN SOMEONE. Because it is not called ignorance, unless when what is not known is that which must be known and which one ought not to be ignorant of. And such an ignorance is a punishment of sin, since the mind is darkened by vice so that it is not able to know the things which it ought to know.

Chapter 6 (121)

1. ON THE TRANSFER OF HUMANKIND TO A BETTER STATE AND ON THE TWO GOODS: THE ONE GIVEN HERE, AND THE OTHER PROMISED. Such was man's establishment before sin according to the condition of his body. But from this state, he was to be transferred with his entire posterity to a better and worthier state, where he would enjoy the heavenly and eternal good which had been prepared for him in the heavens.—For just as man is composed of a double nature, so the Creator prepared for him two goods from the beginning: one temporal, the other eternal; one visible, the other invisible; one for the flesh, the other for the spirit. And because *that which is animal* is *first, and afterwards that which is spiritual*,[1] he

[1] 1 Cor. 15, 46.

gave the temporal and visible good first; but he promised the invisible and eternal one, and made it known that it was to be sought by merits.

2. THAT GOD GAVE TO MAN NATURAL REASON AND A COMMAND SO THAT HE MIGHT PRESERVE THE GOOD WHICH HE HAD RECEIVED AND BECOME WORTHY OF THAT WHICH HE HAD BEEN PROMISED. To preserve what he had given and for the deserving of what he had promised, God added the command of obedience to the natural reason that had been placed in the soul of man at creation, by which he was able to discern between good and evil. By observing this command, man would not lose what he had been given and would obtain what had been promised, so that he might come to his reward through merit.

DISTINCTION XXI

Chapter 1 (122)

1. ON THE DEVIL'S ENVY, BY WHICH HE CAME TO TEMPT HUMANKIND. And so the devil, seeing that human beings were able to ascend by the humility of obedience to that from which he had fallen through pride, envied them. He who through pride had previously become *the devil*, that is, the one who has fallen below, by the jealousy of envy was made *satan*, that is, the adversary.[1]

2. WHY HE CAME TO THE WOMAN FIRST. And so he tempted the woman, in whom he knew that reason was less vigorous than in the man. For his wickedness, fearful of tempting virtue, attacked human nature in that part where it seemed weaker so that, if he should prevail there to some extent, he might afterwards proceed with greater confidence to attack, or rather to subvert, the other and stronger one. And so he first sought out the woman alone, so that he might first exercise the full power of his temptation upon her.

Chapter 2 (123)

1. WHY HE CAME IN A FORM OTHER THAN HIS OWN. But because he could not harm her by violence, he turned to deceit, so that he might overthrow her by fraud whom he could not overcome by power. But lest his deception should become too apparent, he did not come in his own form, lest he should be clearly recognized and so rejected. On the other hand, lest his deceit be so excessively hidden that it would be impossible to guard against and humankind would also seem to suffer a wrong if God allowed it to be tricked in such a way that it would not be able to take any precau-

[1]See above, dist. 10 c2 n1.

tions, the devil was allowed to come in another's form, but in one in which his wickedness could easily be detected. And so, that he not come in his own form was done by his own will; but that he come in a form suitable to his wickedness was done by God.

2. WHY HE CAME IN NO OTHER FORM THAN A SERPENT'S. And so he came to the humans as a serpent, who perhaps, if he had been allowed, would have preferred to come in the shape of a dove. But it was not suitable that the malign spirit should make hateful to humankind that form in which the Holy Spirit was to appear. And so the devil was allowed to tempt only in the form of the serpent, so that the woman should be able to detect the wiliness of the tempter by that which it was outwardly. For the devil tempted through the serpent in whom he spoke.

Chapter 3 (124)

WHY THE SERPENT IS SAID TO BE MORE CUNNING THAN ALL THE OTHER LIVING BEINGS.—AUGUSTINE, IN *ON GENESIS*. And so the serpent is said to be *more cunning than all the other animals of the earth*[1] because, as Augustine says, "the evil angels, although cast down by pride, nevertheless are more excellent by nature than all the beasts because of the eminence of their reason; the serpent, however, might be called most wise, not because of its rational soul, but due to its diabolical spirit. Hence it is not strange if the devil, filling the serpent with his spirit as he filled the diviners, rendered it the wisest of all the beasts."[2]

Chapter 4 (125)

1. THAT HE DID NOT CHOOSE THE SERPENT IN ORDER TO TEMPT THROUGH IT. And so the devil did not choose the serpent for his temptation, but he tempted through whatever animal he was allowed. Hence Augustine, in *On Genesis*: "It is not to be believed that the devil chose the serpent through whom he tempts; but since he desired to deceive, he was not able to do so except through that animal through which he was allowed to do it. For the will to harm exists in each from himself, but the power is from God."[1]

2. STRABUS: "But the devil spoke through the unaware serpent in the same way in which he speaks through the possessed and the insane."[2]

3. AUGUSTINE, IN *ON GENESIS*: "For he used the serpent as an instrument, causing its nature to express the sounds of words and the signs by

[1]Cf. Gen. 3, 1.
[2]Augustine, *De Genesi ad litteram*, bk 11 c2 n4.

[1]Augustine, *De Genesi ad litteram*, bk 11 c3 n5.
[2]Strabo, *In Genesim* 3, 1.

which he might express his will. And so the serpent neither understood the words, nor was made rational. And yet it is called *most cunning*[3] because of the devil's wiliness. But it spoke like Balaam's she-ass;[4] however, the one was done by a devil, the other by an angel. For the good and evil angels work in similar ways."[5]

4. Here it is usual to ask why the woman did not draw back in horror from the serpent.—Because, as she knew it to have been created, she thought that it had also received the power of speech from God.

Chapter 5 (126)

1. ON THE MANNER OF TEMPTATION.—WHY HE BEGAN BY QUESTIONING. And the temptation was done in this way. Standing before the woman, the proud enemy does not dare to come out with words of persuasion, fearing to be discovered. Instead, he approaches her under the guise of questioning so that, from her answer, he might gather how to proceed in his wickedness.

2. THE SERPENT'S WORDS AND THE WOMAN'S RESPONSE. *Why*, he said, *did God command you not to eat of every tree in paradise? The woman answered him: We eat of the fruit of the trees which are in paradise; but of the fruit of the tree which is in the middle of paradise, God has commanded us not to eat of it and not to touch it, lest perhaps we die.*

3. GAINING CONFIDENCE FROM THE WOMAN'S WORDS, THE SERPENT ADDS A FALSE PROMISE. In this speech, she gave room to the tempter, when she said *lest perhaps we die*. And so the devil immediately said to the woman: *You will not die at all: for God knows that, on whatever day you eat of it, your eyes will be opened and you will be like gods, knowing good and evil.*[6]

4. Note well the order and progress of human perdition. First, God had said: *On whatever day you eat of it, you will die the death*;[7] afterwards, the woman said: *Lest perhaps we die*;[8] lastly, the serpent said: *You will not die at all.*[9] God affirmed it, the woman said it as if in doubt, and the devil denied it. Thus, she who doubted distanced herself from the one who affirmed and drew near to the one who denied.

5. ON THE SLYNESS OF THE DEVIL WHO, IN ORDER TO PERSUADE MORE EASILY, REMOVED THE EVIL AND DOUBLED THE GOOD WHICH HE PROMISED. In order to support his inducements more fully, that is, so as to freely

[3]Cf. Gen. 3, 1.
[4]Cf. Num. 22, 28-30.
[5]Augustine, *De Genesi ad litteram*, bk 11 cc27-29 nn34-36.
[6]Gen. 3, 4-5.
[7]Gen. 2, 17.
[8]Gen. 3, 3.
[9]Gen. 3, 4.

persuade her [to do] the evil which he intended, the devil removed the evil which the woman feared by denying it, and added a promise. And he doubled his promise so that his persuasion be received more quickly. Persuading her to take one bite, he set forth two things as a reward, promising likeness to God and knowledge of good and evil.

6. THAT HUMANKIND WAS TEMPTED IN THREE WAYS, NAMELY BY GLUTTONY, VAINGLORY, AND AVARICE.—AUGUSTINE.[10] In this, he tempted humankind in three ways, namely by gluttony in persuading [the woman] to eat, when he said: *On whatever day you eat of it*; by vainglory, promising divinity, when he said: *You will be like gods*; by avarice, promising knowledge, when he said: *Knowing good and evil*. Gluttony is the immoderate craving for food; vainglory is the love of one's own excellence; avarice is the immoderate desire of having, which applies not only to money, but also to high position and knowledge, as when one has excessive ambition for prominence.

Chapter 6 (127)

1. ON THE DOUBLE KIND OF TEMPTATION. Furthermore, it is to be known that there are two kinds of temptation, one exterior and another interior.

2. WHAT AN EXTERIOR TEMPTATION IS AND BY WHOM IT IS DONE. An exterior temptation occurs when an evil extrinsic to us is visibly suggested to us by some word or sign, so that the one to whom the suggestion is made may bend to consent to sin. And such a temptation is done only by the adversary.

3. WHAT AN INTERIOR TEMPTATION IS AND BY WHOM IT IS DONE. But an interior temptation occurs when an evil intrinsic to us is suggested invisibly. And this temptation is sometimes done by the enemy, sometimes by the flesh. Indeed, both the devil invisibly suggests evil, and an unlawful motion and depraved titillation arises from the corruption of the flesh. And for that reason the temptation which is from the flesh does not occur without sin; however, the one which is from the enemy does not cause sin, unless consent is extended to it, but is matter for the practice of virtue. An interior temptation of the flesh is overcome with greater difficulty, however, because, in fighting from within, it is fortified against us by our own [inclinations].

Chapter 7 (128)

1. WHY HUMANKIND WAS ABLE RISE THROUGH ANOTHER, AND THE DEVIL WAS NOT; AND HUMAN SIN WAS REMEDIABLE, BUT THE DEVIL'S WAS NOT. And so humankind, which fell when pressed by exterior temptation alone,

[10]Rather, Gregory, *In Evangelia*, hom. 16 n2.

deserved to be punished the more severely as the pressure by which it had been cast down was the lighter. And yet, because it had some excuse for falling, however small, therefore it could be helped to forgiveness through God's grace so that, having fallen through someone else, it might be raised up through someone else. And so the one who had an inciter to evil not unjustly had a restorer to the good. But because the devil sinned without being tempted by anyone else, he was bound not to be aided by another to rise; he was not able to rise by himself, however, and so his sin was irremediable. But the sin of humankind, as it had its beginning through someone else, so it not unsuitably had its remedy through someone else.

2. WHY HUMANKIND, AND NOT THE ANGEL, WAS REDEEMED. Moreover, because the angelic nature did not entirely perish, but in part remained, it was not redeemed. But all of human nature perished and, so that it should not be entirely lost, it was in part redeemed so that [the numbers lost through] the fall of the angels should be made up from it.—Hence Augustine, in the *Enchiridion*: "It pleased the creator and ruler of the universe that, since the entire multitude of angels had not perished by deserting God, the part which had perished should remain in perpetual perdition. But the part which remained with God when the others deserted should rejoice in their most surely and forever known happiness. But as for the rational creature which was in human beings, because it perished in its entirety by sins and punishments, it should be in part restored so that it should in some part make up for the reduction in numbers which that fall had caused to the angelic fellowship. For this was promised to the saints: that they shall be *equal to the angels of God*."[1,2]

Chapter 8 (129)

1. THAT THE COMMAND WAS NOT GIVEN TO THE MAN ALONE. It is also to be noted that the command does not appear to have been given to the man alone, since the woman herself attests that it was also given to her, saying: *God has commanded us*, etc.[1]—Yet one reads earlier that, before making the woman, God had said to the man: *Of the tree of the knowledge of good and evil, you will not eat*;[2] he did not say: *The two of you will not eat*.—AUGUSTINE, IN *ON GENESIS*. Perhaps because he was going to make the woman, he gave the command in such a way that the mandate would come to the woman through the man: for the woman, who was subject to the man, was bound to receive the divine mandate not otherwise than through

[1]Cf. Lk. 20, 26; Mt. 22, 30.
[2]Augustine, *Enchiridion*, c29.

[1]Gen. 3, 3.
[2]Gen. 2, 17.

the man. Hence the Apostle: *If women wish to learn anything, let them ask their husbands at home.*[3]

2. How they were able to speak or to understand speech.—Augustine, *On Genesis*. If it is asked how they were able to speak or to understand speech, since they never learned by growing up among those who spoke, or by being taught, we say that God made them such that they were able to speak and to learn from others, if these were to exist.[4]

Distinction XXII

Chapter 1 (130)

1. On the origin of that sin. Here it seems that it is to be diligently investigated what the origin and root of that sin was.

2. The opinion of some who say that there was already some pride in the human spirit. Some hold that there was already some pride in the human spirit from which it consented to the suggestion of the devil.

3. An authority of Augustine which seems to support them. Augustine also appears to indicate this, in *On Genesis*, speaking as follows: "It is not to be believed that man would have been cast down, if some pride which needed to be suppressed had not preceded, so that he might learn through the humiliation of sin how falsely presumptuous he had been, and that a nature does not conduct itself well, if it has withdrawn from its maker."[1]—Also, in the same: "How could the woman have believed the tempter's words, that God had forbidden her [the enjoyment of] a good and useful thing, if there were not in her mind that love of her own power and that proud presumption concerning herself which was to be convicted or destroyed by temptation? And so, not satisfied with the serpent's persuasion, she saw the tree was good to eat and beautiful to see;[2] disbelieving that she could suffer death from such a thing, she perhaps believed that God had said those words as a figure of speech. And so she ate, and gave it to her husband, perhaps with some words of persuasion which Scripture has left as understood; or perhaps it was not necessary to persuade him because the man could see that she had not died from that food."[3]

4. Augustine, *On Genesis*: that the devil spoke differently in the woman than in the serpent. "Therefore, just as the devil was not

[3] 1 Cor. 14, 35. Cf. Augustine, *De Genesi ad litteram*, bk 8 c17.
[4] Cf. ibid., bk 8 c16 n35.

[1] Augustine, *De Genesi ad litteram*, bk 11 c5 n7.
[2] Cf. Gen. 3, 6.
[3] Augustine, *De Genesi ad litteram*, bk 11 c30 n39.

allowed to tempt the woman other than through the serpent, so he was not allowed to tempt the man other than through the woman":[4] "so that, as God's command came to the woman through the man, so the devil's temptation passed to the man through the woman."[5] "But in the woman, who was a rational being, he did not himself speak, as he did in the serpent, but his persuasion did so; he assisted interiorly, however, by instigation what he had done externally through the serpent."[6]

5. WHAT MEANING SOME PEOPLE DRAW FROM THE ABOVE WORDS. The manner and progress of temptation is intimated by these words, and also what we said earlier appears to be implied, namely that some pride and presumption existed in the human mind before the temptation.

6. OBJECTION AGAINST THOSE WHO SAY THAT PRIDE PRECEDED IN THE MIND. But if it was so, then humankind did not first sin at another's suggestion. Authority teaches, however, that the devil's sin is incurable because he fell not at another's suggestion, but by his own pride; humankind's sin, on the other hand, is curable because it fell not by itself, but through another, and so it could rise again through another.

7. HE HERE DEFINES HOW THOSE WORDS ARE TO BE UNDERSTOOD. And so the aforesaid words of Augustine pressingly require a pious and diligent reader. We may rightly understand them in this way: 'Humankind would have not been cast down,' namely into the act of that sin, that is, to eat of the forbidden tree, and into these miseries through the temptation of the devil, 'if some pride which needed to be suppressed had not preceded,' not temptation, but the work of sin.

8. NOTE THE ORDER OF TEMPTATION. For this was the order of development: the devil temptingly said: *if you eat of it, you will be like gods, knowing good and evil.*[7] After hearing this, some pride and love of her own power immediately crept into the woman's mind, from which it pleased her to do what the devil suggested, and she certainly did it. And so she sinned by suggestion, because temptation preceded, from which pride arose in her mind, and the sinful deed and the punishment of the sin followed it.

Chapter 2 (131)

WHAT WAS THE WOMAN'S PRIDE. And indeed there was such pride in the woman's mind by which she believed and willed to have likeness to God

[4]Augustine, *De Genesi ad litteram*, bk 11 c27 n34.
[5]Ibid., bk 11 c34 n45.
[6]Ibid., bk 11 c27 n34.
[7]Gen. 3, 5.

with some equality, thinking that what the devil said was true.[1] And so Augustine mentions the woman in particular, saying: 'How could the woman have believed the devil, unless there were in her mind a proud presumption concerning herself?' And what follows, namely 'which was to be convicted or destroyed by temptation,' is to be referred to the woman, in these terms: 'which,' the woman, not the pride, 'was convicted or destroyed by temptation' etc.[2]

Chapter 3 (132)

1. WHAT WAS THE MAN'S PRIDE: WHETHER HE BELIEVED AND WILLED THE SAME AS THE WOMAN. It is usual to ask whether there was the same pride and love of one's power in the man as in the woman.

2. THAT ADAM WAS NOT LED ASTRAY LIKE THE WOMAN, NAMELY SO AS TO BELIEVE THAT WHAT THE DEVIL SAID WAS TRUE; AND YET HE WAS LED ASTRAY IN SOME REGARD, NAMELY SO AS TO BELIEVE THAT THE SIN WAS VENIAL. To this we say that Adam was not led astray in the same way as the woman: for he did not believe that what the devil said was true. And yet it may be believed that he was led astray because he thought that the offense was venial rather than deadly. But he was not led astray first, nor in regard to the same thing as the woman, so as to believe that God had forbidden the touching of that tree because, if they were to touch it, they would become *like gods*.[1] And yet Adam was a transgressor, as the Apostle attests.[2] Therefore, there might have been some pride in his mind immediately after temptation, by which he willed to try the forbidden tree, since he saw that the woman had not died for having eaten of it.

3. HE CONFIRMS WHAT HE HAS SAID BY AUTHORITY. Hence Augustine, *On Genesis*: "The Apostle shows that Adam was a transgressor, saying: *In imitation of Adam's transgression*,[3] and yet denies that he was seduced, where he says: *Adam was not deceived, but the woman.*[4] And so, when questioned, he does not say: *The woman deceived me*, but *she gave it to me, and I ate*;[5] but the woman states: *The serpent deceived me*."[6,7]

4. THE APOSTLE CALLED DECEPTION THAT BY WHICH THE WOMAN, NOT THE MAN, WAS LED ASTRAY.—AUGUSTINE: "The Apostle properly called

[1]Cf. Gen. 3, 5,
[2]Cf. above, c1 n3.

[1]Cf. Gen. 3, 5.
[2]Rom. 5, 14.
[3]Ibid.
[4]1 Tim. 2, 14.
[5]Gen. 3, 12.
[6]Gen. 3, 13.
[7]Augustine, *De Genesi ad litteram*, bk 11 c42 n58.

this a deception because, through it, that which was suggested was believed to be true, even though it was false, namely that God had forbidden them to touch that tree because he knew that, if they had touched it, they would become like gods: as if the one who had made them human had begrudged them divinity. But although, because of some pride in the mind, which could not be hidden from God, a desire to try it influenced the man when he saw that the woman had not died from eating of the fruit, yet I do not think that, if he had already been endowed with a spiritual mind, he would in any way have believed what the devil suggested."[8]

Chapter 4 (133)

1. WHO SINNED MORE, ADAM OR EVE. From this it may be clearly deduced who sinned more, namely Adam or Eve. The woman appears to have sinned more, who willed to seize equality with the divinity and, puffed up with excessive presumption, believed that this would happen. But Adam did not believe that. Instead, even as he humoured the woman and consented to her persuasion, not wishing to sadden her and leave her alienated from himself, lest she should perish, he reflected on penance and God's mercy, and judged that it was a venial, not a mortal, sin.

2. Hence Augustine: "The Apostle says: *Adam was not deceive*d.[1] This may certainly be taken in the sense that he was not deceived, namely first; or not deceived into the same thing as the woman, namely so as to believe that it was true that: *You will become like gods*.[2] But he believed that both things could be: that he indulge his wife, and that he obtain forgiveness through penance. And so he sinned less who thought of penance and God's mercy."[3]

3. AUGUSTINE, *ON GENESIS*: "For after the woman had been deceived and had eaten and gave it to him that they might eat of it together, he did not wish to sadden her whom he believed would waste away without his solace and entirely die if alienated from him. And so he was not vanquished by the concupiscence of the flesh, which he had not yet felt, but by some friendly benevolence, by which it often happens that we offend God so as not to offend a friend. But he ought not to have acted in this way, as the just outcome of the divine sentence indicated."[4]

4. IN WHAT WAS ADAM DECEIVED, AND IN WHAT NOT. "And so he too was deceived in some other way."[5] "For he had no experience of divine

[8]Augustine, *De Genesi ad litteram*, bk 11 c42 n60.

[1]1 Tim. 2, 14.
[2]Gen. 3, 5.
[3]Ordinary gloss, on 1 Tim. 2, 14.
[4]Augustine, *De Genesi ad litteram*, bk 11 c42 n59.
[5]Ibid., bk 11 c42 n60.

severity, and so he could be deceived into believing that the offense was venial."[6] "But I do not at all believe that he could have been deceived by the same guile of the serpent as the woman."[7]

5. From these things, it is given to be understood that the woman sinned more, in whom was the presumption of greater pride. It was also because of this that she sinned against herself, her neighbour, and God; but the man sinned only against himself and God.—THE WOMAN IS PROVEN TO HAVE SINNED MORE ALSO FROM THE PUNISHMENT. That the woman sinned more may also be gathered from her being punished more severely, to whom it was said: *In pain shall you bring forth children*, etc.[8]

6. AN APPARENT OBJECTION TO THE ABOVE VIEW. But what Augustine, in *On Genesis*, says of the man and woman excusing their sin, appears to be contrary to this: "Adam said: *The woman whom you gave to me gave it to me and I ate.*[9] He does not say: *I sinned.* For pride has the ugliness of shame, not the humility of confession."[10] "And the woman does not confess her sin either, but attributes it to another, saying: *The serpent deceived me and I ate*;[11] unequal in sex, but equal in pride!"[12] See, Augustine here says that the woman had equal pride with the man; therefore both equally rose up in pride and equally sinned.

7. DETERMINATION OF THE ABOVE AUTHORITY. But this can be so determined that we say their pride was equal in making excuses for their sin, and also in eating from the forbidden tree; but it was unequal and much greater in the woman, in that she believed and willed to be like God, which the man did not do.

8. BUT OF THE MAN TOO WE READ THAT HE WANTED TO BE LIKE GOD. But even so we read of the man also that he wanted to be like God. For Augustine says on that passage of the Psalm: *I will then restore what I did not steal*: "Adam stole, and Eve [too], presuming, as the devil had done, concerning divinity; they wanted to steal divinity, and lost happiness."[13] Also, on that passage: *God, who is like you?*: "One who, by his own efforts, wants to be like God wants it perversely, like the devil, who was not willing to be subject to God, and also like man, who was not willing to be bound as a servant by God's command, but wanted to be as if God, with none ruling over him."[14]—Also, on that passage of the Epistle: *He*

[6]Augustine, *De civitate Dei*, bk 14 c11 n2.
[7]Ibid., bk 11 c42 n60.
[8]Gen. 3, 16.
[9]Gen. 3, 12.
[10]Augustine, *De Genesi ad litteram*, bk 11 c35 n47.
[11]Gen. 3, 13.
[12]Augustine, *De Genesi ad litteram*, bk 11 c35 n48.
[13]Augustine, *Enarrationes in Psalmos*, on Ps. 68, 5, sermon 1 n9.
[14]Ibid., on Ps. 70, 19, sermon 2 n7.

[i.e. Jesus] did not think it robbery to be equal to God:[15] "Because he did not usurp what was not his, as the devil and the first man did."[16]

9. THE VIEW OF SOME, THAT ADAM HAD THE AMBITION TO BE LIKE GOD, BUT DID NOT BELIEVE IT POSSIBLE. For that reason, it seems to some that Adam also had the ambition to be like God, but did not believe it to be possible; and so he knew that what the devil promised was false. And although he deeply desired equality with the divinity, yet he did not burn so much, nor was he affected by such great ambition as the woman, who believed that it could be done and so rose up in greater pride in her ambition for it. Perhaps some stirring of ambition moved the man, but not to such an extent that he believed it true or possible.

10. THE VIEW OF OTHERS, WHO BELIEVE THAT THIS WAS SAID BECAUSE EVE HAD BEEN DERIVED FROM THE MAN.—THEY SHOW IT BY ANALOGY. But it seems to others that it is said that Adam willed it because the woman who was derived from him willed it; in the same way, they say, sin is said to have *entered into the world,* that is, into human nature, *through one man*,[17] even though the woman sinned before the man, because it entered through the woman who was made from man. Or rather, it is said to have entered through one man because, even if the woman had sinned, if the man had not also done so, humankind would not at all have perished, corrupted by sins. And so the man sinned less than the woman.

11. OBJECTION AGAINST WHAT HAS BEEN SAID, THAT THE MAN SINNED LESS. It is customary to object to this in the following way: As Isidore says, "sin is committed in three ways, namely by ignorance, infirmity, or intention. It is graver to sin by infirmity than by ignorance, and graver still to sin intentionally than by infirmity. And Eve appears to have sinned from ignorance because she was deceived, but Adam with intention because he was not deceived,"[18] as the Apostle says.[19]

12. RESPONSE, IN WHICH EVE'S IGNORANCE IS DISTINGUISHED, NAMELY IN WHAT DID SHE SIN IN IGNORANCE AND IN WHAT NOT. To this we say that, although Eve erred through ignorance in this respect: that she believed to be true what the devil suggested; and yet not in this: that she did not fail to know that it was God's mandate and it was a sin to act against it. And so she could not be excused from sin through ignorance.

[15]Phil. 2, 6.
[16]Cf. Augustine, *Enarrationes in Psalmos*, on Ps. 68, 5, sermon 1 n9.
[17]Cf. Rom. 5, 12.
[18]Isidore, *Sententiae*, bk 2 c17 nn3-4.
[19]Cf. 1 Tim. 2, 14.

Chapter 5 (134)

1. THAT ONE IGNORANCE EXCUSES, ANOTHER DOES NOT. For there is an ignorance which excuses a sinner, and there is an ignorance of such a kind that it does not excuse. For there is an invincible ignorance, and a vincible ignorance. All excuse is removed where the command is not unknown.

2. ON THE THREEFOLD IGNORANCE: WHICH EXCUSES AND WHICH NOT. Ignorance is threefold: namely, that of those who do not wish to know, even thought they are able: this does not excuse because it is itself a sin; that of those who wish to know, but cannot: this excuses, and is the punishment of sin and not itself a sin; and that of those who, as it were, simply do not know, neither refusing nor proposing to learn: this does not excuse anyone fully, except perhaps in the sense that one is punished less. —AUGUSTINE: WHERE THERE IS NO EXCUSE. Hence Augustine, in *To Valentinus*: "The excuse from ignorance which men are accustomed to claim is taken away from those who know God's mandates. And although it is graver to sin knowingly than ignorantly, yet one ought not to take refuge in the darkness of ignorance, so that anybody may find an excuse in it. For it is one thing not to have known, another not to have wanted to know."[1] "Because in those who did not wish to understand, ignorance itself is a sin; in those who were not able to do so, however, it is a punishment of sin."[2] "But the ignorance which is not of those who do not wish to know, but of those who, as it were, simply do not know, does not excuse anyone from burning in the eternal fire, but perhaps that he burn more mildly."[3]—And so the woman did not have an excuse from ignorance, since she knew the mandate and she was not unaware that it would be a sin to act otherwise.

3. FROM WHERE DID THE CONSENT TO THAT SIN COME, SINCE HUMAN NATURE WAS STILL UNCORRUPTED. It is also usual to ask, since human nature was without defect, from where did the consent to that evil come.—RESPONSE. To this it can be answered that it was from the free choice of the will. For the cause of becoming worse existed both in humankind itself and in another. In another, because it was in the devil who persuaded; in humankind itself, because it consented by the will of free choice. And since free choice is a good, that evil consent proceeded from an entirely good thing, and so evil emanated from good. But we shall treat this more fully below, in the investigation of the origin of evil and in what thing it might grow.[4]

[1] Augustine, *De gratia et libero arbitrio*, c3 n5.
[2] Augustine, *Epistola 194* (*ad Sixtum*), c6 n27.
[3] Augustine, *De gratia et libero arbitrio*, c3 n5.
[4] See dist. 34.

Chapter 6 (135)

WHETHER THE WILL PRECEDED THAT SIN. But if it is asked whether the will preceded that sin, we say that that sin consisted in both the will and the act, and that the will preceded the act. But no other evil human will preceded that will itself; and that evil will issued forth from the devil's persuasion and from human choice by which humankind deserted justice and introduced iniquity; and that will itself was iniquity.

DISTINCTION XXIII

Chapter 1 (136)

1. WHY GOD ALLOWED HUMANS TO BE TEMPTED, KNOWING THAT THEY WOULD FALL. AUGUSTINE, IN *ON GENESIS*. Moreover, it is usual to ask "why God allowed humans to be tempted, whom he foreknew would be led astray.—But it would not be praiseworthy for human beings, if they could live well only because none would persuade them to live evilly, since, in their nature, they had the power and, in their power, the will, with the help of God, not to consent to the persuader";[1] "and it is more glorious not to consent than to be unable to be tempted."[2]

2. WHY GOD CREATED THOSE WHO HE FOREKNEW WOULD BE EVIL. "Some are also troubled and say: Why did God create those who he foreknew would be evil?—Because he foresaw that he would draw some good from their evils. For he so made them as to leave them the means to do something; and if they did something culpably, nevertheless they would find him working in a praiseworthy manner in their regard. From themselves, they have an evil will, but from him a good nature and a just punishment."[3] "And so it is vain to say: 'God ought not to have created those who he foreknew would be evil'; for he knew that they would be of use to good persons and would be justly punished for their evil will."[4]

3. They also add: "He ought to have made man such that he would not have been willing to sin at all.—We grant that a nature which would not at all be willing to sin would indeed be better. But let them also grant that a nature is not evil which is so made that it is able not to sin, if it wills; and it is justly punished, if it sinned voluntarily and not by necessity. And since the latter is good and the former is better, why would God not make

[1] Augustine, *De Genesi ad litteram*, bk 11 c4 n6.
[2] Ibid., bk 11 c6 n8.
[3] Ibid., bk 11 c9 n12.
[4] Ibid., bk 11 c6 n8.

both so as to be praised more abundantly from each? For the former is that of the holy angels, the latter of men."[5]

4. They also say: "If God willed it, these too would be good.—We grant this, too; but he better willed that they should be what they willed, and that the good ones should not be without fruit, but the evil ones not without punishment."[6]

5. They also say: "God could change their will to the good, because he is omnipotent.—Indeed, he could. Why did he not? Because he did not will it. Why did he not will it? He alone knows. We must not *know more than is suitable*."[7,8]

Chapter 2 (137)

HERE WHAT [MAN WAS] LIKE IN RESPECT TO THE SPIRIT, AND HE TREATS MAN'S KNOWLEDGE BEFORE SIN. And in respect to the spirit, man was rational, having the ability to discern between good and evil. It is held that, as soon as he was created, he not unsuitably received the knowledge of created things and the knowledge of truth which was suitable to his first perfection; and he did not progress to this by study or any application over the passage of time, but received it by God's gift from the beginning of his existence.

Chapter 3 (138)

1. THAT MAN BEFORE THE FALL HAD A THREEFOLD KNOWLEDGE, NAMELY OF THE THINGS MADE FOR HIS SAKE, OF THE CREATOR, AND OF HIMSELF. And the first man before the fall was endowed with a threefold knowledge, namely of the things made for his sake, of the Creator, and of himself.

2. ON THE KNOWLEDGE OF CREATED THINGS. It is very clear that man received knowledge of created things since it was not the Creator himself or some angel, but man himself, who conferred names on all living things,[1] so that it might be shown that man himself had knowledge of each of them. For the things which had been created for his sake were to be ruled and disposed by him, and so God gave to him the knowledge of all of them and left their provision and care to him because, as the Apostle says, *God is not concerned with oxen*.[2] God left to man the care and provision of these and other animals so that they might be subject to his dominion

[5]Augustine, *De Genesi ad litteram*, bk 11 c7 n9.
[6]Ibid., bk 11 c9 n12.
[7]Rom. 12, 3.
[8]Ibid., bk 11 c10 n13.

[1]Cf. Gen. 2, 19-20.
[2]1 Cor. 9, 9.

and governed by his reason, and that he might know how to provide for the needs of those from which he was bound to receive benefit.

3. SCRIPTURE DID NOT INSTRUCT MAN IN THE KNOWLEDGE OF DISPOSING OF AND PROVIDING FOR THINGS, NOR IN THE KNOWLEDGE OF PROVIDING THE NECESSITIES OF THE FLESH, BUT ONLY IN THE KNOWLEDGE OF THE SOUL, AND WHY. Man did not lose this knowledge by sinning, nor that by which the necessities of the flesh are provided. And so man is not instructed in Scripture about these sorts of things, but about the knowledge of the soul, which he lost by sinning.

4. ON KNOWLEDGE OF THE CREATOR. It is believed that the first man also had knowledge of the Creator. For he knew by whom he had been created, not just by that mode of knowledge in which this is perceived only *from hearing*,[3] by which mode the absent God is now sought by believers, but by some interior inspiration in which he contemplated God's presence. Nevertheless, he did not see either so excellently as the saints will see after this life, or as *darkly*[4] as we do in this life.

5. ON KNOWLEDGE OF HIMSELF. Moreover, the same man appears to have received such knowledge of himself that he was not ignorant of what he owed to his superior and what to his equal and to his inferior. He also understood his own condition and order, namely what he was like at his creation and how he ought to proceed, what he ought to do, what to avoid. If he had not had knowledge of these things, he would not be guilty of transgression, nor would he have known himself.

Chapter 4 (139)

WHETHER MAN HAD FOREKNOWLEDGE OF THE THINGS THAT WERE TO HAPPEN TO HIM.—RESPONSE, IN WHICH IT IS SAID THAT HE DID NOT HAVE FOREKNOWLEDGE OF FUTURE EVENTS. But if it is asked whether man had knowledge of the things that were to happen to him, that is, whether he foreknew his own ruin, and similarly whether he foreknew the goods which he would have had if he had remained in obedience, it can be answered that the things which he ought to do were decreed to him, rather than future things revealed. For he received knowledge and command regarding the things that ought to be done, but he did not have foreknowledge of future things. And so man did not foreknow his own fall, as we also said of the angel; Augustine asserts the same, in *On Genesis*,[5] using the reasoning which we have set out above.[6]—Let it suffice that we

[3]Cf. Rom. 10, 17.
[4]Cf. 1 Cor. 13, 12.
[5]Augustine, *De Genesi ad litteram*, bk 11 cc17-19.
[6]Dist. 4 nn2-4.

have said these things concerning the knowledge of man insofar as it pertains to his primal state.

DISTINCTION XXIV

Chapter 1 (140)

1. ON MAN'S GRACE AND POWER BEFORE THE FALL. Now it is necessary to investigate with diligence what grace or power man had before the fall, and whether or not he was able to stand firm through it.

2. THAT HE WAS CREATED IN GRACE, THROUGH WHICH HE WAS ABLE TO STAND FIRM, BUT NOT TO MAKE PROGRESS, LIKE THE ANGELS. And so it is to be known that, as we said of the angels, through grace help was given to man at creation and a power was granted by which he was able to stand firm, that is, not to fall from what he had received; but he could not make progress so that he could deserve salvation by the grace of creation [alone] without any other. He was certainly able, through that help of the grace of creation, to resist evil, but not to achieve the good.—THAT THROUGH THAT GRACE OF CREATION HE COULD IN SOME WAY LIVE WELL. And yet he was able in some way to live well through that help because he was able to live without sin; but without the additional help of grace, he was not able to live spiritually so as to deserve eternal life.

3. Hence Augustine in the *Enchiridion*: "Man was made upright[1] so that he was able both to remain in that uprightness, although not without divine help, and to become evil by his own choice: whichever of these he might have chosen, God's will would have been done, either by him or concerning him. And because he preferred to do his own will rather than God's, God's will concerning him was done."[2]—Also, in the same: "It was suitable that humankind at first be made in such a way that it would be able to will either well or evilly; not to no end if it willed well, and not with impunity if it willed evilly."[3]

4. AUGUSTINE. The same also says, in the book *On Correction and Grace*: "If this help had been lacking either to the angel or to man, when they were first made (because their nature was not made such as to be able to remain steadfast, if each so willed, without divine help), each would certainly not have fallen by his own fault: indeed, the help would have been lacking without which each could not remain steadfast."[4]—The same: "God gave a good will to man: indeed, he made him upright in it;

[1]Cf. Eccl. 7, 30.
[2]Augustine, *Enchiridion*, c107.
[3]Ibid., c105.
[4]Augustine, *De correptione et gratia*, c11 n32.

he gave him the help without which he could not remain steadfast in that will, if he so willed, and through which he could; but he left it to man's choice to will this, if he so willed."[5]—In the same: "He received the power to will, but he did not have the will by which to exercise that power; for if he had had such a will, he would have persevered."[6] By these testimonies, it is clearly shown that man received uprightness and a good will at his creation, and the help by which he was able to stand firm; otherwise, it would appear that he did not fall by his own fault.

5. WHAT THAT UPRIGHTNESS AND GOODNESS OF WILL IN WHICH HE WAS CREATED WAS LIKE. But how did man have an upright and good will, if through it he was neither able to deserve life, nor did he will to stand firm by it?—Because he did not then will any evil by that will, and for a while willed to stand firm, but not with perseverance; and so, at that time, man's will was upright and good.

6. OBJECTION AGAINST WHAT WAS SAID EARLIER, THAT MAN WOULD NOT HAVE BEEN ABLE TO MAKE PROGRESS. But it is usual to make the following objection against what we said, that man would not have been able to make progress or to have merit through the grace of creation: Through that help of the grace of creation, he was able to stand firm in the good which he had received, and so he was able to resist temptation; but to resist temptations and evil suggestions is a merit and a good worthy of reward; every good merit is a progress, however; and so he was able to make progress through the grace of creation, without the addition of another grace.

7. RESPONSE. To this we say that to resist evil and not consent to temptation would not have gained him any merit, even if he had not consented, because there was nothing in him which might impel him to evil. Similarly, for the angels who did not fall, it was not a merit that they stood firm, that is, that they did not fall to their ruin.

8. THAT TO RESIST EVIL IS SOMETIMES A MERIT AND SOMETIMES NOT. For it is sometimes a merit for us if we do not do evil, but resist it, but only where a cause is present which moves us to commit it, because our steps are prone to fall due to the corruption of sin.[7] But where no cause intervenes to impel us to evil, we gain no merit if we forbear from it. For to resist evil always avoids punishment, but does not always deserve the palm [of victory].

[5]Augustine, *De correptione et gratia*, c11 n32.
[6]Ibid.
[7]Cf. Gen. 8, 21.

Chapter 2 (141)

ON THE HELP GIVEN TO MAN AT CREATION BY WHICH HE WAS ABLE TO STAND FIRM. Here is to be considered what that help given to man at creation was by which he was able to remain steadfast, if he so willed.—That was assuredly a freedom of choice free from all stain and corruption, and an uprightness of will, and a wholeness and liveliness of all the natural powers of the soul.

Chapter 3 (142)

1. ON FREE CHOICE. Free choice, however, is a faculty of reason and will, by which the good is chosen with the assistance of grace, or evil without its assistance. And it is called 'free' in regard to the will, which may turn itself to either of them; but 'choice' in regard to reason, whose faculty or power it is, and to which it also belongs to discern between good and evil. And sometimes someone who has the power to discern between good and evil chooses what is evil; sometimes, that which is good. But he does not choose that which is good except with the help of grace; he chooses evil, however, by himself. For there is in the rational soul a natural will, by which it naturally wills what is good, although weakly and feebly, unless grace assists; at its coming, grace assists that will and builds it up so that it wills the good efficaciously; it is able to will evil efficaciously by itself. And so that power of the rational soul, by which it is able to will good or evil, discerning the one from the other, is called free choice.

2. THAT BRUTE ANIMALS DO NOT HAVE FREE CHOICE, BUT A SENSUAL APPETITE. Brute animals do not have this, because they lack reason; but they have sense and a sensual appetite.

Chapter 4 (143)

ON SENSUALITY. For sensuality is some lower power of the soul, from which comes a motion which is directed to the senses of the body and to the appetites for things that pertain to the body.

Chapter 5 (144)

1. ON REASON, WHICH HAS TWO PARTS IN RESPECT TO ITS FUNCTIONS. Reason, however, is a higher power of the soul, which, so to speak, has two parts or distinguishing attributes: a lower one and a higher. According to the superior one, it attends to the contemplation and observance of the highest things; according to the lower one, it looks after the disposition of temporal things.

2. WHAT PERTAINS TO REASON. And so whatever occurs to us in our soul when we reflect, which we do not have in common with beasts, per-

tains to reason; but whatever you find in it which is common with wild beasts, that pertains to sensuality.

3. WHERE REASON BEGINS IN THE SOUL. And when we proceed to consider step by step all the parts of the soul and we find the first thing which is not common with the beasts, there reason begins.

4. Augustine teaches these things in *On the Trinity*, book 12, where he says as follows: "Let us see where, as it were, some boundary exists between the exterior and the interior man. For whatever we have in our spirit in common with a beast, that is rightly said to pertain to the exterior man. It is not the body alone which is to be considered the exterior man, but also, when some life is added by which the frame of the body and all the senses have their force, he is made fit by these to perceive exterior things."[1] "And so, as we ascend within ourselves gradually to consider the parts of the soul, where something begins to occur which is not common to us and the beasts, there reason begins, and the interior man can now be recognized."[2]

5. ON THE PARTS OF REASON.—AUGUSTINE. "But the higher part of reason cleaves to the contemplation or observance of the eternal reasons; the lower part is turned to the governance of temporal things."[3] And "that gaze of reason by which we contemplate eternal things is considered wisdom; but the one by which we make good use of temporal things is considered knowledge."[4] "But when we discuss the nature of the human mind, we discuss one thing only; we do not separate it into the two things which I have mentioned, except in respect to its functions."[5]—"The carnal or sensual motion of the soul which is directed to the senses of the body is common to us and to the beasts; it is remote from the reason of wisdom, but close to the reason of knowledge."[6]

Chapter 6 (145)

THAT THE ORDER OF SINNING OR FALLING IS THE SAME IN US AS IN THE FIRST HUMANS. It is also not to be passed over that the order and progression of temptation is the same now in a single human person as it was then in our first parents.

[1]Augustine, *De Trinitate*, bk 12 c1 n1.
[2]Ibid., bk 12 c8 n13.
[3]Ibid., bk 12 c7 n12.
[4]Ibid., bk 12 c14 n22.
[5]Ibid., bk 12 c4 n4.
[6]Ibid., bk 12 c12 n17.

Chapter 7 (146)

THAT THE WOMAN, THE MAN, AND THE SERPENT ARE IN US, AND HOW. For at that time, the serpent persuaded the woman to [eat of] the fruit and she consented, then she gave it to her husband, and so the sin was consummated. In the same way now in us, the sensual motion of the soul is like the serpent, the lower portion of reason is like the woman, and the higher one like the man. And the latter is *the man* who, according to the Apostle, is called *the image and glory of God*; and the former is the woman who, according to the same, is called *the glory of man*.[1]

Chapter 8 (147)

1. ON THE SPIRITUAL MARRIAGE OF THE MAN AND THE WOMAN IN US. And between this man and this woman there is, as it were, a spiritual marriage and a natural contract by which the higher portion of reason, the man, as it were, is to go first and dominate; but the lower one, the woman, as it were, is to be subject and obey. And so the man, according to the Apostle, is not to wear a veil, but the woman must.[1]

2. ON A HELPER LIKE HIMSELF. And just as among all the animals there was not found for man *a helper like himself*,[2] but one taken from him, who might be joined to him in marriage; similarly, among the parts of the soul which we have in common with the beasts, there is no like helper for our mind.

3. HE SHOWS THIS TO BE THE CASE BY THE TESTIMONY OF AUGUSTINE. Hence Augustine, in the same: "That [faculty] of ours which is engaged in the management of temporal things in such a way that it is not common to us with the beasts is indeed rational. But it is drawn, as it were, from that rational mind by which we cleave to the intelligible and unchangeable truth, and it is deputed to deal with and govern the lower things. For just as among all the animals there was not found for the man *a helper like himself*,[3] but only one taken from him, who might be joined to him in marriage, similarly, from among the parts of the soul which we have in common with the beasts, there is no like helper for our mind, by which we observe supernal truth, which might help in making use of temporal things in a manner sufficient for the nature of man. And so our rationality, not separated so as to breach its unity, but branched off, as it were, to aid the partnership, is divided up to fulfil its function. And just as the flesh of the two is one in the male and female, so the one nature of our mind embraces our intellect

[1]Cf. 1 Cor. 11, 7; Augustine, *De Trinitate*, bk 12 c7 n10.

[1]Cf. 1 Cor. 11, 7-10.
[2]Cf. Gen. 2, 18.
[3]Cf. Ibid.

and action, or reason and the rational appetite, or whatever other way there is in which this may be stated more meaningfully. Just as it was said of them: *They shall be two in one flesh*,[4] so of these it can be said: two in one mind."[5]—See, by these words, it can be understood how there is an image of that marriage in the human soul, and how in each of us those three are present spiritually, namely the man, the woman, and the serpent.

Chapter 9 (148)

1. HOW TEMPTATION IS CONSUMMATED IN US THROUGH THOSE THREE. Now it remains to show how sin is consummated in us through these three, whereby it could be recognized, if we attend with diligence, what a mortal or a venial sin is in the soul.

2. For just as there the serpent persuaded the woman, and the woman the man, similarly in us, when the sensual motion has perceived the attraction of sin, it suggests it, like the serpent to the woman, namely to the lower part of our reason, that is, to the reason of knowledge; if the latter consents to the attraction, the woman eats the forbidden fruit. Afterwards, she gives of the same to the man, when [the lower part] suggests the same attraction to the higher part of our reason, that is, to the reason of wisdom; if the latter consents, then the man also tastes the forbidden fruit together with the woman.

3. WHEN SIN IS VENIAL. Therefore, if the attraction of sin is confined only to the sensual motion, then the sin is venial and very light.

Chapter 10 (149)

WHEN THE WOMAN ALONE EATS OF THE FORBIDDEN FRUIT. But if the lower part of our reason has consented, so that it is confined only to the pleasure of thought, without the will of fulfilling [the desire], the woman alone eats, not the man, by whose authority the will is restrained from achieving the deed itself.

Chapter 11 (150)

WHEN THE MAN ALSO EATS, THEN IT IS A MORTAL SIN. But if there is present a full will to fulfil [the desire], so that, if the occasion arises, the deed is done, then the man also eats, because the higher part of our reason consented to the attraction; and then it is a grave and damnable sin.

[4]Gen. 2, 24.
[5]Augustine, *De Trinitate*, bk 12 c3 n3.

Chapter 12 (151)

1. In the woman's tasting distinguish: sometimes it is mortal, sometimes venial. But when the woman tastes without the man, sometimes it is a mortal sin, sometimes venial. For as we said,[1] then the woman tastes without the man, when the sin is confined to the pleasure of thought in such a way that it is not decreed to be done; or when some limit and measure is placed by the man on the sin, so that the woman is not allowed to go further into sin by an unbridled freedom.—He repeats about the woman tasting without the man, where he shows when it is venial and when mortal. And so if the sin is not kept long in the pleasure of thought, but is repelled by the man's authority as soon as it has touched the woman, it, it is venial. But if it is kept for a long time in the pleasure of thought, even though there is no will to complete it, it is mortal; and because of it the man and the woman will be damned together, that is, the whole man, because then the man did not restrain the woman as he ought to have done; and so he may be said to have consented.

2. Repetition and summary. And so to present a brief summary of the above, when sin is conceived in the soul so that it decides to commit it, or does commit it, whether frequently or only once, or even when it is kept for a long time in the pleasure of thought, it is mortal. But when it is only in the sensual motion, as we said earlier,[2] then it is very light because the reason does not then delight in it.

3. Why he said 'frequently' or 'once.' And above I said: 'whether frequently or only once,' because there are some things which damn even if they are done, or proposed to be done, only once; but there are some things which do not do so, unless they are done or determined to be done more frequently, as in the case of needless speech and suchlike.

4. Augustine confirms it to be so in his authority. Augustine teaches these things, in *On the Trinity*, book 12, in the following terms: "Just as in that marriage of the first humans, the serpent persuaded to eat, and the woman did not eat alone, but gave it to her husband and they ate together, similarly in the secret marriage which is made and discerned in every man, when the animal sense introduces the attraction [of sin] to the reason of knowledge, which is engaged in the management of temporal things by the liveliness of ratiocination, then it is like the serpent speaking to the woman. To consent to this pleasure is to eat of the forbidden tree."—When the woman alone tastes. "But if this consent is contained only within the pleasure of thought, and the members are restrained by higher authority so as not to become *weapons of iniquity in sin*,[3] then I

[1] Under c10.
[2] In c9 n3.
[3] Cf. Rom. 6, 13.

judge this to be as if the woman alone had eaten the forbidden fruit."—WHEN THE WOMAN TASTES WITH THE MAN. "But if in that consent it is decreed that any sin, if there be the power, will be completed also in deed, then it is to be understood that the woman gave the unlawful food to her husband for them to eat of it together. For it is not possible for sin to be decreed by the mind not only to be considered with pleasure, but also committed effectively, unless that intention of the mind, which has the supreme power to move its members to the deed or to restrain them from it, also gives in to the evil action."—WHETHER THAT WHICH IS CONFINED ONLY TO THE PLEASURE OF THOUGHT IS MORTAL. "It is certainly not to be denied that it is a sin when the mind takes pleasure in unlawful things in thought alone, while not decreeing that they are to be done, and yet holding on to them and gladly considering things which ought to have been spat out as soon as they touched the spirit, but much less so than if it were also decided to complete it in deed. And so forgiveness is also to be sought for such thoughts, and the breast is to be struck while saying: *Forgive us our debts, as we also forgive our debtors*.[4] For it is not as with those first two humans, where each was responsible only for one's own person, and so, if the woman alone had eaten of the forbidden fruit, she alone would certainly have been punished with the penalty of death. In the case of the single human being, however, it cannot be said that, if thought alone freely feeds upon unlawful delights, from which it ought to turn away immediately, and evils are not decreed to be done, but are only kept pleasurably in the memory, the woman can, as it were, be damned without the man. Far be it from us to believe this! For this is a single person, a single human being, who will be entirely damned, unless those things which are felt to be only sins of thought without the will to do them, yet with the will to give pleasure to the spirit by them, are remitted by the grace of the Mediator."[5]

5. AUGUSTINE. The same also speaks of this in *Against the Manichees*, book 2, saying: "The Apostle says: *According to the prince of power of this air, the spirit who now works in the children of faithlessness*.[6] Does he then appear visibly to them, or enter, as it were, the physical places in which they are and do his work? [Not at all], but he suggests whatever he can by thought in remarkable ways. We must resist these suggestions: *For we are not unaware of his deviousness*.[7] How did he approach Judas, when he persuaded him to betray the Lord? Did he appear to him in [physical] places, or as visible to his eyes? No; he merely, as it is said,

[4]Mt. 6, 12.
[5]Augustine, *De Trinitate*, bk 12 c12 nn17-18.
[6]Eph. 2, 2.
[7]2 Cor. 2, 11.

entered into his heart.[8] But man repulses him, if he would preserve paradise. For God placed man in paradise *to work and keep it,*[9] because, as it is said of the Church in the Song of Songs: *an enclosed garden, a marked fountain,*[10] where that persuader of perversity is not at all allowed. But he deceived through the woman nevertheless. For our reason cannot be brought to consent to sin, except when pleasure is moved in that part of our spirit which ought to be subject to reason as [woman] to the rule of the man.—Also, in each of us nothing else happens, when each falls into sin, than what was then done in those three: the serpent, the woman, and the man. For first comes suggestion, either by thought or by the senses of the body: seeing, or touching, or hearing, or tasting, or smelling. When this suggestion has occurred, if our cupidity is not moved to sin, the serpent's wiliness is kept out. But if it is moved, then it is as if the woman had already been persuaded. Sometimes, however, the reason manfully holds back and restrains cupidity; when this happens, we do not fall into sin, but are crowned with some struggle. But if our reason consents and decrees that what desire moved is to be done, man is expelled from all blessed life, as if from paradise. For it is already imputed a sin, even if the deed does not follow, when conscience is found guilty of consent."[11]

6. WHY HE HAS SAID THESE THINGS ABOUT THE PARTS OF THE SOUL. We have inserted these things about the parts of the soul so that the nature of the soul itself may be known more fully and free choice be understood in respect to that part of the soul it resides in, namely in respect to reason. For it is by free choice that every mortal sin is done, but not every venial one, namely that which consists in the movement of sensuality alone.

Chapter 13 (152)

THAT IN SCRIPTURE SENSUALITY IS OFTEN TAKEN OTHERWISE THAN ABOVE, NAMELY THAT THE LOWER PORTION OF REASON IS ALSO UNDERSTOOD BY THAT TERM. But it is not to be passed over in silence that in Scripture[1] by the term sensuality is often understood not only that in our soul which is common to us and the beasts, but also the lower portion of reason which oversees the disposition of temporal things.[2] Let the reader vigilantly note this in the passages of Scripture where it is mentioned.

[8]Cf. Lk. 22, 3; Jn. 13, 2.
[9]Gen. 2, 15.
[10]Song 4, 12.
[11]Augustine, *De Genesi contra Manichaeos*, bk 2 c14 nn20-21.

[1]Cf. Augustine, *De Trinitate*, bk 12 c13 n20.
[2]See above, cc4-5.

DISTINCTION XXV

Chapter 1 (153)

1. HE RETURNS TO THE CONSIDERATION OF FREE CHOICE. But let us now return to our subject,[1] namely to treating free choice.

2. DEFINITION OF FREE CHOICE ACCORDING TO THE PHILOSOPHERS, WHICH AGREES WITH WHAT WAS SET OUT EARLIER. In defining it, the philosophers called it "a free judgement concerning the will"[2] because the very power and ability of will and reason, which we said above free choice to be,[3] is free toward either [good or evil], since it can be freely moved to the one or to the other. And so choice is called free in regard to the will, because it can be moved voluntarily and it can be led by a spontaneous appetite to those things which the will judges, or can judge, to be good or evil.

3. THAT FREE CHOICE PERTAINS ONLY TO THE FUTURE, BUT NOT TO ALL THAT IS FUTURE. And this is to be known, that free choice does not refer to the present or past, but to future contingencies. For what is in the present is already determined; and it is not in our power that it should then be or not be, when it already is. For it can afterwards not be, or be otherwise; but it cannot not be while it is, or be otherwise while it is what it is. But whether it will be this or something else in the future pertains to the power of free choice.—And yet, not all future things come under the power of free choice, but only those things which can be done or not done through free choice. For if one wills or disposes to do such a thing that is not at all in one's power, or that would equally happen without one's disposition, then one does not have free choice in this.

4. THAT THE DESCRIPTION OF FREE CHOICE POSITED ABOVE DOES NOT APPLY TO GOD, OR TO THOSE WHO ARE ALREADY IN GLORY. According to the above description, free choice appears to be only in those who can change their will and bend it to contrary things, that is, in those whose power it is to elect good or evil, and to do or leave undone either of these according to their election. According to this, there cannot be free choice either in God, or in all those who are strengthened by such grace of blessedness that they are already unable to sin.

5. THAT THERE IS FREE CHOICE IN GOD. But Augustine teaches that God has free choice; in *On the City of God*, book 22, he speaks as follows: "Is God really to be said not to have free choice, simply because

[1]See dist. 24 c3.

[2]Boethius, *In libro Aristotelis de interpretatione, editio secunda seu maiora commentaria*, 3.

[3]Dist. 24 c3.

he cannot sin?"[4]—Ambrose too, in the book *On the Trinity*, asserts: "Paul says that *one and the same Spirit works all things, who distributes them to each as he wills*,[5] that is, according to the choice of free will, not in subjection to necessity."[6]

Chapter 2 (154)

HOW FREE CHOICE IS UNDERSTOOD IN GOD. But free choice is understood otherwise in the Creator than in the creature. For God's most wise and omnipotent will, which does all things as it wills, and not by necessity, but by free goodness, is called free choice.—And so Jerome, noting that free choice is not in God in the same way as it is in creatures, appears to deny that there is free choice in God; in a homily *On the Prodigal Son*, he says: "God is the only one in whom no sin happens or can happen; all others, since they have free choice, can bend to either side."[1] When he says 'all others,' he implies that free choice is not in God as it is in all others.

Chapter 3 (155)

THAT THE ANGELS AND SAINTS WHO ARE ALREADY BLESSED HAVE FREE CHOICE. The angels and saints, however, who already live happily with the Lord, and are already so confirmed in the grace of blessedness that they neither can, nor wish to bend to evil, do not lack free choice.—Hence Augustine, in *On the City of God*, book 22, says: "Just as the first immortality, which Adam lost by sinning, consisted in being able not to die, so the first free choice consisted in being able not to sin, but the last will consist in not being able to sin."[1]—The same in the *Enchiridion*: "It was suitable that man first be made so that he could will both good and evil; but afterwards he shall be such that he will not be able to will evil, nor will he lack free choice thereby."[2]

Chapter 4 (156)

1. THAT THE CHOICE SHALL BE FREER WHEN HE WILL NOT BE ABLE TO SIN. —AUGUSTINE: "In fact, the choice shall be much freer for his being entirely unable to be subject to sin. Nor is it not a will, or said not to be a free will, by which we so will to be blessed that not only do we not will to

[4]Augustine, *De civitate Dei*, bk 22 c30 n3.
[5]1 Cor. 12, 11.
[6]Ambrose, *De fide*, bk 2 c6 n48.

[1]Jerome, *Epistola 21* (*ad Damasum*), n40.

[1]Augustine, *De civitate Dei*, bk 22 c30 n3 .
[2]Augustine, *Enchiridion*, c105.

be miserable, but are entirely unable to do so. Therefore, just as even now our soul has the inability to will unhappiness, so [in the future] it will always have the inability to will iniquity. But an order had to be preserved, by which God willed to show how good a rational animal is that is even able to sin, although it would be better not to be able to sin."[1]—See, by these words, it is clearly affirmed that, after the confirmation of blessedness, there will be in man a free choice by which he will be unable to sin, as it already now is in the angels and saints who are with the Lord; and certainly the choice will be so much the freer the more immune it is from sin and the more prone to good. For the further removed one is kept by such choice from that slavery to sin, of which it is said: *He who commits sin is a slave to sin*,[2] the freer the judgement one has in electing the good.

2. CLEAR AND SUFFICIENT REASON WHY IT IS SAID TO BE A FREE CHOICE. And so, if the matter is diligently examined, choice is seen to be called 'free' because, without compulsion or necessity, it is able to desire or elect what it has decreed by reason.

Chapter 5 (157)

ON THE DIFFERENCE IN FREEDOM OF CHOICE AT DIFFERENT TIMES. From what has been said, it has become very clear that the first freedom of choice was greater than the second, and the third will be much greater than the second or the first. For the first freedom of choice was that in which there was the power to sin and not to sin; but the last will be that in which there be the power not to sin, and no power to sin; and the middle one is that in which there is the power to sin, and no power not to sin: before restoration [of grace], even mortally; after restoration, not even venially.[1]

Chapter 6 (158)

ON THE FOUR STATES OF FREE CHOICE. And four states of free choice can be noted in man. For before sin, nothing impeded man from the good, nothing impelled him to evil; he did not have a weakness toward evil, and had a help toward the good. Then, reason was able to judge without error, and the will was able to desire the good without difficulty.—But after sin, before the restoration of grace, he is pressed down and overcome by concupiscence; he has weakness toward evil, but does not have grace toward good; and so he can sin and cannot not sin, even damnably.—After the restoration and before confirmation, however, he is pressed down by concupiscence, but not overcome; and he also has weakness toward evil, but

[1]Augustine, *Enchiridion*, c105.
[2]Jn. 8, 34.

[1]On this chapter and the next, see Augustine, *De correptione et gratia*, c12 n33.

grace toward good, so that he is able to sin because of his freedom and weakness, and he is able not to sin unto death because of his freedom and the help of grace. Nevertheless, he does not yet have the power not to sin entirely or the inability to sin, because his weakness has not yet been entirely removed and grace has not yet been entirely perfected.—But after the confirmation, when the weakness will have been entirely destroyed and grace achieved, he will have the power to be neither overcome nor pressed down, and then he shall have the inability to sin.

Chapter 7 (159)

1. ON THE CORRUPTION OF FREE CHOICE THROUGH SIN. And so it is manifest that, in addition to other penalties, because of that sin man incurred a punishment in the corruption and suppression of free choice. For by that sin, natural goods became corrupt in man and the goods of grace were taken away. Indeed, he is the one who was wounded and despoiled by robbers:[1] *wounded* in his natural goods, of which he was not deprived, otherwise reparation could not occur; but *despoiled* of the goods of grace, which had been added to the natural ones through grace. These are the *very best* grants and the *perfect* gifts,[2] some of which were corrupted by sin, that is, the natural ones, such as ingenuity, memory, intellect; others were taken away, that is, the goods of grace. Although the natural gifts are also from grace (for they pertain to the general grace of God), yet this kind of distinction is often made when the term grace is taken specifically, not generically.

2. And so freedom of choice was corrupted through sin and was in part lost. Hence Augustine in the *Enchiridion*: "By making an evil use of his free choice, man lost both himself and that choice. For when he sinned by free choice, and sin had overcome him, free choice was also lost: *For a man becomes the bond servant of the one by whom he is overcome.*"[3,4] See, he says that man lost free choice: not because he did not have free choice after sin, but because he lost the freedom of choice, not indeed all of it, but only the freedom from misery and sin.

Chapter 8 (160)

1. ON THE THREE MODES OF FREEDOM OF CHOICE. Indeed, freedom is threefold, namely from necessity, from sin, from misery.

[1]Cf. Lk. 10, 30.
[2]Cf. James 1, 17.
[3]2 Pet. 2, 19.
[4]Augustine, *Enchiridion*, c30.

2. ON FREEDOM FROM NECESSITY. Choice is equally free from necessity both before and after sin. For just as it could not be compelled then, so it cannot be now. And so it is rightly concluded that there is a will in God which is always free from necessity and can never be compelled. Where there is necessity, there is no freedom; where there is no freedom, there is no will; and so there is no merit. This freedom is in all, both good and evil.

3. ON FREEDOM FROM SIN. There is also another freedom, namely from sin, of which the Apostle says: *Where the Spirit of the Lord is, there is freedom*;[1] and Truth says in the Gospel: *If the Son has freed you, you will be truly free*.[2]—This freedom frees us from the servitude of sin and renders us servants of justice, just as conversely the servitude of sin frees us from justice. Hence the Apostle: *Freed from sin, you have become servants of justice*;[3] and also: *When you were slaves of sin, you were free from justice*.[4]—Man lost this freedom by sinning; and so Augustine says that "by making an evil use of his free choice, man lost both himself and that choice,"[5] because the freedom [that] was lost through sin, was not freedom from necessity, but from sin: *For one who commits a sin is a slave of sin*.[6]

4. WHO HAVE THIS FREEDOM, NAMELY FROM SIN, AND THROUGH WHAT. Those alone whom the Son frees and restores through grace now have this freedom, which is from sin: not in such a way that they are entirely without sin in this mortal flesh, but that sin will neither dominate, nor rule in them.—And this is the true and good freedom, which gives birth to the good servitude, namely of justice. Hence Augustine in the *Enchiridion*: "No one shall be free to do justice unless, freed from sin, he will have begun to be a servant of justice; and that is the true liberty because of joy in the righteous deed, and also pious servitude because of obedience to God's command."[7]

5. There is another freedom that is not true, attached to the evil servitude, which is that of doing evil: where reason dissents from the will, judging that what the will desires is not to be done. But in doing good, reason agrees with the will, and so there is a true and pious freedom.—And concerning the freedom to do evil and the evil servitude, Augustine says in the *Enchiridion*: "What can the freedom of a bond servant be, ex-

[1]2 Cor. 3, 17.
[2]Jn. 8, 36.
[3]Rom. 6, 18.
[4]Rom. 6, 20.
[5]Above, c7 n2.
[6]Jn. 8, 34.
[7]Augustine, *Enchiridion*, c30.

cept when it pleases him to sin? For he freely serves who does his lord's will with pleasure. And so he is free to sin who is the servant of sin."[8]

6. QUESTION REGARDING THE FREEDOM TO DO EVIL, WHETHER THIS IS THE FREEDOM OF A FREE CHOICE OR SOMETHING ELSE. Here it can be asked whether this freedom, by which one is free to do evil, is freedom of choice. For if it is freedom of choice, then it is a good, because freedom of choice is a natural good.—RESPONSE ACCORDING TO SOME. It seems to some that this is freedom of choice, which is always good; but because of the servitude of sin, it becomes freer and more prone to sin, and so it is said not to be true freedom, because it is for evil.—ACCORDING TO OTHERS. But it seems to others that this freedom to do evil, which Augustine has recalled above,[9] is not freedom of choice itself, but is some proneness and bent toward sinning, which is from sin and is evil.

7. ANOTHER QUESTION, ON THE FREEDOM TO DO GOOD, WHETHER IT IS FREEDOM OF CHOICE OR NOT. Similarly, it is also usual to ask whether that true liberty, which is the one to do justice, is freedom of choice itself.—RESPONSE ACCORDING TO SOME.—AUGUSTINE. Some say that it is the very same, but restored through grace, with whose help it is free toward the good; but without grace, it is not free toward the good. Hence Augustine in the *Enchiridion*: "Whence will come this freedom to do good to the man who is bound and sold, unless he is redeemed by the one who says: *If the Son has freed you, you will be truly free?*[10] And before this begins to be done in a man, how will anyone boast of free choice, who is not yet free to do what is good?"[11] See, he plainly shows that free choice is freed through grace, so that one may do what is good through it. And so they say that that true freedom, which is for doing good and which Augustine has recalled above,[12] is freedom of choice itself, freed and helped by God's grace.—ACCORDING TO OTHERS. But others hold that it is not freedom of choice itself, but something else, which from grace and free choice begins to be in the mind of man when it is restored by the working of God.

8. A CERTAIN DETERMINATION OF BOTH QUESTIONS, IN WHICH IT IS SAID THAT FREEDOM OF CHOICE IS FREEDOM TOWARD GOOD AND TOWARD EVIL. But it pleases us more that freedom of choice itself be both that by which one is free to do evil, and that by which one is free to do the good. For it is called different things because of different causes. It is called freedom to do evil before it is restored through grace; but once it has been restored through grace, it is called freedom to do good, because before grace, the will is free toward evil, but through grace it is made free toward the good.

[8]Augustine, *Enchiridion*, c30.
[9]Above, n5.
[10]Jn. 8, 36.
[11]Augustine, *Enchiridion*, c30.
[12]In n4.

And so the will of man is always in some manner free, but it is not always good: for it is not good, unless it is freed from sin; and yet it is free from necessity. Hence Augustine in the book *On Grace and Free Choice*: "The will is always free in us, but it is not always good. For either it is free from justice when it serves sin, and then it is evil; or it is free from sin when it serves justice, and then it is good."[13]

9. ON FREEDOM FROM MISERY. There is likewise a freedom from misery, of which the Apostle says: *And the creature itself will be freed from the servitude of corruption into the liberty of the glory of the children of God.*[14] Man had this freedom before sin, because he lacked all misery and was touched by no trouble; and he shall have it more fully in his future blessedness, where he will not be able to be miserable. But in this life, which is between the first sin and the final confirmation, no one is free from misery, because no one lacks the punishment of sin.

10. HE AGAIN ADDRESSES THE CORRUPTION OF FREE CHOICE IN ORDER TO ADD SOME THINGS. From the above, it is already apparent [what it was] in which free choice was diminished or corrupted through sin: because before sin there was no difficulty and no impediment in man toward the good regarding the law of the members, no impulsion or instigation toward evil. But now he is impeded from the good by the law of the flesh, and he is instigated toward evil, so that he cannot will and achieve the good, unless he is freed and assisted through grace, because, as the Apostle says, *sin lives in the flesh.*[15]

11. THAT CHOICE IS NOT EQUALLY FREE IN GOOD AND EVIL PERSONS, NOR TOWARD GOOD AND EVIL THINGS. And so free choice, although it is always free in every person, yet is not equally free in both the good and evil ones, nor toward good and evil things. For it is freer in good people, in whom it has been freed, than in evil ones, in whom it has not been freed; and it is freer toward the evil which it can do by itself than toward the good which, unless it is freed and helped by grace, it cannot do.

Chapter 9 (161)

1. ON FREEDOM: WHICH IS FROM GRACE AND WHICH FROM NATURE. And so freedom from sin and from misery is through grace, but freedom from necessity is through nature. The Apostle signifies both freedoms, namely of nature and of grace, when he speaks in the person of the man who is not redeemed: *To will is in me, but I cannot find how to achieve it*;[1] as if

[13]Augustine, *De gratia et libero arbitrio*, c15 n31.
[14]Rom. 8, 21.
[15]Rom. 7, 17-18.

[1]Rom. 7, 18.

to say: I have the freedom of nature, but I do not have the freedom of grace, and so the achievement of the good is not in me.

2. WHAT THE WILL OF MAN IS UNABLE TO DO BY ITSELF, AND WHAT IT CAN DO THROUGH GRACE. Indeed, the will of man, which he has naturally, is not able to raise itself to will the good efficaciously or to fulfil it in deed, unless it is freed and aided by grace: freed in order to will, and aided in order to achieve; because, as the Apostle says, to will *is not of the one who wills, nor to run*, that is, to work, *of the one who runs*,[2] but *of the merciful God, who works in us to will and work the good.*[3] It is not the will or work of man which calls upon God's grace, but grace itself first comes to the will, preparing it to will the good, and then aids the prepared will to achieve it.

DISTINCTION XXVI

Chapter 1 (162)

1. ON OPERATING AND CO-OPERATING GRACE. This is operating and co-operating grace. For operating grace prepares the will of man to will the good; co-operating grace helps it not to will in vain. Hence Augustine in the book *On Grace and Free Choice*: "By co-operating, God achieves in us what he had begun by operating; because he begins by working that we will, and he achieves by co-operating with those who do will. And so he works that we will; once we do will, and so will that we proceed to doing, he co-operates with us. Yet without him, either operating that we will or co-operating when we do will, we can do nothing toward the good works of piety."[1]

2. WHICH IS THE OPERATING GRACE AND WHICH THE CO-OPERATING ONE. See, by these words, it is sufficiently revealed which is the operating grace and which the co-operating one. The operating one is that which goes ahead of the good will, for it is by it that man's will is freed and prepared in order to be good and to will the good efficaciously; and co-operating grace accompanies the will which is already good in order to aid it.

3. AUGUSTINE. Hence *Against Julian the Heretic*, who said that a good will was from free choice alone, and who asserted that man can will the good through free choice and work it without grace, Augustine says: "The Apostle offered a clear statement in commendation of grace when he said: *It is not of the one who wills, or of the one who runs, but of the*

[2]Rom. 9, 16.
[3]Phil. 2, 13.

[1]Augustine, *De gratia et libero arbitrio*, c17 n33.

merciful God.[2] If you were to attend to this, O Julian, you would not extend the merits of the human will against grace. For God does not have mercy on someone because that person has willed and run, but he willed and ran because God has had mercy on him. For the human *will is prepared by the God*,[3] and *the steps of man are directed by the Lord*;[4] and so fittingly does he say: *It is not of the one who wills, or of the one who runs, but of the merciful God*."[5]—AUGUSTINE, *ON THE PERFECTION OF RIGHTEOUSNESS*: "It is not that this is done without our will, but that our will can do nothing good without divine assistance."[6]—AUGUSTINE, *TO PAULINUS*. Hence the Apostle says elsewhere: "*And not I, but the grace of God in me*.[7] He does not say this because he was doing nothing good, but because he would have done nothing good if that grace were not aiding him."[8]—By these testimonies, it is plainly indicated that the will of man is first visited and prepared by the grace of God so that it may be made good, not so that it may be made a will, because it was a will even before grace, but it was not a good and righteous will.

Chapter 2 (163)

1. WHAT THE WILL IS. In the book *On the Two Souls*, Augustine defines the will itself in the following terms: "The will is a movement of the spirit, without the compulsion of anyone, toward not committing something or toward gaining it."[1]

2. HE CONTINUES HIS TREATMENT OF OPERATING AND CO-OPERATING GRACE AND OF THE WILL OF MAN. But this [will] is first visited and prepared by God's grace so that it may not commit evil and may gain the good.—AUGUSTINE, IN THE *ENCHIRIDION*: Hence the Apostle, offering a commendation of prevenient and subsequent grace, that is, of operating and co-operating grace, vigilantly said: *It is not of the one who wills, or of the one who runs, but of the merciful God*,[2] and not the converse: It is not of the merciful God, but of the one who wills and of the one who runs. Indeed, "if, as it has pleased some, when it is said: *It is not of the one who wills, or of the one who runs, but of the merciful God*,[3] it should be taken as if it said: The will of man alone does not suffice, if the mercy of God is

[2]Rom. 9, 16.
[3]Prov. 8, 35, Septuagint.
[4]Cf. Ps. 36, 23.
[5]Augustine, *Contra Julianum opus imperfectum*, bk 1 c141.
[6]Augustine, *De perfectione iustitiae hominis*, c19 n40.
[7]1 Cor. 15, 10.
[8]Augustine (rather, Alypius), *Epistola 186* (*ad Paulinum*), c10 n36.

[1]Augustine, *De duabus animabus*, c10 n14.
[2]Rom. 9, 16.
[3]Ibid.

not also present; we would say, on the contrary, that even the mercy of God is not sufficient, if the will of man is not also present. And so, if the first is rightly said, because the will of man alone cannot fulfil it, then why is the converse not rightly said: It is not of the merciful God, but of the man who wills, because God's mercy alone does not fulfil it? For man would not be able to believe or hope unless he wills to do so, nor to gain the palm [of victory] unless he runs willingly. And so it remains that what was said be rightly understood so as to ascribe everything to God, who first comes and prepares the good will of man to receive aid and aids it when it is prepared. God first comes to the unwilling to make him willing, then follows the willing so that he should not will in vain."[4]—See, by these words and the earlier ones, it is clearly taught that the will of man is first visited and prepared by God's grace in order to will the good; then it is helped so as not to will it in vain.

3. THAT GOOD WILL GOES WITH GRACE. And so good will goes with grace, not grace with the will. Hence Augustine, in *To Pope Boniface*, writing against the Pelagians, says: "When faith obtains justification, *according to the measure of faith which God* has shared out *to each*,[5] it is not that something of human merit precedes God's grace; but that grace itself deserves to be increased, so that once increased it may deserve to be perfected, while the will goes with it and does not lead, going after it and not before."[6] See, here you expressly have it that grace goes before the merit of good will, and good will itself goes after, not before, grace.

Chapter 3 (164)

1. WHAT THE GRACE THAT GOES BEFORE THE WILL IS, NAMELY FAITH WITH LOVE. And if you contemplate it with diligence, it will likewise be shown to you what the grace that goes before and prepares the will is, namely faith with love.[1]—And so Augustine, in the same treatise, discussing how we are justified by faith and yet freely (for the Apostle asserts both), says: "The Apostle who says: *Justified by faith*,[2] says elsewhere: *Freely justified through grace*.[3] For he said this so that faith itself should not become proud; lest it should say to itself: If justified from faith, then how freely? For if faith deserves something, why [should it not be said] to be repaid rather than given? (PAY ATTENTION!) Do not let the faithful man say such things, for when he says: I have faith so I deserve justifica-

[4]Augustine, *Enchiridion*, c32.
[5]Cf. Rom. 12, 3.
[6]More correctly, Alypius, in Augustine, *Epistola 186* (*ad Paulinum*), c3 n10.

[1]Cf. Gal. 5, 6.
[2]Rom. 5, 1.
[3]Rom. 3, 24.

tion, it is answered to him: *What do you have which you have not received?*[4] For the faith by which you are justified has been freely given to you."[5] Here it is plainly shown that faith is the cause of justification.

2. ON THE BENEFIT BY WHICH THE WILL IS FREED. And grace itself is also the benefit by which the will of man is first visited and prepared. Hence Augustine in the *Retractations*, book 1: "The will is that by which we both sin and live righteously. But unless the will itself is freed by God's grace from servitude, by which it is made a servant to sin, and is helped to overcome the vices, it is impossible for mortals to live righteously and piously. And unless this benefit, by which the will is freed, were given before the will becomes good, then it would be given because of merits and would not be grace, which is given entirely freely."[6] And so the good will of man is first visited by that benefit of grace by which it is freed and prepared.

3. And that benefit is rightly understood as the faith of Christ, as Augustine clearly shows in the *Enchiridion*, saying: "After that fall, the faculty of choice required liberation from servitude to sin. And it is not at all freed by itself, but exclusively through God's grace, which rests in the faith of Christ, so that the will itself may be prepared."[7] See, he plainly says that the grace by which choice is freed and the will is prepared rests in the faith of Christ. As he says in the same: "For the faith of Christ obtains what the law commands."[8]

Chapter 4 (165)

1. THAT THE GOOD WILL WHICH IS PRECEDED BY GRACE PRECEDES SOME GIFTS OF GOD. And yet it itself precedes some gifts of grace. Hence Augustine, in the *Enchiridion*: "The good will of man precedes many of God's gifts, but not all. Indeed, the good will itself must be counted among the gifts it does not precede and which it aids. And so in holy Scripture we read both, *his mercy shall precede me*,[1] and *his mercy shall follow me*.[2] It goes ahead of the unwilling to make him willing, it follows the willing so that he not will in vain. For why are we urged to pray for our enemies who do not will to live piously,[3] unless so that God should work willingness in them? And also, why are we urged to ask that we

[4]1 Cor. 4, 7.
[5]Augustine, *Epistola 186* (*ad Paulinum*), c3 nn9-10.
[6]Augustine, *Retractationes*, bk 1 c9 n4.
[7]Augustine, *Enchiridion*, c106.
[8]Ibid., c117.

[1]Ps. 58, 11.
[2]Ps. 22, 6.
[3]Cf. Mt. 5, 44.

may receive,[4] unless so that what we will may come from him from whom has come that we will?"[5] And so the Apostle says: *It is not of the one who wills, or of the one who runs, but of the merciful God.*[6]—From these words, it appears that the good will of man precedes some of God's gifts because helping grace goes with it; and it is preceded by some others because operating grace, that is, faith with love, precedes it.

2. SOME APPARENT CONTRADICTIONS TO THE FOREGOING, NAMELY THAT FAITH SEEMS TO BE SAID TO BE FROM THE WILL. And yet we must not ignore that elsewhere Augustine appears to signify that faith is from the will; namely in *On John*, discussing that phrase of the Apostle, *Belief in the heart is for justification*,[7] he says: "And so the Apostle does not simply say *belief*, but *belief in the heart*, because man can do other things unwillingly, but he cannot believe unwillingly; he can enter a church and approach the altar unwillingly, but not believe."[8]—Also, on the passage in Genesis where Laban and Bathuel said: *Let us call the girl and seek her will*,[9] the expositor says: "Because faith pertains to the will, not to necessity."[10]

3. RESPONSE WITH DETERMINATION. In response to these contradictions, we say that they are not to be taken in such a way that faith is understood to come from the will of man since, as the Apostle says, faith properly is the gift of God,[11] and in it the good merits of man have their beginning. As Augustine says on Psalm 67: "For it is through faith that the impious is justified, that is, he is made pious from being impious, so that afterwards faith itself begins to work through love";[12] and so all good merits begin from it.—But rather these things have been so said in the sense that faith does not reside in anyone except him who wills to believe, whose good will faith precedes not in time, but according to cause and nature. Hence Augustine fittingly said above that 'the good will itself must be counted among the gifts it does not precede and which it aids':[13] because it aids the things by which it is preceded when it consents with them to achieve the good, and it is among them because it is not preceded by them in time.

4. HE ADDS SOME OTHER THINGS WHICH MAKE THE QUESTION MORE DIFFICULT, NAMELY THAT THOUGHT OF THE GOOD PRECEDES FAITH. Moreover, the words of Augustine make this question more pressing and pointed; in the book *On the Predestination of the Saints*, discussing that phrase of the

[4]Cf. Mt. 7, 7-8; Lk. 11, 9.
[5]Augustine, *Enchiridion*, c32.
[6]Rom. 9, 16.
[7]Rom. 10, 10.
[8]Augustine, *In Ioannem*, tr. 26 n2.
[9]Gen. 24, 57.
[10]Interlinear gloss, on Gen. 24, 57; from Ambrosiaster on 2 Cor. 1, 23.
[11]Cf. Eph. 2, 8.
[12]Augustine, *Enarrationes in Psalmos*, on Ps. 67, 32-33, n41.
[13]Above, at the beginning of n1.

Apostle: *Not that we are sufficient to think anything as coming from ourselves,*[14] he says: "As for those who hold that the beginning of faith comes from ourselves and that the strengthening of faith comes from God, let them pay attention and weigh these words. For in his commendation of this grace, which is not granted according to any merits, but renders all good things meritorious, the Apostle says: *Not that we are sufficient to think anything*" good, that is, "*as coming from ourselves*. But who does not see that thinking comes before believing? For no one believes anything without first thinking that it ought to be believed. (WHAT IT IS TO BELIEVE.) And so, if to think about the good is not from ourselves, as the Apostle teaches here, then to believe is not either, since to believe itself is nothing other than to think with the assent of the mind."[15]—Here he seems to imply that good thought precedes faith, and so good will precedes faith and is not preceded by it; this appears to contradict what was said above.

5. DETERMINATION. And to this we say that sometimes good thought or will precedes faith, but it is not that good thought or will by which we live righteously. For that one does not exist without faith and charity. Indeed, as Augustine says in *To Anastasius*, "the will of man is not free without the Spirit because it is overcome by desires."[16] It is not free to the good, unless it has been freed; but it is not freed unless *charity is poured into our hearts through the Spirit.*[17]—AUGUSTINE, IN *ON THE BAPTISM OF CHILDREN*. The will is not free, "unless grace frees it *through the law of faith*,"[18] that is, it is not free without faith *working in love*;[19] and [only] that will is sufficiently and truly good. "For there is no good fruit which does not grow from the root of charity; but if there is also faith working through love, then there is delight in the good."[20]

Chapter 5 (166)

HE DISCUSSES FULLY THAT THOUGHT OF THE GOOD WHICH PRECEDES FAITH. But that thought or will, which precedes faith and charity and the other sources of justification, does not suffice for salvation, nor does one live righteously by it. The good will which is a great good is desired by this [preceding] will, but not this by that one; and so this will or thought is one thing, and that will another.

[14] 2 Cor. 3, 5.
[15] Augustine, *De praedestinatione sanctorum*, c2 n5.
[16] Augustine, *Epistola 145*, nn2-3.
[17] Cf. Rom. 5, 5.
[18] Rom. 3, 27.
[19] Cf. Gal. 5, 6.
[20] Augustine, *De peccatorum meritis et remissione et de baptismo parvulorum*, bk 2 cc18-19.

Chapter 6 (167)

THAT UNDERSTANDING PRECEDES BOTH THOUGHT OF THE GOOD AND GOOD WILL. And as the one will precedes the other, so understanding precedes the first will. Hence Augustine, on the place of the Psalm: *My soul burned to desire your judgements*,[1] draws a distinction in these terms: "He says *burned to desire*, not *I desired*. For we often see with our reason how useful are God's judgements, and yet, impeded by weakness, we sometimes do not desire them. Therefore, our understanding flies ahead, but our affection follows late or not at all. We know the good, but have no delight in doing it; and we desire that it delight us. Thus, the psalmist once burned to desire those things which he saw to be good, desiring to find pleasure in the things the reason for which he was able to see. And so he shows the degrees, as it were, by which we come to them: for first we must see that they are useful and worthy; afterwards, that we desire a desire for them; finally, that, with the assistance of grace, doing those things should delight us whose reason alone had already delighted us."[2]

2. HE EXPOUNDS THE ORDER OF GRACES ACCORDING TO THE WORDS OF AUGUSTINE. Note the order of graces which Augustine here distinctly sets out: namely, how an understanding of good things precedes desire for them, and desire itself precedes delight, which comes about through faith and charity. Once delight is had, the will is truly the good one by which we live righteously; and such a will goes with faith, but does not precede it.

Chapter 7 (168)

1. THAT MANY OTHER GOODS PRECEDE THE GRACE OF JUSTIFICATION IN MAN: SOME COME FROM GRACE AND FREEDOM OF CHOICE, OTHERS ONLY FROM FREEDOM OF CHOICE. One who considers the above words of Augustine[1] in the light of this distinction will conclude that there is no contradiction. And he will not be unaware that, even before preceding and operating grace, by which a good will is prepared in man, some goods precede from God's grace and from freedom of choice, some others only from freedom of choice; and yet by these, he does not merit life, nor the grace by which he is justified.—AUGUSTINE, IN *ON THE SPIRIT AND THE LETTER; TO SIXTUS:* "No merits precede the reception of that grace which heals the will of man so that, in its healed state, it may fulfil the law. For that is the grace by which the impious is justified, that is, the one who used to be impious is made pious. But what the impious duly deserves is punishment, not grace; and it would not be grace, if it were not given

[1]Ps. 118, 20.
[2]Augustine, *Enarrationes in Psalmos*, on Ps. 118, 20, sermon 8 nn4-5.

[1]Above, in c4 n1.

freely."[2] And it is given freely because we had done no good beforehand by which we deserved this.

2. THAT THERE ARE SOME GOOD THINGS WHICH ARE DONE BY MAN EVEN THROUGH FREE CHOICE ALONE. And yet we do not deny that there are many good things which are done by man through free choice before this grace and apart from this grace. Augustine states the same in the *Responses against the Pelagians*, where he says that men, through free choice, cultivate fields, build houses, and do many other good things without co-operating grace.[3]

Chapter 8 (169)

1. WHETHER THE GRACE WHICH IS CALLED OPERATING AND CO-OPERATING IS ONE AND THE SAME. It has been said above[1] that, through operating and prevenient grace, the will of man is freed and prepared to will the good, and through co-operating and subsequent grace it is aided so as not to will in vain. And so we must consider here whether it is one and the same grace, that is, one freely given gift which operates and co-operates, or whether they are different, one operating and the other co-operating.

2. HERE HE SAYS THAT IT IS ONE, BUT THAT IT TAKES DIFFERENT NAMES BECAUSE OF ITS DIFFERENT EFFECTS. It seems not unreasonably to some that the grace is one and the same, the same gift, the same virtue which operates and co-operates, but, because of its different effects, it is called operating and co-operating. For it is called operating insofar as "it frees and prepares the will of man to will the good," and co-operating insofar as it "aids him lest he will in vain," namely to do a good work. For this grace is not fruitless, "but deserves to be increased so that, once increased, it may also deserve to be perfected."[2]

Chapter 9 (170)

IT IS ASKED WHAT THIS GRACE IS AND HOW IT MAY DESERVE TO BE INCREASED. But if it is asked how this prevenient grace may deserve to be increased, since there is no merit without free choice, and what this grace is, whether a virtue or not and, if a virtue, whether an act or not, in order that all this may be indicated clearly, we must first set forth that there are three kinds of goods.

[2]Augustine, partially from *Epistola 194* (*ad Sixtum*), c3 n7; partially from *De spiritu et littera*, c9 n15.
[3]*Hypognosticon*, bk 3 c4 n5, among the works attributed to Augustine.

[1]Dist. 25 c9 and dist. 26 cc2-4.
[2]See Augustine's statements, above, cc1-2 of this Distinction.

Chapter 10 (171)

BEFORE RESOLVING THE QUESTION, HE SETS FORTH THE THREE KINDS OF GOODS. For some goods are great, some very small, some middling, as Augustine says in book 1 of his *Retractations*, where he states: "The virtues by which we live righteously are great goods; the forms of bodies, without which it is possible to live righteously, are very small goods; and the powers of the soul, without which it is not possible to live righteously, are middling goods."[1]—Also: "No one makes an evil use of the virtues; but as for the other goods, that is, the middling and very small ones, everyone can use them not only well, but also evilly. And the reason why no one uses virtue evilly is that the work of virtue is the good use of these other goods, which we can also use not well; but no one, in using them well, uses them evilly. And it is the goodness of God which arranged that not only the great ones, but also the middling and very small goods should exist."[2] See, you have the three kinds of goods distinguished.

Chapter 11 (172)

1. AMONG WHICH GOODS IS FREE CHOICE. But it is asked among which goods free choice is found.—Concerning this, Augustine, in book 1 of his *Retractations*, says as follows: "The free choice of the will is found among the middling goods because we can also use it evilly; and yet it is such that we cannot live righteously without it. For its good use is already a virtue which is found among the great goods which no one can use evilly. And because goods, whether great, middling, or very small, are from God, it follows that the good use of free will, which is a virtue and is counted among the great goods is also from God."[1]

2. HE TELLS [THE READER] TO CONSIDER AND COMPARE THE ABOVE AUTHORITIES IN ORDER TO RESOLVE THE QUESTION THAT WAS RAISED EARLIER. Note diligently the things which have been said and compare them to each other, for in this way what was asked above will become clear.[2] For he did indeed say that the good use of those goods which we can also use not well, that is, of the middling goods, is a work of virtue; among these, he placed free choice, good use of which he also said is a virtue. If it is so, then it is not the work of virtue which he spoke of above, because virtue is one thing and its work another.

[1]Augustine, *Retractationes*, bk 1 c9 n4.
[2]Ibid.

[1]Augustine, *Retractationes*, bk 1 c9 n6.
[2]See c9.

DISTINCTION XXVII

Chapter 1 (173)

1. ON VIRTUE: WHAT IT IS AND WHAT ITS ACT IS. Here we must examine what virtue is and what an act or work of virtue is. As Augustine says, "virtue is a good quality of the mind by which we live righteously and of which no one makes an evil use; God alone works virtue in man."[1]

2. HE CITES THE EXAMPLE OF JUSTICE, WHICH IS TO BE UNDERSTOOD EQUALLY OF THE OTHER VIRTUES. That virtue is the work of God alone Augustine teaches with regard to the virtue of justice. He teaches this on that passage of the Psalm: *I have done judgement and justice*,[2] saying as follows: "Justice is a great virtue of the spirit, which no one but God can bring about in man. And so, when the Prophet says, in the person of the Church, *I have done justice*, he did not wish the virtue itself to be understood, which man does not do, but its work."[3] See, it is plainly indicated here that justice in man is not the work of man, but of God. This is to be understood equally of the other virtues.

3. HE SPEAKS SIMILARLY CONCERNING FAITH, THAT IT IS NOT FROM MAN, BUT FROM GOD ALONE. Indeed, writing to the Ephesians on the grace of faith, the Apostle similarly asserts that faith is not from man, but from God alone; he says: *By grace, you were saved through faith, and this not from yourselves, for it is a gift of God*.[4] This is expounded as follows by the Saints: "*This*, that is, faith, *is not from yourselves*, that is, from the power of your nature, because *it is* purely *a gift of God*."[5] See, here too it is clearly taught that faith is not from freedom of choice or from the choice of the will.—This is in keeping with what was set out above,[6] where it was said that prevenient or operating grace is the virtue which frees and heals the will of man. Hence Augustine, in the book *On the Spirit and the Letter*, says: "We are justified not through free will, but through the grace of Christ: not that this happens without our will, but, through the law [of the Old Testament], our will is shown to be infirm, so that grace may heal the will, and the healed will may fulfil the law."[7]

[1] See above, dist. 26 c10.
[2] Ps. 118, 121.
[3] Augustine, *Enarrationes in Psalmos*, on Ps. 118, sermon 26 n1.
[4] Eph. 2, 8.
[5] Interlinear gloss, on Eph. 2, 8.
[6] Dist. 26 c8.
[7] Augustine, *De spiritu et littera*, c9 n15.

Chapter 2 (174)

1. ON THE GRACE WHICH FREES THE WILL, AND THAT, IF IT IS A VIRTUE, THEN VIRTUE IS NOT FROM FREE CHOICE, AND SO IT IS NOT A MOTION OF THE MIND. And so, if the grace which heals and frees the will of man is a virtue, whether one or several, since grace itself is not from a choice of the will, but rather heals and prepares the will so that it may be good, it follows that virtue is not from free choice, and so it is not a motion or disposition of the mind, since any motion or disposition of the mind is from free choice: but a good one is from grace and free choice, and an evil one from free choice alone.—For as Augustine says in book 1 of the *Retractations*, "man was able to fall freely and from free choice, but not to rise again."[1] Also, in the book *On the Two Souls*: "If souls lack a free movement of the spirit toward doing and not doing, if, in short, they are not granted any power to abstain from their work, we cannot hold them guilty of their sin."[2]—Here it is plainly shown that the motion of the spirit, whether toward good or evil, is from free choice; and so, if grace or virtue is a movement of the mind, it is from free choice; but if it is wholly or in part from free choice, then it is not God alone who works it, without man.

2. HERE HE REVEALS TO WHAT THE FOREGOING WERE POINTING, NAMELY THAT IT SHOULD BECOME CLEAR WHETHER VIRTUE IS A MOVEMENT OF THE MIND OR NOT. Moreover, not unlearnedly, some teach that virtue is a good quality or form of the mind which informs the soul. And it is not a movement or disposition of the mind, but free choice is aided by it in order to move and raise itself up toward the good. And so from virtue and free choice is born a good movement or disposition of the mind, and from this a good work proceeds outward.

3. HE SHOWS IT BY ANALOGY, AND HERE THERE IS A MANIFEST COMPARISON BETWEEN TWO THREES. The earth is bathed by the rain in order to germinate and produce fruit, but the rain is neither the earth, nor the seed, nor the fruit; the earth is neither the seed, nor the fruit; the seed is not the fruit. (APPLICATION OF THE COMPARISON.) In the same way, the rain of divine blessing is freely poured into the earth of our mind, that is, the choice of our will, that is, it is inspired by grace—which God alone does, and not man with him. By this grace, the will of man is bathed so as to germinate and produce fruit, that is, it is healed and prepared to will the good, according to which the grace is called operating; and it is assisted to do the good, according to which the grace is called co-operating. And that grace is not unsuitably termed 'virtue,' because it heals and aids the infirm will of man.

[1]Augustine, *Retractationes*, bk 1 c9 n6.
[2]Augustine, *De duabus animabus*, c12 n17.

Chapter 3 (175)

1. IN WHAT SENSE GOOD MERITS ARE SAID TO BEGIN FROM GRACE AND OF WHICH GRACE THIS IS UNDERSTOOD. And so, when good merits are said to be and begin from grace,[1] either the grace that freely gives, that is, God, is meant; or better, the grace that is freely given, which precedes the will of man; for it would not be a great thing if these things were to be said to be from God, from whom are all things. It is rather his freely given grace, from which good merits have their beginning, that is meant.

2. HOW 'SINCE THEY ARE SAID TO BE FROM GRACE ALONE' IS UNDERSTOOD. But when they are said to be from grace alone, free choice is not excluded, because there is no merit in man which is not through free choice. But in deserving goods, principality of cause is attributed to grace because the principal cause of good merits is grace itself, by which free choice is roused, and the will of man is healed and aided so that it may be good.

Chapter 4 (176)

1. THAT GOOD WILL IS PRINCIPALLY OF GRACE, AND EVEN IS GRACE, JUST LIKE ALL GOOD MERIT. This [good will] itself is also a gift of God and a merit of man, or rather of grace, because it is principally from grace, and is grace. Hence Augustine, in *To the Priest Sixtus*: "What is the merit of man before grace, since nothing but grace makes for any good merit in us?"[1]

2. HE IN PART SHOWS HOW THE GOOD IS ESTABLISHED IN MAN THROUGH GOOD MERIT, AND WHAT THE FIRST GOOD MERIT IS. As has been said,[2] from the grace which precedes and heals the choice of man and from free choice itself, a good disposition or a good movement of the mind is engendered in the soul, and this is the first good merit of man. Just as, for example, from the virtue of faith and the choice of man, some good and rewardable movement is generated in the mind, namely belief itself, so too from charity and free choice comes another movement, namely to love, which is very good. The same is to be understood of the other virtues. And these good movements or dispositions are merits and gifts of God, by which we deserve both their increase and the other things which are conferred on us as a consequence here and in the future.

[1]See above, dist. 26 c4 n3.

[1]Augustine, *Epistola 194*, c5 n19.
[2]Above, c2 nn1-2.

Chapter 5 (177)

BY WHAT REASON FAITH IS SAID TO DESERVE JUSTIFICATION AND OTHER THINGS. And so, when faith is said to deserve justification[1] and eternal life, it is taken to be said for this reason: because those things are deserved by the act of faith. It is taken similarly in regard to charity, justice, and the other virtues. For if faith, the prevenient virtue itself, were to be said to be an act of the mind, which is a merit, then it would have its origin in free choice; because it is not, it is said to be a merit because an act of virtue is a merit, so long as charity is present, without which neither to believe, nor to hope, is deserving of life. Hence it truly seems that charity is the Holy Spirit.[2] Charity informs and sanctifies the qualities of the soul so that the soul may be informed and sanctified in them; without charity, a quality of the soul is not called a virtue because it is not able to heal the soul.

Chapter 6 (178)

1. ON THE GIFTS OF THE VIRTUES AND ON GRACE, WHICH IS NOT ITSELF MERIT, BUT PRODUCES IT. And so it is from the gifts of the virtues that we are good and live justly. And from grace, which is not itself merit, but produces it, and yet not without free choice, come our merits, namely our good dispositions and their development and good works, which God rewards in us.—And these things too are gifts of God. Hence Augustine, in *To the Priest Sixtus*: "When he crowns our merits, he crowns nothing other than his own gifts. So it is that eternal life itself, which is restored at the end by God for those merits that went before, is called 'grace' because it is given gratis. It is rightly so called because the very merits for which it is given are not from ourselves, but are done in us through grace. And it is given freely not because it is given without reference to merits, but because the very merits for which it is given are also given through grace."[1]

2. EPILOGUE, WHERE HE ADDS SOME OTHER THINGS. From the foregoing, it can already be somewhat clear to us how prevenient grace deserves to be increased, and other things; and what it is, whether a virtue or something else, and if a virtue, whether it is an act or not.[2] For it has been shown above,[3] on the part of some, that it is a virtue, and that a virtue is not an act, but its cause, and yet not without free choice.

[1]Above, dist. 26 c2 n3. and c3 n1.
[2]As was shown above, Bk 1 dist. 17.

[1]Augustine, *Epistola 194*, c5 n19.
[2]All this was asked above, dist. 26 c9.
[3]See c2 n2.

3. HE EXPOUNDS HOW THE STATEMENT: 'VIRTUE IS THE GOOD USE OF FREE CHOICE' IS TO BE UNDERSTOOD. And so what Augustine said above,[4] that virtue is the good use of free choice, may be taken as follows: that is, it is an act of virtue. Otherwise he would seem to contradict himself, since he also said above that the work of virtue is the good use of those things which we can use not well;[5] among these, he included free choice.[6] But if the good use of free choice is a work of virtue, then it is certainly not a virtue. And so, when he said that its good use is a virtue, by the term virtue, he meant its use.

Chapter 7 (179)

1. THAT THE USE OF VIRTUE AND OF FREE CHOICE IS THE SAME, BUT IT IS PRINCIPALLY OF VIRTUE. To be sure, good use from virtue and from free choice is the same, but it is principally from virtue; and that good use is to be numbered among the great goods.[1]

2. THAT PREVENIENT GRACE, WHICH IS UNDERSTOOD TO BE A VIRTUE, IS NOT THE USE OF FREE CHOICE, BUT THE GOOD USE OF FREE CHOICE AND ALL GOOD MERITS COME FROM IT. And that prevenient grace, which is also a virtue, is not the use of free choice, but rather the good use of free choice comes from it. It is ours from God, not from ourselves. But the good use of choice is from both God and ourselves; and so it is a good merit. In the one case, God alone works; in the other, God and man [work together]. —This merit has its provenance in that most pure grace. The Apostle noted this, saying: *By the grace of God, I am what I am, and his grace was not empty in me.*[2]—AUGUSTINE, IN *ON GRACE AND FREE CHOICE.* Commenting on that passage, Augustine speaks as follows: "Rightly does he call it grace. For at first, God gives by grace alone, and he gives nothing but grace, since only bad merits have gone before; but afterwards, through grace, begin the good merits. And in order to indicate free choice as well, he adds: *And his grace was not empty in me.*"[3]—THE SAME: "And lest the will itself be thought able to do anything good without God's grace, he immediately adds: *But it was not I* alone, namely without grace, *but God's grace in me*, that is, with free choice.[4] Plainly, when grace has been given,

[4]Dist. 26 c11 n1.
[5]Dist. 26 c10.
[6]Dist. 26 c11 n1.

[1]Dist. 26 c11 n1.
[2]1 Cor. 15, 10.
[3]Augustine, *De gratia et libero arbitrio*, c5 n12.
[4]Cf. 1 Cor. 15, 10.

our merits begin to be good; and yet through that grace, because, if it is lacking, man falls."[5]

Chapter 8 (180)

1. HERE IS SHOWN THE VIEW OF OTHERS, WHO SAY THAT THE VIRTUES ARE GOOD USES OF FREE CHOICE, THAT IS, ACTS OF THE MIND. But others say that the virtues are good uses of natural powers, and yet not all such uses, but only the interior ones, which are in the mind. Exterior acts, which are done by the body, are not said to be virtues, but works of the virtues.

2. HOW THE WORDS OF AUGUSTINE ABOVE AGREE WITH THIS VIEW. And so, when Augustine says that 'the work of virtue is the good use of natural powers,'[1] they take it as referring to exterior use; but when he says that 'the good use of free choice is a virtue and is to be numbered among the great goods,'[2] they understand it as referring to interior use. And they assert that the virtues are nothing other than good dispositions or movements of the mind. It is God, not man, who makes these in man because, although those movements pertain to the free choice, yet they cannot come to be unless God frees and aids the choice with his operating and cooperating grace. They take this grace to be the free will of God, because *it is God who works in us to will* and work the good.[3]

3. WITH WHAT AUTHORITIES THEY SUPPORT WHAT THEY SAY. And they support with the testimonies of the Saints the view that the virtues are movements of the mind. For Augustine says, in *On John*: "What is faith? To believe what you do not see";[4] and so to believe is a movement of the mind.—The same, in *On the Trinity*, book 3: "And I call charity a movement of the spirit."[5] But if charity and faith are movements of the spirit, then the virtues are movements of the spirit.

4. HOW OTHERS RESPOND TO THESE [AUTHORITIES], WITH A DETERMINATION OF THE FOREGOING. Some others, responding to these [authorities], say that the foregoing words of Augustine are to be understood as follows: 'Faith is to believe what you do not see,' that is, faith is a virtue by which what is not seen is believed. Also, 'charity is a movement of the spirit,' that is, a grace by which the spirit is moved to love.

5. THEY CONFIRM THEIR DETERMINATION WITH AUTHORITIES.—AUGUSTINE. And that these and similar statements are to be taken as they say is suggested by what Augustine says elsewhere. For in book 1 of *Questions*

[5]Augustine, *De gratia et libero arbitrio*, c5 n2.

[1]Above, dist. 26 c10.
[2]Dist. 26, c11.
[3]Cf. Phil. 2, 13.
[4]Augustine, *In Ioannem*, tr. 40 n9.
[5]Augustine, *De doctrina christiana*, bk 3 c10 n16.

on the Gospel, he says: "There is a faith by which things are believed which are not seen, and this is properly called faith."[6]—Also, in *On the Trinity*, book 13: "The things which are believed are one thing, the faith by which they are believed is another thing."[7]

6. Arguing from the above words, they proceed as follows: To believe is one thing, that by which one believes is another; but it was said earlier that faith is that by which one believes; and so to believe is not faith because to believe is not that by which one believes.—They also add: Virtue is the work of God alone, which he alone does in us; therefore, it is not the use or act of free choice. But to believe is an act of the free choice; and so it is not a virtue.

7. HE LEAVES THE JUDGEMENT OF THESE VIEWS TO THE READER. Both the above views are supported by the foregoing and by other reasons and authorities. But I leave the judgement of these to the examination of the diligent reader; I move on to other things.

DISTINCTION XXVIII

Chapter 1 (181)

1. HE REPEATS WHAT WAS ALREADY SAID IN ORDER TO ADD OTHER THINGS, SETTING OUT A DEFINITE DESCRIPTION OF GRACE AND FREE CHOICE AGAINST THE PELAGIANS. But let us hold firmly and unhesitatingly that free choice, without prevenient and aiding grace, does not suffice for the obtaining of justice and salvation, and that God's grace is not sought by our preceding merits, as the Pelagian heresy has taught. Indeed, as Augustine says in his *Retractations*, book 1, "the new Pelagian heretics make such assertions on behalf of the free choice of the will as not to leave any room for God's grace, which they claim is given according to our merits."[1]

2. WHAT THE HERESY OF THE PELAGIANS IS CONCERNING GRACE AND FREE CHOICE.—AUGUSTINE, IN HIS BOOK *ON HERESIES*: "The heresy of the Pelagians, which is the most recent of all, has arisen from the monk Pelagius. These are such enemies of God's grace, by which we are predestined and by which we have deserved to be snatched *from the power of darkness*,[2] that they believe man to be able to fulfil all divine mandates without grace. Moreover, Pelagius, upon being reproved by his brethren for attributing nothing to the aid of God's grace in fulfilling his mandates, did not place grace ahead of free choice, but, with faithless slyness, made

[6]Augustine, *Quaestiones Evangeliorum*, bk 2 q39, on Lk. 17.5.
[7]Augustine, *De Trinitate*, bk 13 c2 n5.

[1]Augustine, *Retractationes*, bk 1 c9 n3.
[2]Cf. Col. 1, 13.

it subject [to it]. He said that grace was given to men so that they may more easily fulfil through grace those things which they are commanded to do through free choice. At any rate, by saying 'they may more easily,' he wanted it to be believed that, although with greater difficulty, men can nevertheless do what is divinely commanded without grace. As for the grace of God, without which we cannot do anything good, they say that it does not exist apart from the free choice which our nature, without any preceding merits of its own, received from God. And God only helps us through his law and doctrine so that we may know the things which we must do and for which we must hope; but he does not help us through the gift of the Holy Spirit to do the things which we have learned that we must do. And by this, they confess that we have been divinely given knowledge, by which ignorance is repelled; but they deny that we are divinely given the charity by which to live piously; in other words, that *knowledge*, which without charity *puffs up,* is a gift of God; but that *charity* itself, which *builds up* so that knowledge may not puff up, is not a gift of God.[3] They also destroy the prayers which the Church offers, whether for the infidels and those who resist the God's teaching, that they may be converted to God; or for the faithful, that their faith may increase and they may persevere in it. Indeed, they contend that these things are not received from God, but that men have them from themselves, since they say that the grace of God, by which we are freed from impiety, is given according to our merits. They also assert that little children are born without any bond of original sin."[4]

Chapter 2 (182)

1. HERE HE SETS OUT THE THINGS BY WHICH THEY CONFIRM THEIR OWN ERROR AS THEY USE AUGUSTINE'S WORDS AGAINST HIM. As for their saying that man can fulfil all mandates through free choice and without grace, they support it by inductive reasonings like the following.

2. TESTIMONY OF AUGUSTINE WHICH PELAGIUS ADDUCES IN HIS OWN SUPPORT. If man cannot do the things which are commanded, they say, it is not to be imputed a capital offense for him, as you yourself assert, Augustine, in the book *On Free Choice*, where you say: "Who sins in that which could in no way be avoided? But there is sin, therefore it can be avoided."[1]—AUGUSTINE'S RETRACTATION. Pelagius made use of this testimony of Augustine in disputing against him, or rather against grace, as Augustine himself recalls in the book of *Retractations*, where he reexamines the text above and others like it, saying: "In these and other words of

[3]Cf. 1 Cor. 8, 1.
[4]Augustine, *De haeresibus*, n88.

[1]Augustine, *De libero arbitrio*, bk 3 c18 n50.

mine like them, because God's grace (which was not then at issue) is not mentioned in them, the Pelagians believe that we held their view. But they believe this in vain. The will is indeed that by which we sin and live righteously, and this is what we had in mind in these words. But unless the will is freed by God's grace and is aided to overcome the vices, it is not possible for mortals to live righteously."[2] See, he openly determines in what sense he said those words, refuting the enemies of grace.

3. HE SETS OUT ANOTHER TESTIMONY OF AUGUSTINE WHICH PELAGIUS HAD ALSO USED IN HIS OWN SUPPORT. Similarly, Pelagius also found support against grace in the words which Augustine speaks in the book *On the Two Souls*, stating: "To hold anyone guilty of sin because he did not do what he was not able to do is the height of iniquity and senselessness."[3] —PELAGIUS' QUESTION. Hearing this, Pelagius jumped up, saying: Why, then, are little children and those who do not have grace, without which they cannot do the divine mandates, held to be guilty?

Chapter 3 (183)

1. DETERMINATION OF AUGUSTINE. In the book of *Retractations*, responding to Pelagius, Augustine reveals the circumstances in which he had said the above.[1] For he said it against the Manichees, who contend that there are two natures in man: a good one from God, and an evil one from the nation of darkness, which was never good and is not able to will the good; if it were so, it would seem that man ought not to be held guilty if he does not do the good.

2. HE ADDS SOMETHING ELSE WHICH APPEARS TO CONTRADICT GOD'S GRACE. Elsewhere too, Augustine says things which appear to contradict this grace by which we are justified. For he says, in the book *Against Adamantus*, a disciple of the Manicheans: "Unless each of us changed his will, he cannot work the good. God teaches that this is placed in our power, where he says: *Either make the tree good [and its fruit will be good]*,"[2] etc.[3]—AUGUSTINE'S DETERMINATION IN HIS *RETRACTATION*. In his *Retractations*, Augustine shows that "this statement is not against the grace of God which we preach. It is indeed in man's power to change his will for the better, but that power is nothing unless it is given by God, of whom it is said: *He gave them the power to become children of God.*[4] For since it is in our power that when we will we do, nothing is more in our

[2]Augustine, *Retractationes*, bk 1 c9 nn3-4.
[3]Augustine, *De duabus animabus*, c12 n17.

[1]Augustine, *Retractationes*, bk 1 c15 nn1 and 6.
[2]Mt. 12, 33.
[3]Augustine, *Contra Adimantum*, c26.
[4]Jn. 1, 12.

power than the will itself; but *the will is prepared by the Lord.*[5] And so, in that way, he gives the power."[6]

3. ANOTHER TESTIMONY OF THE SAME WHICH SEEMS CONTRADICTORY. —AUGUSTINE, IN THE BOOK *ON THE TWO SOULS*; IN THE *RETRACTATIONS*. "Also it similarly is to be understood" what he says in the same place,[7] namely "that it is in our power that we deserve either to be grafted into God's goodness, or to be cast out by his severity. Because there is nothing in our power other than that which follows our will; when this will is prepared by the Lord, the work of piety, even that which had been impossible and difficult, becomes easy."[8]

4. ANOTHER TESTIMONY. Also, in his *Exposition of Some Propositions in the Epistle to the Romans*, Augustine interspersed some things which seem to oppose this teaching of grace. For he says: "That we believe is ours; but that we do good belongs to him who gives the Holy Spirit to believers."[9] And a little later: "It pertains to us to believe and to will; but it pertains to him to give to those who believe and will the faculty of doing the good through the Holy Spirit."[10]—RETRACTATION AS TO HOW THESE [WORDS] ARE TO BE TAKEN. Augustine makes clear how these [words] are to be understood in the book of *Retractations*, saying: "It is indeed true that it is from God that we do the good, but the same rule pertains to both, namely to willing and doing. And both are God's, because he prepares the will; and both are ours, because neither happens without our willingness. Undoubtedly, I would not have said those things, if I had already known that faith itself is also included among the gifts of the Holy Spirit."[11]

5. HE ADDS YET ANOTHER TEXT WHICH APPEARS CONTRADICTORY. That is also to be examined with diligence which Augustine says in the book of *The Sentences of Prosper*, namely that "the power to have faith, like the power to have charity, belongs to men by nature; but to have faith, as to have charity, belongs to the faithful by grace."[12]—DETERMINATION. But this was not said as if faith or charity can be had by free choice, but because the human mind has a natural aptitude for believing and loving. With the prevenient grace of God, the mind believes and loves; it is not able to do this without grace.

[5]Prov. 8, 35, Septuagint.
[6]Augustine, *Retractationes*, bk 1 c22 n4 .
[7]Augustine, *Contra Adimantum*, c27.
[8]Augustine, *Retractationes*, bk 1 c22 n4.
[9]Augustine, *In Epistolam ad Romanos quaedam propositiones*, n60.
[10]Ibid., n61.
[11]Augustine, *Retractationes*, bk 1 c23 nn2-3.
[12]Prosper of Aquitaine, *Sententiae ex Augustino delibatae*, n316.

Chapter 4 (184)

HE SETS FORTH A TESTIMONY OF JEROME, ADDING WHAT IS TO BE HELD CONCERNING GRACE AND FREE WILL, WHERE A THREEFOLD HERESY IS REVEALED, NAMELY OF JOVINIAN, MANICHAEUS, AND PELAGIUS. And so, concerning grace and free will, let us hold without doubt that which Jerome teaches in his *Explanation of the Catholic Faith to Pope Damasus*, where he strikes at the errors of Jovinian, Manichaeus, and Pelagius, saying: "We acknowledge that choice is free so as to say that we are always in need of God's aid; and that both those are in error who say with Manichaeus that man cannot avoid sin, and those who assert with Jovinian that man cannot sin. Each of them takes away freedom of choice. But we say that man is always able to sin and not to sin, so that we confess ourselves to be ever free in our choice. This is the faith which we learned in the Catholic Church and which we have always held."[1]

DISTINCTION XXIX

Chapter 1 (185)

1. WHETHER MAN BEFORE SIN WAS IN NEED OF OPERATING AND CO-OPERATING GRACE. After these matters, it is to be considered whether man before sin was in need of operating and co-operating grace.

2. THAT HE WAS IN NEED OF OPERATING AND CO-OPERATING GRACE, BUT HE DID NOT NEED THE OPERATING ONE IN EVERY WAY IN WHICH IT OPERATES NOW. To this we briefly say that he was in need not only of co-operating, but also of operating grace; but not in every way in which operating grace operates now, for it operates by freeing and preparing the will of man to the good.[1] And so man [before sin] needed it not in order to free his will, which was not a slave to sin, but in order to prepare it to will the good efficaciously, which he was not able to do by himself.—For he was not able to deserve the good without grace, as Augustine clearly teaches in the *Enchiridion*, saying: "Human nature, through free choice, lost that immortality by which it was able not to die; as for its [future] immortality, by which it will be unable to die, it will receive that through grace which it would have received through merit, if it had not sinned. And yet, even then, there could not have been any merit without grace because, although sin could only have been brought about by free choice, yet the same free choice was not sufficient to have or retain righteousness

[1]Actually, Pelagius, *Libellus fidei ad Innocentium Papam*, nn13-14.

[1]See above, dist. 26 c1.

without the imparting of divine aid."[2]—See, by these words it is sufficiently shown that man before sin was in need of operating and co-operating grace. For he was not able to take a step without the aid of operating and co-operating grace; yet he was able to stand straight.[3]

Chapter 2 (186)

1. THAT MAN HAD VIRTUES BEFORE THE FALL. Moreover, it is usual to ask whether man had virtue before the fall.—It seems to some that he did not have it, and they strive to prove it by saying as follows: He did not have righteousness, because he held God's command in contempt; nor prudence, because he made no provision for himself; nor temperance, because he desired what belonged to another; nor fortitude, because he surrendered to a depraved suggestion.—In response to these, we say that he certainly did not have these virtues when he sinned, but that he had them before, and then he lost them.

2. BY THE TESTIMONIES OF THE SAINTS, HE SHOWS THAT THE FIRST MAN HAD VIRTUES. This is proved by many testimonies of the Saints. For Augustine says in one of his homilies: "Adam, after losing his charity, was found to be evil."[1] Also: "In overcoming Adam, who had been made in God's image from the mud of the earth, armed with chastity, adorned with temperance, resplendent in charity, the prince of vices destroyed our first parents and despoiled them of those gifts and of such great goods."[2] —On this same matter, Ambrose, in *To Sabinus*, says: "When Adam was alone, he did not transgress, because his mind adhered to God."[3] The same, commenting on the Psalm, also says that "man was most blessed before sin and tasted the ethereal air";[4] but how could he be most blessed without virtue?—Augustine too, in *On Genesis*, says that Adam before sin "was endowed with a spiritual mind."[5] And so it is not to be doubted that man before sin shone with the virtues, but he was despoiled of them through sin.

Chapter 3 (187)

ON THE EJECTION OF MAN FROM PARADISE. And also as a punishment for that sin, he was ejected from paradise into this place of miseries, as we

[2]Augustine, *Enchiridion*, cc105-106.
[3]See above, dist. 24 cc1-2.

[1]Rather, Quodvultdeus, *Sermo 4, Contra Iudaeos, paganos, et Arianos*, c2.
[2]Ibid.
[3]Ambrose, *Epistola 49* (*ad Sabinum*) n2.
[4]Ambrose, *In Psalmum 118, 25*, sermon 4 n3.
[5]Augustine, *De Genesi ad litteram*, bk 11 c42 n58.

read in Genesis: *And so now, lest he stretch out his hand and take and eat of the tree of life, and live forever, God cast him out of the garden of delight.*[1] By these words, it seems to be implied that he would never have died, if he had afterwards taken from that tree.

Chapter 4 (188)

HOW 'LEST HE STRETCH OUT HIS HAND AND TAKE AND EAT OF THE TREE OF LIFE, AND LIVE FOREVER' IS TO BE UNDERSTOOD. But because, through sin, he already had *a dead body*,[2] those words may be taken in the following sense: God, speaking in the manner of one who has been angered, says of the proud man: *Beware lest he stretch out his hand*, etc.,[3] that is, beware, you angels, lest he eat of the tree of life, of which he is unworthy: if he had remained faithful, he would have eaten of it and would have lived forever, but now, because of his disobedience, he is not worthy to eat it. And as God had said by his word, he also showed by his deed: for *God cast him out of the garden of delight*,[4] "into a place suitable for him; similarly, when a man who is mostly evil has begun to live among good people, if he does not will to change for the better, he is expelled from the assembly of the good," weighted down "by the weight of an evil custom."[5]

Chapter 5 (189)

ON THE FLAMING SWORD PLACED IN FRONT OF PARADISE. But so that man should not be able to enter it, *God placed the Cherubim before paradise and a flaming sword, which turned every way, to guard the way of the tree of life.*[1]—STRABUS. According to the letter, this may be taken in this way: that "through the ministry of angels, a fiery guard was established there."[2] —AUGUSTINE, *ON GENESIS*: "For this is to be believed to have been done in the visible paradise through the celestial powers, that some fiery guard was there through the ministry of angels; we must not think that this was in vain, since it signifies something regarding the spiritual paradise."[3]— "For Cherubim is interpreted as the fullness of knowledge; this is charity, because *love is the fullness of the law*.[4] And the flaming sword are the temporal punishments, which turn everywhere because the times are change-

[1]Gen. 3, 22-23.
[2]Cf. Rom. 8, 10.
[3]Cf. Gen. 3, 23.
[4]Gen. 3, 22-23.
[5]Augustine, *De Genesi contra Manichaeos*, 2 c22 n34.

[1]Gen. 3, 24.
[2]Strabo, *In Genesim*, 3, 24.
[3]Augustine, *De Genesi ad litteram*, bk 11 c40 n55.
[4]Rom. 13, 10.

able." And so they were placed before paradise to guard the tree of life, because "there is no return to life other than through the Cherubim, namely the fullness of knowledge, that is, charity, and through the sword that turns in every direction, that is, the bearing of temporal sufferings."[5]

Chapter 6 (190)

1. WHETHER MAN BEFORE SIN HAD EATEN OF THE TREE OF LIFE. It may be asked whether man before sin had eaten of the tree of life. In the book *On the Baptism of Children*, Augustine speaks as follows concerning this: "Surely, the first humans are rightly understood to have abstained from the forbidden fruit before the malign persuasion of the devil, and to have made use of what was allowed to them."[1] By these words, it is shown that they took of the tree of life before sin, since they had been commanded to eat of every tree of paradise, other than the tree of the knowledge of good and evil.[2]

2. WHY THEY WERE NOT MADE IMMORTAL, IF THEY ATE OF THE TREE OF LIFE. But why, then, were they not clothed in perpetual soundness and blessed immortality, so that they should not be changed for the worse by any infirmity or age? For that tree is said to have had this natural power.[3] —SOLUTION. But perhaps it did not confer this, unless there were repeated eatings from it. And so it may have been that he ate of that tree only once, and not more often, although he is understood to have remained in paradise for some time, since Scripture says that he was asleep there when a rib was taken from his side and the woman was formed from it;[4] and the animals were brought before him and he conferred names on them.[5]

DISTINCTION XXX

Chapter 1 (191)

THAT THROUGH ADAM SIN AND PUNISHMENT CAME TO HIS POSTERITY. It has been indicated in the above[1]—if only partially, because we are not

[5]Isidore, *Quaestiones de veteri et novo Testamento*, on Gen., c5 n14; remotely, from Augustine, *De Genesi contra Manichaeos* bk 2 c23 nn35-36.

[1]Augustine, *De peccatorum meritis et remissione et de baptismo parvulorum*, bk 2 c21 n35.
[2]Cf. Gen. 2, 16-17; cf. above, dist. 19 c4 n3.
[3]Above, dist. 17 c6.
[4]Cf. Gen. 2, 21-22.
[5]Cf. Gen. 2, 19-20.

[1]In dist. 21, 22,

fully sufficient [to the task]—how the first man sinned, and what punishment he suffered for his sin. To these matters, it is to be added that sin and punishment both came to his posterity through him, as the Apostle shows by saying: *Just as sin entered into this world through one man, so death also passed into all men.*[2]

Chapter 2 (192)

WHETHER THAT SIN WAS ORIGINAL OR ACTUAL. Here it is first to be seen what that sin was, namely whether original or actual; and if it is understood to be original, then it is next to be diligently investigated what original sin is, and why it is called original, and how it passed or passes into all.

Chapter 3 (193)

SOME UNDERSTAND IT TO BE ACTUAL. It has pleased some to understand that text to refer to the actual sin of Adam; they say this is what the Apostle meant, since he says later: *Just as through the disobedience of one man, many were made sinners, so also* etc.[3] They say that the Apostle clearly expresses, even by the term itself, the sin which *through one man entered into the world*,[4] namely disobedience; but disobedience is an actual sin.

Chapter 4 (194)

1. HOW THEY SAY THAT IT ENTERED INTO THE WORLD. And they say that it entered into the world not by the transmission of origin, but by similarity of transgression;[1] and they say that all sinned in that one man because he was an example of sinning to all.

2. THE PELAGIANS SAY THIS. Some heretics wrongly reached this conclusion, and they are called Pelagians, whom Augustine mentions in the book *On the Baptism of Children*, saying: "It is to be known that some heretics, who are called Pelagians, said that the sin of the first transgression passed into other men not by propagation, but by imitation. Hence they also refuse to believe that original sin is absolved in children through baptism, because they contend no such sin exists in infants. But we say to them that, if the Apostle had wanted this sin to be understood to be one of imitation, and not of propagation, he would have named as its originator not Adam, but the devil, of whom it is said in the book of Wisdom: *By the devil's envy, death entered into the world.*[2] And because Scripture does

[2]Rom. 5, 12.
[3]Rom. 5, 19.
[4]Rom. 5, 12.

[1]Cf. Rom. 5, 14.
[2]Wis. 2, 24.

not wish this to be understood to have been done by propagation, but by imitation, it immediately added: *And they that are on his side imitate him [i.e. the devil].*[3] Certainly, they imitate Adam as often as they transgress God's mandate through disobedience; but it is one thing that he is an example to those who sin willingly, and another that he is the progenitor those who are born with sin."[4] And so the sin of Adam is not to be taken to have passed into all only by the example of imitation, but also by the vice of propagation and origin.

Chapter 5 (195)

HERE HE MAKES EXPLICIT THAT THE SIN WHICH PASSES TO POSTERITY IS ORIGINAL SIN. As Augustine plainly attests, the original sin is that which through Adam passed into all those who were begotten with concupiscence through his vitiated flesh.[1]

Chapter 6 (196)

1. HERE IT IS ASKED WHAT ORIGINAL SIN IS. And it is to be diligently investigated what it is. For the holy doctors have spoken of this very obscurely, and the doctors of the schools have reached different conclusions.

2. THE OPINION OF SOME CONCERNING ORIGINAL SIN. For some hold that original sin is a liability to punishment for the sin of the first man, that is, the debt or subjection to punishment by which we are made liable and bound to temporal and eternal punishment for the actual sin of the first man; because, they say, eternal punishment is due to all for that sin, unless they are freed through grace.—According to their view, it is fitting to say that original sin is neither fault, nor punishment. They profess that it is not fault. And according to them, it cannot be a punishment either because, if original sin is a debt of punishment, since a debt of punishment is not a punishment, original sin is not a punishment either.—Some of them even admit this, saying that in Scripture original sin is frequently called a liability; and they there understand by 'liability,' as has been said, subjection to punishment. And for this reason they assert that original sin is said to be in children, because children are liable to punishment for that first sin, just as, according to the justice of the courts, children are sometimes exiled for the sin of an evil parent.

[3]Wis. 2, 25.
[4]Augustine, *De peccatorum meritis et remissione et de baptismo parvulorum*, bk 1 c9 nn9-10.

[1]Augustine, as cited in the preceding chapter and below, c10, nn1-2.

Chapter 7 (197)

1. HE PROVES BY AUTHORITIES THAT ORIGINAL SIN IS A FAULT. But that original sin is a fault is taught by several testimonies of the Saints.—GREGORY. On Exodus, where it says: *The first-born of an ass you shall redeem with a sheep*,[1] Gregory says: "We have all been born in sin, and, conceived from the pleasure of the flesh, we have all contracted the original fault in ourselves; so it is that we embroil ourselves in sin also by our own will."[2] See, he says that we contract the original fault; and so it is clear that original sin is a fault.

2. AUGUSTINE. Augustine too, in the book *On Nature and Grace*, speaking of this same subject, says: "As the Apostle says, *all sinned*:[3] certainly either in themselves, or in Adam, because they are not without sin, either the one which they originally contracted, or the one which they added by their own evil practices."[4] "For the sin of the first man harmed not only him, but the whole human race, because from it we received condemnation and fault together."[5]

3. AUGUSTINE. The same, on Psalm 50: "What is sown from a dead body is born with the bond of original sin and of death. And that is why David describes himself as conceived *among iniquities*, because all contract from Adam iniquity and the bond of death: for no one is born without contracting punishment and the deserving of punishment."[6] Now, what deserves punishment is sin; and so anyone who is born through the concupiscence of the flesh contracts sin.

4. Therefore, original sin is the fault which all contract who are conceived through concupiscence. Hence in *On Ecclesiastical Dogmas* it is written: "Hold most firmly and do not at all doubt that any man who is conceived by the sexual joining of a man and a woman is born with original sin, subject to impiety and liable to death, and because of this is born *by nature a son of wrath*;[7] from this, no one is freed except through the faith *of the mediator of God and men*."[8,9]—By these and other authorities, it is clearly shown that original sin is a fault, and that it is contracted by all who are born from their parents through concupiscence.

[1]Exod. 13, 13.
[2]Rather, Paterius, *Liber testimoniorum Veteris Testamenti ex opusculis S. Gregorii*, on Exod. 13, 13.
[3]Rom. 3, 23.
[4]Augustine, *De natura et gratia*, c4 n4.
[5]Pseudo-Augustine, *Hypognosticon*, bk 2 c4 n4.
[6]Augustine, *Enarrationes in Psalmos*, on Ps. 50, 7, n10.
[7]Cf. Eph. 2, 3.
[8]1 Tim. 2, 5.
[9]Rather, Fulgentius, *De fide ad Petrum*, c26 n67.

Chapter 8 (198)

1. WHAT IT IS THAT IS CALLED ORIGINAL SIN: NAMELY THE INCENTIVE TO SIN, THAT IS, CONCUPISCENCE. Now it remains to see what is original sin itself. And since it is not actual sin, it is not an act or movement of the soul or of the body. For if it is an act of the soul or of the body, it is certainly an actual sin. But it is not actual; and so it is not an act or movement. What then is it?

2. Original sin is called the incentive to sin, namely concupiscence or the attraction to pleasure, which is called the law of the members, or the weakness of nature, or the tyrant who is in our members, or the law of the flesh.—Hence Augustine in the book *On the Baptism of Children*: "Concupiscence is in us, which must not be allowed to reign. There are also its desires, which are actual concupiscences: these are the weapons of the devil and come from the weakness of nature."[1] "This weakness is a tyrant which causes our evil desires. And so, if you wish to overcome the tyrant,"[2] and to find the enemy defenseless,[3] do not obey evil concupiscence.—By these words, it is sufficiently shown that the incentive to sin is concupiscence.

Chapter 9 (199)

1. THAT BY THE TERM CONCUPISCENCE IS UNDERSTOOD AN INCENTIVE, WHICH IS CALLED THE INCENTIVE TO SIN. But by the term concupiscence, [Augustine] signified not the act of desiring, but the first vice, when he called it 'the law of the flesh.'[1] Hence the same, in his treatise *On the Words of the Apostle*, says: "There is always a battle *in the body of this death*,[2] because the very concupiscence with which we are born cannot be ended for so long as we live; it can be diminished each day, but it cannot be ended."[3] What is the concupiscence with which we are born? Surely, it is the vice which makes the child able to become concupiscent, and which renders the adult [actually] concupiscent.

2. HE SHOWS IT BY ANALOGY. At night, there is blindness in the eye of a blind person, but it is not readily apparent, and one cannot discern between one who sees and one who is blind until the arrival of the light. In

[1]Rather, Augustine, *De continentia*, c3 n8.
[2]Rather, Augustine, *Sermo 30*, c5 n6.
[3]Ambrosiaster, on Rom. 6, 13.

[1]Namely, Augustine, *De peccatorum meritis et remissione et de baptismo parvulorum*, bk 2 c28 n45.
[2]Rom. 7, 24.
[3]Augustine, *Sermo 151*, c5 n5.

the same way, this vice is not apparent in a child, until the arrival of a more advanced age.

Chapter 10 (200)

1. THAT THROUGH ADAM, ORIGINAL SIN, THAT IS, CONCUPISCENCE, ENTERED INTO ALL. From these statements, it is given to be understood what original sin is, namely the vice of concupiscence, which entered into all who were born from Adam through concupiscence and made them all sharers in its stain.—Hence Augustine, in the book *On the Baptism of Children*: "Apart from the example of imitation, Adam also corrupted in himself, by the hidden disease of carnal concupiscence, all those who were to come from his stock. Hence the Apostle rightly says: *In which all sinned.*"[1,2]

2. HOW 'IN WHICH ALL SINNED' IS TO BE UNDERSTOOD. "The Apostle said this with circumspection and without ambiguity: for whether *in which* is understood to refer to the man or to the sin, it is equally well said."[3] "For in Adam all sinned in the very matter of which they are composed, not only by his example, as the Pelagians say.[4] For all were that one man,"[5] that is, they were in him materially.—AMBROSE: "And so it is manifest that all sinned in Adam, as if [forming] a mass. For once he had been corrupted by sin, all those whom he begot were born under sin, and so from him all are sinners."[6]—AUGUSTINE, REPLYING TO HILARY'S QUESTIONS. Therefore, in that one sin which entered into the world, all are rightly said to have sinned:[7] because "just as from that one man, so from that one sin, they cannot be free, unless they are released from that liability through the baptism of Christ."[8]—AUGUSTINE, *ON THE BAPTISM OF CHILDREN*: "And so our own sins, in which each is responsible only for the sins which he commits, are one thing; but this one sin, in which all sinned,"[9] that is, from which all *have been made sinners*,[10] "is another thing."

[1]Rom. 5, 12.
[2]Augustine, *De peccatorum meritis et remissione et de baptismo parvulorum*, bk 1 c9 n10.
[3]Ibid., bk 1 c10 n11.
[4]See above, c4.
[5]Ordinary gloss, on Rom. 5, 12, partially from Augustine, loc. cit.
[6]Ambrosiaster, on Rom. 5, 12.
[7]Cf. Rom. 5, 12.
[8]Augustine, *Epistola* 157 (*ad Hilarium*), c3 n18.
[9]Augustine, *De peccatorum meritis et remissione et de baptismo parvulorum*, bk 1 c10 n11.
[10]Cf. Rom. 5, 19.

Chapter 11 (201)

THAT THIS IS THE SIN IN WHICH ALL SINNED, NAMELY THE ORIGINAL ONE, WHICH PROCEEDED FROM DISOBEDIENCE. This is the original sin, by which all are born sinners who are conceived in concupiscence, and it issued from Adam or from his disobedience and passed on to his posterity.—Hence the Apostle suitably says that *through the disobedience of one man, many were made sinners*:[1] this [disobedience] is actual sin; when earlier he said that *through one man sin entered into the world*, and *in him all sinned*,[2] this must be taken as referring to original sin.

Chapter 12 (202)

IN WHAT SENSE IT IS SAID 'THROUGH THE DISOBEDIENCE OF ONE, MANY WERE MADE SINNERS.' And so the statement, *through the disobedience of one, many were made sinners*,[1] is to be understood to have been said in this sense: that from Adam's disobedience, namely from Adam's actual sin, proceeded the original sin by which all are born sinners, so that it was in him and passed into all.[2]

Chapter 13 (203)

1. THAT ORIGINAL SIN WAS IN ADAM AND IS IN US. Julian the heretic contended that there is no sin in little children. In reply, Augustine plainly states that original sin proceeded from Adam's will and entered into the world through his disobedience.[1]

2. JULIAN'S QUESTION. For Julian asks through what is sin found in a child, saying as follows: "The infant does not sin; the one who begot does not sin; the one who created does not sin. Among so many guarantees of innocence, through what secret openings do you imagine that sin has entered?"—AUGUSTINE'S RESPONSE: "The sacred page answers him: *Through one man sin entered into the world: through one man's disobedience*,[2] says the Apostle. What more does he seek? What greater clarity?"

3. ANOTHER QUESTION OF JULIAN. Julian also says: "If sin entered into the world through a man, sin is either from the will or from nature. If it is from the will, the will that commits sin is evil; but if it is from nature,

[1]Rom. 5, 19.
[2]Rom. 5, 12.

[1]Rom. 5, 19.
[2]See below, at the end of c13.

[1]Augustine, *De nuptiis et concupiscentia*, bk 2 cc27-28, nn47-48, from which come also cc2-3, below.
[2]Rom. 5, 12.

nature is evil."—RESPONSE OF AUGUSTINE. To him "I respond: Sin is from the will. Perhaps he asks whether original sin is from the will. I say that even original sin is from the will because it was sown from the will of the first man so that it was in him and passed into all."

Chapter 14 (204)

1. THE OBJECTION OF SOME AGAINST WHAT WAS SAID ABOVE, THAT ALL MEN WERE IN ADAM. As to what we said earlier about all men having been in Adam,[1] some literalists make an objection, saying as follows: All the flesh which has come down from Adam could not have existed in him simultaneously because it is a much greater quantity than was Adam's body; there were not even as many atoms in it as there are men descended from him. By this, they assert that it is not true that the substance of each had been in the first parent.

2. RESPONSE, WHERE IT IS REVEALED HOW THEY WERE IN ADAM ACCORDING TO SEMINAL REASON, AND HOW THEY DESCENDED FROM HIM, NAMELY BY THE LAW OF PROPAGATION. To this it can be answered that all which naturally exists in human bodies is said to have been in the first man materially and causally, not formally.[2] And it descended from the first parent by the law of propagation, and it was increased and multiplied in itself, without the introduction of any exterior substance into it; and it will rise again in the future. It finds nourishment in foods, but foods are not converted into human substance, and it is that which descends from Adam by propagation.

3. HOW IT DESCENDS BY PROPAGATION. For Adam transmitted some little portion of his own substance to the bodies of his children when he procreated them, that is, some little portion of the mass of his substance was divided and from it was formed the body of the child, and it was increased by its own multiplication, without the addition of anything extrinsic. And from that body so increased, some little portion is separated in the same way, from which are formed the bodies of posterity. And so the order of procreation proceeds in this manner by the law of propagation until the end of humankind. In this way, it is evident to those who understand it diligently and clearly that all were in Adam in respect to their bodies through seminal reason, and they descended from him by the law of propagation.

[1]Cf. above, at the end of c10.
[2]Cf. above, c10 n2.

Chapter 15 (205)

1. IT IS PROVEN BY AUTHORITY AND REASON THAT NOTHING EXTRINSIC IS CONVERTED INTO THE HUMAN SUBSTANCE WHICH COMES FROM ADAM.—AUTHORITY. And that nothing extrinsic passes into the nature of the human body is indicated by Truth, who says in the Gospel: *All that enters into the mouth goes into the belly and is cast into the sewer.*[1]—REASON. This may also be shown by reason in this way: A child who dies soon after birth will rise again in that stature which it would have had if it had lived until the age of thirty and had not suffered any defect of body.[2] From where comes that substance, which was so small at birth and will be so great at the resurrection, if not from itself by its own multiplication? From this, it is clear that, even if the child had lived, that substance would have increased from itself and not from anything else, like the rib from which the woman was made[3] and like the loaves in the Gospel.[4]

2. THAT FOODS PASS INTO THE FLESH, BUT NOT INTO THAT WHICH DESCENDS FROM ADAM. And yet we do not deny that foods and liquids pass into the flesh and blood, but not into that truth of the human nature which descends from the first parents: this alone will exist at the resurrection. But the rest of the flesh, into which foods pass, will be laid aside at the resurrection as superfluous; nevertheless, it grows with the nourishment of foods and other things.

DISTINCTION XXXI

Chapter 1 (206)

HOW ORIGINAL SIN PASSES FROM FATHERS TO CHILDREN: WHETHER ACCORDING TO THE SOUL, OR ACCORDING TO THE FLESH. Now it remains to investigate how that sin is passed from fathers to children, namely whether according to the soul alone, or according to the flesh, or according to both.

Chapter 2 (207)

THE OPINION OF SOME WHO WRONGLY BELIEVE THAT THE SOUL IS TRANSMITTED. Some have held that original sin is contracted according to the soul, and not only according to the flesh, because they concluded that not

[1]Mt. 15, 17.
[2]Cf. Augustine, *De civitate Dei*, bk 22 cc14 and 19; see also below, Bk 4 dist. 44 cc1-3.
[3]Gen. 2, 21-22.
[4]Mk. 6, 35-44; Jn. 6, 5-13.

the flesh alone, but also the soul is transmitted. For just as in the generation of offspring, flesh is taken substantially from the paternal flesh, so also they judge that the soul of the begotten is taken essentially from the soul of the begetter. And so they say that, just as corrupt flesh is sown from corrupt flesh, so also a sinful soul is derived from a sinful soul infected by the original corruption.

Chapter 3 (208)

1. HE CONDEMNS THE ABOVE OPINION, AND SAYS THAT SIN IS TRANSMITTED THROUGH THE FLESH, AND HE SHOWS HOW. But the Catholic faith utterly rejects this and condemns it as opposed to truth since, as we said above,[1] that faith admits that the flesh alone, and not souls, is transmitted. And so it is not according to the soul, but only according to the flesh, that original sin is derived from parents.

2. WHY CONCUPISCENCE IS SAID TO BE IN THE FLESH. For original sin, as we said above,[2] is concupiscence, not the act, but the vice. Hence Augustine in *To Valerius*: "Concupiscence itself is the law of the members or of the flesh, which is some morbid disposition or weakness that arouses unlawful desire, that is, carnal concupiscence, which is called the law of sin."[3,4] This is said to remain in the flesh not because it is not in the soul, but because it occurs in the soul through the corruption of the flesh.

Chapter 4 (209)

HE SHOWS THE CAUSE OF THE CORRUPTION OF THE FLESH, FROM WHICH SIN OCCURS IN THE SOUL. For the flesh became corrupt in Adam through sin. Before sin, a man and a woman could join together without the incentive of lust and the burning of concupiscence, and there was *a marriage bed without stain*;[1] but after sin, there cannot be carnal joining without lustful concupiscence, which is always a flaw, and even a fault, unless it is excused by the goods of marriage. And so it is in concupiscence and lust that the flesh is conceived which is to be formed into the body of the offspring. And so the flesh itself, which is conceived in vicious concupiscence, is polluted and corrupted. From contact with such flesh, the soul, as it is infused, derives the stain by which it is polluted and becomes guilty, that is, the vice of concupiscence, which is original sin.

[1]Dist. 18 c7.
[2]Dist. 30 cc8-9.
[3]Cf. Rom. 7, 23.
[4]Augustine, *De nuptiis et consupiscentia*, bk 1 cc30-31 nn34-35

[1]Cf. Hebr. 13, 4.

Chapter 5 (210)

1. THAT BECAUSE OF THE CORRUPTION OF THE FLESH, WHICH IS THE CAUSE OF SIN, SIN IS SAID TO BE IN THE FLESH. And that is why sin is said to be in the flesh. And so the flesh which is sown in the concupiscence of lust has neither guilt nor the action of guilt, but its cause. Therefore, in that which is sown, there is corruption; in that which is born by concupiscence, there is vice.

2. Hence Ambrose, on the words of the Apostle, says as follows: "How does sin live in the flesh, since it is not a substance, but a privation of the good? In this way: the body of the first man was corrupted through sin, and that corruption remains in the body through the nature of the offense, preserving the force of the divine sentence promulgated against Adam, by association with whom the soul is stained by sin. And so it is because the cause of the deed remains that sin is said to live in the flesh."[1] This is the law of the flesh.—The same: "Sin does not live in the spirit, but in the flesh, because the cause of sin is from the flesh, not from the soul; because the flesh is, from its origin, of the flesh of sin, and through its transmission all flesh becomes [flesh] of sin."[2] But the soul is not transmitted, and so it does not have the cause of sin in it.

3. Augustine too, in a sermon *On the Words of the Apostle*, shows that the soul contracts sin from the flesh; he says: "The vice of concupiscence is what the soul contracted, but from the flesh. For human nature was not first established with vice by God's work, but it was wounded by vice coming from the choice of the will of the first humans,"[3] so that there is not *good in the flesh*,[4] but vice, by which the soul is corrupted.

Chapter 6 (211)

1. ON THE CAUSE OF ORIGINAL SIN WHICH IS IN THE FLESH: WHETHER IT IS A FAULT OR A PUNISHMENT. Here it is usual to ask whether the cause of original sin, which is said to be in the flesh, is a fault or a punishment, or something else.—It cannot be a fault because there is no fault in an irrational thing. For if there were a fault in the flesh before the infusion of the soul, it would be either actual or original. But there is no actual fault there; nor is it the original fault because it is the cause of original sin.—But if it is a punishment, what is it? Passibility, or mortality, or some other corruption? For it is clear that these defects are in the flesh.

[1]Ambrosiaster, on Rom. 7, 18.
[2]Ibid., on Rom. 7, 22.
[3]Rather, Augustine, *De continentia* c8 n19.
[4]Rom. 7, 18.

2. HERE IS REVEALED WHAT IT IS, NAMELY AN UNCLEANNESS DERIVED FROM THE LUST OF THOSE WHO JOINED TOGETHER, WHICH CAN BE CALLED A VICE OR CORRUPTION. To this it can be said that the cause of original sin is a manifold defect of the flesh, and especially some pollution which the flesh contracts in its conception from the burning of the parents' joining and their lustful concupiscence; and it can rightly be called a vice or corruption of the flesh. This uncleanness appears to be greater in the flesh which has been begotten in concupiscence than in that from which it is begotten. And that a vice or corruption exists in the flesh before the joining of the soul to it is proven by the effect at the infusion of the soul: it is stained from the corruption of the flesh, just as a defect is recognized to be in the vessel when the wine placed in it turns to vinegar.

3. BY THE DRAWING OF ANALOGIES, HE SHOWS THAT IT IS NOT ABSURD TO SAY THAT CHILDREN DERIVE ORIGINAL SIN FROM PARENTS WHO HAVE BEEN CLEANSED FROM IT. But lest we wonder and be troubled in our mind in hearing that children derive original sin from parents who have already been cleansed of that sin through baptism, Augustine indicates by the drawing of a number of analogies that this can be so. In his book *On the Baptism of Children*, he says as follows: "How is it that the foreskin, which is removed by circumcision, nevertheless remains in the son of a circumcised man? How is it that the chaff, which human labour removed with such diligence, nevertheless remains in the grain which issues from the winnowed wheat? In the same way, the sin which is cleansed in the parents through baptism remains in those whom they have begotten."[1]—"For they beget insofar as they still retain their ancient nature, not from that which has promoted them in newness among the children of God."[2] For parents do not beget children according to that generation by which they have been born anew,[3] but rather according to that by which they themselves were first begotten carnally.

Chapter 7 (212)

1. HERE IT IS STATED WHY IT IS CALLED ORIGINAL, WITH AN EPILOGUE. It has already been shown what original sin is, and how it passes from parents to children and into the soul through the flesh. From these comments, it also becomes clear why it is called original sin: namely, because it is transmitted by the vicious law of our origin in which we are conceived, namely by the lustful concupiscence of the flesh, as was said

[1]Augustine, *De peccatorum meritis et remissione et de baptismo parvulorum*, bk 3 c8 n16.
[2]Ibid., bk 2 c9 n11.
[3]Cf. Jn. 3, 6-7.

above.[1] For it is not because we are conceived from the flesh drawn from Adam that we derive this sin. The body of Christ was also formed from the same flesh which descends from Adam, but his conception did not occur by the law of sin, that is, by the concupiscence of the flesh, but by the operation of the Holy Spirit, and so his flesh was not sinful. But our own conception does not occur without lust, and so it is not without sin.

2. AUGUSTINE. Augustine clearly shows this, in the book *On Faith to Peter*; he says as follows: "When husband and wife come together in this manner, the intercourse of parents is not without lust and, because of this, the conception of their children born from their flesh cannot be without sin. And here it is not propagation which transmits sin to their children, but lust. Nor is it the fecundity of human nature which causes men to be born with sin, but the uncleanness of lust, which men have from the most just condemnation of that sin. Therefore, blessed David, because of the original sin by which the *children of wrath*[2] are naturally bound, says: *I was conceived amid iniquities, and my mother conceived me among sins*."[3,4] And so from this, it is clear that original sin is transmitted by the law of conception because, unless conception occurred in this manner in the flesh, the soul would not contract the vice of concupiscence from its becoming joined with the flesh.

3. THE OBJECTION OF SOME WHO STRIVE TO PROVE THAT SIN IS NOT DERIVED FROM THE LAW OF COITION. But an objection to this is made in the following way: The flesh is propagated in the [act of] conception itself, in which the sin is said to be transmitted, but the soul is not infused then, according to the natural philosophers, but in an already formed body. Moses too signifies this clearly in Exodus, when he speaks of the striking of a pregnant woman, saying: *If anyone strikes a pregnant woman and causes a miscarriage, if the child was still unformed, he shall pay a money fine; but if the child was formed, let him render a soul for a soul.*[5] But *formed* is understood to mean animated by its own soul, and *unformed* as not yet having a soul.[6] And so in the [act of] conception itself, when the flesh is propagated, the soul is not yet infused. How then can sin be transmitted there, since there cannot be a sin where there is not a soul?

4. RESPONSE WITH SOLUTION. To this it can be said that sin is said to be transmitted in that conception not because original sin is there, but because the flesh there draws that from which the sin comes to be in the soul

[1]In c4.
[2]Cf. Eph. 2, 3.
[3]Ps. 50, 7.
[4]Rather, Fulgentius, *De fide ad Petrum*, c2 n16.
[5]Exod. 21, 22-23, in part according to the Vulgate, in part according to the Old Latin version.
[6]Cf. ordinary gloss, on Exod. 21, 22-23.

when it is infused. And each of these is called conception, namely when the flesh is propagated and receives the form of the human body, and when the soul is infused. This is also sometimes called birth; hence: *What is born in you*;[7] but the bringing forth into the light is properly called birth.

DISTINCTION XXXII

Chapter 1 (213)

1. HOW ORIGINAL SIN IS REMITTED IN BAPTISM, SINCE THAT CONCUPISCENCE WHICH IS CALLED ORIGINAL SIN REMAINS EVEN AFTERWARDS. Because it has been said above that original sin is the vice of concupiscence,[1] and it has been described how it is derived from parents and is called original, it remains to investigate how it is remitted in baptism since, even after baptism, that concupiscence remains which had been there before. So it seems that either the original sin is not concupiscence, or that it is not remitted in baptism.

2. AUGUSTINE IN THE BOOK *ON MARRIAGE AND CONCUPISCENCE*: As Augustine says: "For in fact there remains in *the body of this death*[2] a carnal concupiscence, whose vicious desires we are commanded not to obey; and yet this concupiscence is diminished each day in those who make progress and remain continent."[3] But although concupiscence remains after baptism, yet it does not dominate and reign as before; indeed, by the grace of baptism, it is mitigated and diminished, so that it is not able to dominate afterwards, unless one restores vigour to the enemy by going *after concupiscences*.[4] Nor does it remain after baptism in regard to guilt, because it is not imputed as a sin, but is only a punishment of sin; but before baptism, it is punishment and fault.

3. THAT ORIGINAL SIN IS REMITTED IN TWO WAYS, NAMELY BY ITS ATTENUATION AND BY ABSOLUTION FROM GUILT. And so original sin is said to be remitted in baptism by a double reason: because through the grace of baptism, the vice of concupiscence is weakened and attenuated, so that it will no longer reign, unless its vigour is restored by our consent; and because the guilt for it is absolved.

4. AUTHORITY REGARDING ONE MANNER OF REMISSION. Hence Augustine, in the book *On the Baptism of Children*: "By grace through baptism it is brought about that *the old man is crucified* and *the body of sin is de-*

[7]Cf. Mt. 1, 20.

[1]Dist. 30 c8 n2.
[2]Cf. Rom. 7, 24.
[3]Augustine, *De nuptiis et concupiscentia*, bk 1 c25 n28.
[4]Cf. Eccli. 18, 30; Rom. 6, 12-14.

stroyed:[5] not in such a way that the concupiscence which is diffused and innate in the living flesh is suddenly taken away and no longer exists, but so that what was in him when he was born should not be an obstacle to the one who has died [to sin in baptism]. For if he lives after baptism, he has a concupiscence in his flesh with which he can struggle and which, with God's aid, he overcomes, so long as he has received God's grace *not in vain*.[6] And so it is not granted in baptism, apart perhaps from an ineffable miracle of the Creator, that *the law of sin which is in our members*[7] is entirely extinguished and no longer exists; but that whatever evil has been done, said, and thought by man is entirely abolished and is regarded as if it had not been done. But concupiscence itself remains in the battle, even though the bond of the guilt by which the devil held the soul and separated it from its Creator has been loosened."[8]—See, here he shows plainly that it is remitted in baptism for this reason: not because it does not remain after baptism, but because the guilt is abolished in baptism.

5. AUTHORITY REGARDING THE OTHER [MANNER]. Then, he shows that it is also remitted in the sense that, by the grace of baptism, concupiscence itself is mitigated and diminished; in the same book, he speaks as follows: "The law of the flesh, which the Apostle calls *sin* when he says: *Do not let sin reign in your mortal body*,[9] does not so remain in the members of those who are reborn *from water and the Spirit*[10] as if its remission had not happened; indeed, there is an entirely full remission of sins [in baptism]. But it does remain in our old flesh as something overcome and destroyed, unless it is in some way revivified by our unlawful consent, and recalled to its own reign and domination."[11] Here he plainly indicates that concupiscence is weakened in baptism: on account of this, too, it is said to be remitted, and not only because guilt is absolved there.

6. Scripture teaches this latter manner of remission in many other testimonies. For Augustine says, in *Against Julian*: "The law which is in our members is a vice of the flesh, which comes from the punishment of sin and the transmission of death."[12] "But this law *which is in our members*,[13] is remitted by spiritual regeneration, and [yet] remains in our mortal flesh. It is remitted because the guilt is absolved by the sacrament in which the

[5]Cf. Rom. 6, 6.
[6]Cf. 2 Cor. 6, 1.
[7]Cf. Rom. 7, 23.
[8]Augustine, *De peccatorum meritis et remissione et de baptismo parvulorum*, bk 1 c39 n70.
[9]Rom. 6, 12.
[10]Cf. Jn. 3, 5.
[11]Augustine, *De peccatorum meritis et remissione et de baptismo parvulorum*, bk 2 c28 n45.
[12]Cf. Augustine, *In Ioannem*, tr. 3 n12.
[13]Cf. Rom. 7, 23.

faithful are reborn; but it remains because it causes the desires against which even the faithful struggle."[14]—The same, in a sermon *On the Concupiscence of the Flesh*: "Through the grace of baptism and the washing of regeneration, the guilt of concupiscence with which you were born is absolved, as is also whatever consent you gave before to evil concupiscence, whether in thought, speech, or action."[15]—The same, in the book *On Marriage and Concupiscence*: "Although the concupiscence of the flesh is no longer held to be a sin in those who have been born again, nevertheless, every offspring that is born is bound by original sin."[16]—Also: "The concupiscence of the flesh is remitted in baptism not so that it no longer exists, but so that it is not accounted a sin."[17] "Not to have sin means not to be guilty of sin. Therefore, just as other sins pass away in act and remain in guilt, such as homicide and suchlike, so it can conversely happen that concupiscence passes away in guilt and remains in act."[18] From the above, it is plainly shown how original sin is remitted in baptism.

Chapter 2 (214)

1. ON THE UNCLEANNESS WHICH THE FLESH CONTRACTS FROM THE LUST OF INTERCOURSE: WHETHER IT IS WASHED AWAY IN BAPTISM. But it is usual to ask here whether even the flesh itself is purged in baptism of that uncleanness which it contracted at its conception from lustful concupiscence.

2. SOME SAY THAT THE FLESH IS CLEANSED THERE FROM THAT POLLUTION. It seems to some that, just as the soul is purified from guilt, so also the flesh is purged of that pollution. In this view, just as the mystery of baptism is accomplished by two things, namely water and the Spirit, so also two things are purged there, namely the soul of guilt and the flesh of that contagion. This view is very probable.—OTHERS SAY NOT. But others hold that the soul alone is cleansed there, but the flesh is not purged of that uncleanness.

3. HE SHOWS THE UNSUITABLENESS OF THE VIEW OF THOSE WHO DENY IT. But if that uncleanness remains until the procreation of children which is done in the concupiscence of the flesh, it seems that the nature of the flesh becomes more and more corrupt, and the flesh of the offspring seems to be more corrupt than that of the parents. For the flesh of the offspring is derived in a polluted state from flesh that retains the pollution that it had from its conception; and it is conceived in concupiscence, from which it is also polluted, and so it is contaminated from a double cause.

[14]Augustine, *Contra Iulianum*, bk 2 c3 n5.
[15]Augustine, *Sermo 152,* n3.
[16]Augustine, *De nuptiis et concupiscentia*, bk 1 c24 n27.
[17]Ibid., bk 1 c26 n29.
[18]Ibid.

Hence it seems that the pollution of the flesh is greater in the offspring than it was in the parent.

4. THEIR ANSWER. To this they say that, although the flesh of the offspring is inseminated from unclean flesh and is conceived in concupiscence, yet it does not derive a greater uncleanness than was had by the flesh from which it is inseminated. And they add that, even if the flesh of the offspring were more fetid and unclean, and so more corrupt than the flesh of the parent, no prejudice to truth follows from this. For it is not absurd, they say, if the nature of the flesh derived by posterity were more corrupt, and yet the soul is not more corrupted by such a more corrupt nature.

Chapter 3 (215)

FROM WHICH AUTHOR THAT CONCUPISCENCE IS, WHETHER FROM GOD OR ANOTHER. Moreover, it is usual to ask whether the concupiscence which remains after baptism and is a punishment only, but which was punishment and fault before baptism, has God as its author or another.—RESPONSE. Replying briefly to this, we say that, insofar as it is a punishment, it has God as its author; but insofar as it is a fault, it has the devil or man as its author.

Chapter 4 (216)

1. BY WHAT JUSTICE THAT SIN IS IMPUTED TO A SOUL CLEAN FROM CREATION, SINCE IT CANNOT AVOID IT. It is also usual to ask by what justice a soul created innocent by God is bound by that sin, since it is not in its power to avoid it, for it is not committed through free choice, because no sooner does the soul exist than it is subject to that sin.

2. THE FALSE ANSWER OF SOME. Regarding this, some say that the soul is guilty of that sin because, although it is created clean by God, yet it shares pleasure with the flesh when it is infused in the body, and it contracts the sin from this.—But if it were so, then it would not be called original sin, but actual sin.

3. A SUITABLE AND TRUE ANSWER. Therefore, it is rather to be rightly said that that sin which it unavoidably derives from the corruption of the body is imputed to that soul, because, as Augustine says in the book *On the City of God*, "the corruption of the body, which *weighs down the soul*,[1] was not the cause of the first sin, but its punishment; nor was it the

[1]Cf. Wis. 9, 15.

corruptible flesh which made the soul sinful, but a sinful soul which made the flesh corruptible."[2]

Chapter 5 (217)

1. WHETHER THAT SIN IS VOLUNTARY OR NECESSARY. It may also not undeservedly be asked whether original sin ought to be called voluntary or necessary.

2. THAT IT CAN BE CALLED VOLUNTARY AND NECESSARY. On the one hand, it can be called necessary because it cannot be avoided; and so the Prophet says: *Rescue me from my necessities.*[1] On the other hand, it is not incongruously called voluntary because it proceeded from the will of the first man, as Augustine shows in book 1 of the *Retractations*, saying: "That which in children is called original sin, although they do not yet use the free choice of the will, may without absurdity be called voluntary because it is contracted from the first evil will of man and was made in some way hereditary."[2]

Chapter 6 (218)

1. WHY GOD JOINS THE SOUL TO THE BODY, KNOWING THAT IT WILL BE STAINED THEREBY AND SO DAMNED. But if it is asked why God joins the soul to the body, since he made the soul itself without stain, and knows that it draws the stain of sin from being joined to the body, and that sometimes it is separated from that body before baptism and so is damned, we answer that this proceeds from the loftiness of God's judgements, and it is not done unjustly by God. For it is not incongruous that he continuously preserves without change the mode of human generation which he established in the beginning, even though human sins have since intervened. And so God forms bodies from the matter which was made without defect from the beginning, and he creates souls from nothing, and he completes man by the joining of the two. Therefore, since each nature of man was established by God without defect, although it was afterwards vitiated by man's own sin, the unchangeable God was not for that reason bound to change the first law of human generation, or to desist from the multiplication of humans.

[2]Augustine, *De civitate Dei*, bk 14 c3 n2.

[1]Ps. 24, 17.
[2]Augustine, *Retractationes*, bk 1 c13 n5.

Chapter 7 (219)

1. WHETHER THE SOUL IS AS IT IS CREATED BY GOD.—HOW SOME PROVE THAT IT IS NOT. Here it is usual for some to ask whether the soul before baptism is as it is created by God. They strive to prove that this is not the case in the following way: The soul is created in the body, in being joined to which it is stained by sin. And so, as soon as it exists, it has sin, and no sooner did it exist than it had sin. Therefore, it is not as it is created by God, for it is created by God innocent and without vice, and it never is like that.

2. SOLUTION. To this it can be said that it is not entirely as God made it, for God made it good, and gave to it goodness without corruption. And that which it received from the Creator at creation is called a natural goodness; and it did not entirely lose that goodness through sin, but had it in a vitiated form: and yet God had made it without vice. For if the soul were not a good thing, evil could not be in it, since there cannot be evil, except in the good, as will be discussed below.[1] And so the soul is not entirely as it was created by God, just as a person with dirty hands does not receive a fruit as I gave it to him with my clean hands, but it was clean when I gave it.

Chapter 8 (220)

WHETHER SOULS FROM CREATION ARE EQUAL IN THEIR NATURAL GIFTS. It is also usual to ask, not unsuitably, whether all souls are equal from creation, or whether some are more excellent than others.—Not unreasonably, it seems to many that, from creation itself, some souls excel others in natural gifts, as in their essence; one is more acute than another and better able to understand and remember, in as much as it is endowed with a sharper mind and a more far-seeing intellect.—This is said not improbably, as it is clear that such was the case with the angels.[1] And although some have greater natural gifts than others, yet, in departing from the body, if before baptism, they receive an equal punishment and, if after baptism, they are immediately allotted an equal crown, because sharpness or dullness of intellect does not determine the reward or punishment in future.

[1] Dist. 34 c4.

[1] As was shown above, dist. 3 c2.

DISTINCTION XXXIII

Chapter 1 (221)

1. WHETHER CHILDREN ORIGINALLY CONTRACT THE SINS OF ALL THEIR FOREFATHERS AS THEY DO THE SIN OF ADAM. It seems that we must add to the above whether the sins of forefathers pass down to children, as we have said that that crime of the first man redounded against all who were carnally procreated; and if the sins of parents pass to their children, whether those of all those who existed from Adam all the way down to them, or those of some, but not of others.

2. WHAT AUGUSTINE SEEMS TO SAY CONCERNING THIS IN THE *ENCHIRIDION*. Augustine speaks about this ambiguously in the *Enchiridion.*[1] For he seems to approve [the view] that the sins of their ancestors are imputed to children; yet not of all those who were from Adam, lest children be burdened by an unbearable and excessive burden unto eternal punishment, but only those of their ancestors from the fourth generation. And he confirms this by the words which the Lord speaks in Exodus: *I am God, visiting the iniquities of the fathers unto the third and fourth generation*;[2] as if only the sins of their nearest ancestors were imputed to children, but not other sins; this happens by the moderation of divine mercy.

3. HE SETS FORTH THE EVIDENCE OF THOSE WHO SAY THAT THE CRIMES OF PARENTS PASS DOWN TO THEIR CHILDREN. As for the view that it is not the crime of the first man alone which binds children, but also other crimes, those who hold this view confirm it by the fact that children too, and not only older people, are said to be baptized 'for the remission of sins,' in the plural, and not in the singular: 'for the remission of sin.' And David, who was the issue of a legitimate marriage, says: *I was conceived amid iniquities, and my mother conceived me among sins*;[3] he does not say: in iniquity or sin. And so they hold that not only that one original sin is imputed to children, but also many others which can be found in Adam's sin as well as the other sins of their parents.

Chapter 2 (222)

1. THAT IN THAT ONE FIRST SIN, MANY OTHERS ARE FOUND. But Augustine, in the *Enchiridion*, indicates that many sins can be identified in the actual sin of Adam, saying: "Many sins can be noted in the one transgression of Adam, if it is divided, as it were, into its members. For there was pride in it, because man loved more to be in his own power than in God's;

[1]Augustine, *Enchiridion*, c47.
[2]Exod. 20, 5.
[3]Ps. 50, 7.

and sacrilege, because he did not believe God; and homicide, because he hurled himself into death; and spiritual fornication, because the integrity of the human mind was corrupted by the persuasion of the serpent; and theft, because he usurped the forbidden food; and avarice, because he desired more than ought to have sufficed for him; and whatever other sin can be found in this one sin."[1]

2. ON THE SINS OF PARENTS, WHETHER THEY BIND CHILDREN.—AUGUSTINE. He next discusses the sins of the ancestors who have gone before and whether they are imputed to children; he does so more by way of offering an opinion than by assertion, saying as follows: "It is not improbably said that children are bound by the sins not only of the first humans, but also of those of their own parents from whom they themselves were born. Indeed, that divine sentence: *I shall visit the sins of the fathers upon their children*,[2] binds them before their regeneration, so that even one who was born of a lawful marriage says: *I was conceived amid iniquities, and my mother conceived me among sins*.[3] He did not say *in iniquity* or *in sin*, although he could rightly have said so, but preferred to say *iniquities* and *sins* because, as I discussed above,[4] many sins are found in that one sin, which passed into all men and is so great that human nature was changed by it. And the other sins of parents, which cannot change nature in such a way, bind their children by guilt, unless God's grace comes to their help."[5]

3. SEE THE DIFFERENT OPINIONS. "But regarding the sins of other parents, through whom each [of us] descends from Adam himself to our own father according to their generations, it is not pointless to raise the question: whether each person who is born is bound by the evil actions and the multiplied original faults of all of them, so that the later each is born, the worse one is. Or does God threaten to visit the sins of parents on their posterity *until the third and fourth generation*[6] because, by a merciful moderation, he does not extend his anger any further in regard to the faults of their ancestors, lest those on whom the grace of regeneration is not conferred be crushed unto eternal damnation by such an excessive burden, if they were compelled to derive as original sins the sins of all their forefathers from the very beginning of humankind and to satisfy the penalties due for them. Whether this or something else may, or may not, be found concerning such a great matter by a more diligent examination and interpretation of the holy Scriptures I do not dare boldly to assert."[7] See, it is

[1]Augustine, *Enchiridion*, c45.
[2]Num. 14, 18; Deut. 5, 9.
[3]Ps. 50, 7.
[4]In c1.
[5]Augustine, *Enchiridion*, c46.
[6]Exod. 20, 5.
[7]Augustine, *Enchiridion*, c47.

made very clear to the reader that Augustine said the above things not by way of assertion, but by reporting the opinions of different people.

4. HE SHOWS THAT AUGUSTINE WOULD BE CONTRADICTING HIMSELF, IF HE HELD THE ABOVE OPINION. Otherwise, he would be shown to be contradicting himself since, in the same book, he says in these words that the punishment of children who are bound by original sin alone is the mildest of all: "Indeed, their punishment will be mildest for those who, apart from the original sin which they derived, added none other on top of it; and as for the rest who did add sins, each will have a more bearable damnation there insofar as his iniquity was lesser here."[8] See, he here says plainly that the punishment of children is the lightest of all other punishments.

5. If this is so, then they are not bound by the sins of their forefathers other than Adam. For if they were punished eternally for the actual sins of their parents as well as for their own original one, they would not be punished any less, but perhaps more than their own parents. And so children will not be damned for the actual sins of their parents, nor even for the actual sins of the first parent, but for the original one which is derived from parents; for it, they will not feel any other punishment of material fire or of the worm of conscience, except that they will perpetually lack the vision of God. And so children are bound by one sin, and not by many.

6. DETERMINATION OF THE ARGUMENTS WHICH THEY ADVANCED TO BOLSTER THEIR OWN OPINION. And so even those things by which their opinion seems to be supported, namely the fact that Scripture at times signifies that there are sins and iniquities in children, using the plural, Augustine determines in this way in the same book: because in Scripture "the plural number is often signified through the singular, as there: *And so pray to God that he take away the serpent from us*;[9] it does not say *serpents*, which the people were afflicted. And conversely, the singular number is signified by the plural, as in the Gospel: *For they are dead who sought the life of the child*;[10] it does not say, *he is dead*, although Herod is the one who is being spoken about. And in Exodus: *They made gods of gold*,[11] although they made one calf, of which they said: *These are your gods, Israel*.[12] And so, that one original sin is signified by the plural number, when we say that children are baptized for the remission of sins, and are conceived amid sins and iniquities."[13]

[8]Augustine, *Enchiridion*, c93.
[9]Num. 21, 7, according to the Septuagint.
[10]Mt. 2, 20.
[11]Exod. 32, 31.
[12]Exod. 32, 4.
[13]Augustine, *Enchiridion*, c44.

Chapter 3 (223)

1. WHETHER THE ACTUAL SIN OF ADAM IS GRAVER THAN THE REST. Here it is usual to ask whether the sin of Adam's transgression, from which proceeded original sin and in which many sins were identified above,[1] was graver than other sins.

2. WHY IT SEEMS TO SOME TO BE GREATER THAN THE REST. Such seems to be the case to some, because that sin changed all of human nature, as Augustine says in the *Enchiridion*: "That one sin, committed in a place and state of life of such felicity, is so great that in one man as at its origin and, as it were, at its root, all of humankind was damned."[2]—The same in the book *On the City of God*: "The injustice by which that mandate was violated was so much the greater injustice the easier was the observance by which it could be kept. For desire did not yet stand in the way of the will: this followed afterwards from the punishment of the transgression."[3] Those who say that that sin was graver than the rest of the sins of other men support their view with these and other authorities.

3. AFTER THE AUTHORITIES, HE SETS OUT THEIR REASONING. They labour to show this also by reason, in this way: That sin was more harmful than any sin of other people because it vitiated all of humankind and made it subject to both kinds of death; this was done by no other sin. And so that sin had a greater evil effect than any other.

4. RESPONSE AGAINST THEM, WHERE OTHER SINS ARE SHOWN TO BE GREATER THAN IT. To this it can be said that, although that sin changed human nature in regard to the necessity for death and diffused guilt throughout all of humankind, yet it is not to be held to have been graver than the sin against the Holy Spirit, which is remitted *neither* here *nor in the future*, as Truth says.[4]—And that it corrupted all of human nature is not because it was graver than all other sins, but because it was committed by man when the whole of human nature resided in one man, and so all of it was corrupted in him.

5. IN WHAT REGARD DID IT HAVE A GREATER EVIL EFFECT THAN OTHERS, AND IN WHAT REGARD IT DID NOT, BUT [RATHER] A LESSER ONE. And it brought about a greater evil effect in regard to the manifold defects that emanated from it, but not in regard to eternal punishment, for he did not deserve a graver punishment than many afterwards deserved through other sins; indeed, we believe that others deserved a graver wrath than Adam did.

[1]In c2 n1.
[2]Augustine, *Enchiridion*, c48.
[3]Augustine, *De civitate Dei*, bk 14 c12.
[4]Mt. 12, 32.

Chapter 4 (224)

WHETHER THAT SIN WAS REMITTED TO THE FIRST PARENTS. But if it is asked whether that sin was remitted to the first parents, we say that they received forgiveness through penance. Hence Augustine, in the book *On the Baptism of Children*: "Just as those first parents, by living justly afterwards, are believed to have been freed from the final punishment through the blood of the Lord, and yet did not deserve to be restored to paradise during their life on earth, so too sinful flesh, even if man live justly in it after the remission of sins, does not necessarily deserve not to suffer that death which it has derived from the propagation of sin."[1]

Chapter 5 (225)

1. THAT THE SINS OF PARENTS ARE VISITED ON THEIR CHILDREN, AND THAT THERE IS NO CONTRADICTION BETWEEN WHAT GOD SAYS IN EXODUS AND IN EZECHIEL. And although children are not bound by the sins of parents, other than Adam's, nevertheless it is not to be denied that the sins of parents redound upon their children, as the Lord says to Moses in Exodus: *For I am God, strong and jealous, visiting the iniquities of the fathers upon the children, unto the third and fourth generation of those who hate me.*[1] By these words, it is plainly indicated that God inflicts punishment for the sins of the fathers upon their descendants in the third and fourth generation.

2. AUTHORITY OF EZECHIEL, WHICH SEEMS TO CONTRADICT THE LAW. But against this seems to stand what the Lord says in Ezechiel: *What does it mean that, among yourselves, you turn the following phrase into a proverb, saying: 'The fathers ate sour grapes, and the teeth of their children are set on edge?' As I live, says the Lord, this parable will no longer be as a proverb among you. All souls are mine: as the father's soul is mine, so also the son's soul is mine. And the soul that sins, it shall die.*[2] *The son shall not bear the iniquity of the father, and the father shall not bear the iniquity of the son. The justice of the just man shall be his, and the impiety of the impious one shall be his.*[3]—JEROME. By these words, it seems that "God corrects through the Prophet what he had said badly"[4] in the Law: "For if he inflicts punishment for the sins of the fathers unto the third and fourth generation, there seems to be injustice in

[1]Augustine, *De peccatorum meritis et remissione et de baptismo parvulorum*, bk 2 c34 n55.

[1]Exod. 20, 5.
[2]Ezech. 18, 2-4.
[3]Ezech. 18, 20.
[4]Jerome, *In Ezechielem* 18, 2.

God in that one sins and another is punished. For how is it just that one sins and another bemoans the sins?"[5]

3. DETERMINATION, SHOWING THE CONSONANCE OF THE ABOVE AUTHORITIES. But, as Jerome says, lest "it seem that the Law and the Prophets, that is, Exodus and Ezechiel, or rather, God himself, who spoke in both places, speak discrepantly,"[6] let us note the end of that authority from Exodus. For after saying: *I visit the iniquities of the fathers upon the children*, he adds: *of those who hate me*.[7] By this, he shows clearly "that the children are not punished because their fathers sinned, but because, like their fathers, by some hereditary evil, they hated God."[8]—And so, as Jerome teaches, what the Lord says in Exodus does not mean what many believe, nor is it like the proverb: *The fathers ate sour grapes*, etc. For both Jerome, in *On Ezechiel*, and Augustine, on the Psalm, *God, do not pass over my praise in silence*, hold that the text of Exodus is to be taken with regard to children who imitate their fathers' sins: God is said to visit the sins of their fathers upon them because he punishes them for imitating their fathers' sins, not because their fathers sinned.[9] And so the Lord does not correct in the Prophet what he had said before in the Law, but he reveals how it is to be understood. And so he reproves those who understood it wrongly, who said: *The fathers ate*, etc.[10]

4. WHY HE SAID: UNTO THE THIRD AND FOURTH GENERATION, AND WHY FATHERS ALONE WERE MENTIONED. And yet, if that statement is to be taken of the imitators of evil people, why did he mention only the third and fourth generation, since those who imitate their fathers' sins are held guilty in every generation? And why did he mention fathers alone, since all who imitate the sins of any evil people are evil?—HE RESOLVES IT. But he named fathers especially because sons mostly imitate their fathers, whom they particularly love. And he mentioned the third and fourth generation, because fathers sometimes live so long that they have descendants to the third and fourth generation; these, seeing the iniquities of their fathers, are made the heirs of their impiety through imitation. In this way, what is said in Exodus is rightly understood according to its letter.

5. HOW THAT TEXT OF EXODUS IS TO BE UNDERSTOOD ACCORDING TO THE MYSTERY.—JEROME. It is clear that it is also to be understood mystically from the fact that it is called a parable. "For," as Jerome says, "if it is a parable, it says one thing literally, but contains another meaning."[11] And

[5]Jerome, *In Ezechielem* 18, 2.
[6]Ibid.
[7]Exod. 20, 5.
[8]Jerome, *In Ezechielem* 18, 2.
[9]Ibid.; Augustine, *Enarrationes in Psalmos*, on Ps. 108, 14, n15.
[10]Cf. Ezech. 18, 2, above, in n2.
[11]Jerome, *In Ezechielem* 18, 2.

so some others "carefully explained it as follows: They say that the father in us is the light pricking of the senses," namely the first movement of suggestion or thought; "the son, however, is if thought conceived the sin": in this is signified the consent and delight of the woman; "the grandchild is, if what you have thought and conceived, you have accomplished in deed" or have decided to accomplish in deed: in this is signified the man's consent or the execution of the sin; "but the great-grandchild is, if you have not only done it, but gloried in it; and this is the fourth generation": not because three preceded it, but it is called the fourth because it is numbered fourth from the first movement, which is, as it were, the father. "And so God will not punish eternally the first and second goads of thoughts, which the Greeks call 'propatheias' and without which no man can exist; but only if one has decreed to do what he has thought and has not willed to correct what he has done":[12] these are mortal sins and the third and fourth generation.

6. BY WHAT MAY IT BE PROVED THAT THE FIRST MOVEMENT IS NOT PUNISHED ETERNALLY. As Jerome says: "To prove that the first impulse of thought is not punished eternally by God, that text of Genesis is to be adduced:[13] For Cham sinned by ridiculing his father's nakedness, and not he, but his son Chanaan, received the punishment: *Cursed be Chanaan, he shall be a slave of his brothers*.[14] For what is the justice, that the father sinned and the son was punished?"[15] But that was said according to the mystery [allegorically].

DISTINCTION XXXIV

Chapter 1 (226)

WHAT THINGS ARE TO BE INVESTIGATED REGARDING SIN. After what has been said above, some things are to be considered by diligent investigation regarding actual sin, namely what the origin and first cause of sin was, whether a good or an evil thing; afterwards, in what thing does sin exist; then, what sin is, and in how many ways it is done, and of the difference among specific sins.

[12]Jerome, *In Ezechielem* 18, 2.
[13]Cf. Gen. 9, 22-25.
[14]Gen. 9, 25.
[15]Jerome, *In Ezechielem* 18, 2.

Chapter 2 (227)

1. WHAT WAS THE ORIGIN AND FIRST CAUSE OF SIN. The cause and first origin of sin was a good thing, because before the first sin there was nothing evil from which it might arise. For since it had an origin and cause, either it had it from good, or from evil. But there was no evil before; and so it arose from good. For sin first arose in the angel, and afterwards in man; and what was the angel other than a good nature of God? It was not from God that the evil which was in the angel arose; it was not from anyone other than the angel, and so it arose from good.

2. Hence in his responses against Julian the heretic, who had said: "If sin is from nature, then the nature is evil," Augustine says: "I ask that he answer me, if he can: It is manifest that all evil deeds arise from an evil will, like evil fruits from an evil tree.[1] But from where does he say that the evil will itself has arisen, other than from good? For if from an angel, what is an angel, other than a good work of God? If from man, what was man himself, other than a good work of God? Indeed, what were these two before an evil will arose in them, other than a good work of God and a good and praiseworthy nature? And so evil arises from good, and it could not arise from anything other than good. Therefore, I say that no evil preceded the evil will,"[2] but that it had its origin from good.—Here it is plainly said that a good nature was the first cause and origin of evil; and it is also shown to what the cause of sin belonged, namely to an evil will.

Chapter 3 (228)

THAT AN EVIL WILL WAS THE SECONDARY CAUSE OF EVILS. And that evil will, of the angel and of man, is also the cause of subsequent evils, namely of evil deeds and evil wills.—Hence Augustine in the *Enchiridion*: "We must not at all doubt that the cause of the good things that pertain to us is nothing else than the goodness of God; but the cause of evil things is the falling away from the unchangeable good of the will of a changeable good, first of the angel and then of man." "This is the first evil of the rational creature, namely the first privation of good."[1]—See, you have here that the first will of a changeable good, that is, of the angel or of man, falling away from the unchangeable good, that is, from God, is the cause of the evil things which pertain to us, because it is the cause of both the sins and the punishments by which human nature is oppressed. And so the first origin and cause of sin was a good; and the second, an evil which had arisen from the good.

[1]Cf. Mt. 7, 17-18.
[2]Augustine, *De nuptiis et concupiscentia*, bk 2 c28 n48.

[1]Augustine, *Enchiridion*, cc23-24.

Chapter 4 (229)

1. IN WHAT THING EVIL EXISTS, WHETHER IN A GOOD THING OR IN AN EVIL ONE, AND IT IS SAID THAT IT ONLY EXISTS IN A GOOD THING. After the origin of evil has been shown, it remains to see in what thing evil exists, whether in a good thing or in an evil thing.

2. One who knows rightly and acutely, understands evil to be in nothing other than a good, that is, in a good nature. For evil is the corruption or privation of the good; and where there is not a good, there cannot be a corruption or privation of the good; and so sin cannot exist in anything other than a good thing.—AUGUSTINE. As Augustine says in the *Enchiridion*: "Just as bodies are weakened by illnesses and wounds, which are privations of that good which is called health, so also whatever vices of spirits there are, are privations of natural goods. What, indeed, is it that is called an evil, other than a privation of good?"[1]—"For good to be diminished is an evil; although, however much it is diminished, it is necessary that something of it remain, if its [God-created] nature is still there. For the good which is a nature cannot be consumed, unless its nature itself is consumed. But when it is corrupted, its corruption is an evil because it deprives that nature of some good. (EXPLICATION OF THE ARGUMENT.) Indeed, if it does not deprive it of any good, it does not harm it; but it does harm it, and so it takes away the good. Therefore, for so long as a nature is being corrupted, there is in it the good of which it is being deprived."[2]— "And so it is that there is nothing which is called evil, if there is nothing good. A good which entirely lacks evil is an uncorrupted good; but when there is some evil in it, it is a vitiated or defective good. There cannot be any evil, where there is no good. Hence we have a curious conclusion: that since every nature, insofar as it is a nature, is a good, nothing else seems to be said, when we say that 'a nature is defective' or 'evil,' than that what is good is evil, and that evil is nothing other than what is good."[3]—By the weaving of all this, it is clearly indicated that evil cannot exist in anything other than a good thing; and although it seems absurd,[4] it is also manifestly said that what is good is evil."

3. WHAT FOLLOWS FROM THE FOREGOING, NAMELY THAT WHEN MAN IS CALLED EVIL, HE IS CALLED AN EVIL GOOD. From this it is gathered that, when man is called evil, nothing else is meant than an evil good. Hence Augustine adds, in the same place: "What is an evil man, if not an evil nature, because man is a nature? Now, if man is a good thing because he is a nature, what else is an evil man, if not an evil good? Yet, when we

[1]Augustine, *Enchiridion*, c11.
[2]Ibid., c12.
[3]Ibid.
[4]Cf. Ibid.

distinguish between these two things, we find that he is not evil because he is a man, nor is he good because he is iniquitous; but he is called good because he is a man, evil because iniquitous. And so each nature, even if it is defective, insofar as it is a nature, is good; insofar as it is defective, it is evil."

Chapter 5 (230)

1. THAT THE RULE OF THE DIALECTICIANS REGARDING OPPOSITES FAILS IN THESE, NAMELY IN REGARD TO GOOD AND EVIL.—AUGUSTINE. And so, "in these opposites which are called good and evil, that rule of the dialecticians fails, by which they say that two opposites cannot be in the same thing at the same time. For no drink or food is at the same time sweet and bitter; nothing is at the same time and place black and white. And this is found in many things and in almost all contraries, that they cannot be at the same time in the same thing. But although no one doubts that goods and evils are opposites, not only can they exist at the same time, but evils are entirely unable to exist without goods, or in anything other than goods."[1]

2. THAT EVIL ARISES FROM GOOD AND EXISTS IN NOTHING OTHER THAN THE GOOD. "And these two opposites exist at the same time in such a way that, if the good did not exist in which evil might exist, evil could not exist at all, because not only would corruption not have a place to stay, but it would have no source from which to arise, unless there were something that could be corrupted, because corruption is nothing other than the extermination of the good. And so evils have arisen from goods, and cannot exist in anything other than good things."[2] "Therefore, there was no source at all from which an evil nature could arise, except from the good nature of angel and man, from which the evil will first arose."[3]

3. HE COMPOSES AN EPILOGUE IN ORDER TO MOVE ON TO OTHER THINGS. From these arguments is revealed what we said above was to be investigated first and second,[4] namely what the origin of evil was and in what thing it exists. By the testimonies cited above, it is proven that it arose from a good thing and exists in a good thing.

4. OPPOSED TO THAT SENTENCE IN WHICH IT WAS SAID THAT EVIL IS GOOD IS THE ONE FROM THE PROPHECY WHICH SAYS: WOE TO THOSE WHO SAY THAT EVIL IS GOOD. But some make the following objection to the statement 'evil is that which is good':[5] If we say that evil is good, we fall

[1]Augustine, *Enchiridion*, c14.
[2]Ibid.
[3]Ibid., c15.
[4]Above, c1.
[5]Cf. Augustine, *Enchiridion*, c13.

under that sentence of the Prophet where we read: *Woe to those who say that evil is good and good is evil.*[6] And so, if we wish to avoid this curse, we must not at all say that good is evil and vice versa.—DETERMINATION ACCORDING TO AUGUSTINE. But Augustine determines this in the same book, saying that what is said in the prophecy "is to be understood of those very things by which men are evil, not of men themselves. And so it is the one who calls adultery good upon whom the prophet's detestation falls,"[7] as well as upon him who "says that man is evil, or that the good is iniquitous."[8] For he who says that man as man is evil, and that iniquity is goodness, "faults God's work, which is man; and praises a vice of man, which is iniquity."[9]

DISTINCTION XXXV

Chapter 1 (231)

1. WHAT SIN IS. After these things, we must see what sin is.—AUGUSTINE, TO FAUSTUS: As Augustine says, "sin is every word or deed or desire which happens against the law of God."[1]—AUGUSTINE. ANOTHER DESCRIPTION. The same, in the book *On the Two Souls*: "Sin is the will to obtain or retain what justice forbids."[2]—In either description, what is discussed is actual and mortal sin, not venial sin. By the first description, it is shown that sin is an evil will, or depraved speech and deed, that is, an evil action, whether interior or exterior. By the second, it is shown to be only an interior action, for the will, as was said above,[3] is a movement of the spirit; and so the action is interior.

2. Ambrose too, in the book *On Paradise*, says: "What is sin, except a transgression of the divine law and disobedience of heavenly commands? And so there is sin in the transgressor, but there is no fault in the one who mandated the commands. For there would be no sin, if there had been no prohibition. But if there were no sin, not only wickedness, but perhaps not even virtue would exist, which, if there had not been some seeds of wickedness, might either not exist, or not rise in excellence above it."[4] See, Ambrose defines sin to be transgression of the law and a disobedience.

[6] Is. 5, 20.
[7] Augustine, *Enchiridion*, c19.
[8] Ibid. c13.
[9] Ibid.

[1] Augustine, *Contra Faustum*, bk 22 c27.
[2] Augustine, *De duabus animabus*, c11 n15.
[3] Dist. 26 c2 n1.
[4] Ambrose, *De paradiso*, c8 n39.

3. John says: *The one who sins commits iniquity, and sin is iniquity.*[5] On this passage, Augustine says: "Law is *lex* in Latin and *nomos* in Greek; iniquity is *anomia,* which is against the law or is lawless. And so he says: *Sin is iniquity*: whatever sin we commit, we act against God's law. Hence: *I counted all sinners of the earth to be transgressors*:[6] not only those who hold the written law in contempt, but also those who corrupt the innocence of the natural law."[7]

Chapter 2 (232)

1. HE CITES THE SENTENCES OF DIFFERENT AUTHORS ON SIN. By reason of the diversity of these statements,[1] many have thought different things concerning sin.—THREEFOLD OPINION ON SIN. For some said that an evil will alone is sin, and not exterior actions; others that it is the will and the acts; others that it is neither, saying that all actions are good and by God and from God as their source, while evil is nothing, as Augustine says, in *On John*: "*All things were made through him, and without him was made nothing,*[2] that is, sin, which is nothing; and men are made into nothing when they sin."[3]

2. Above,[4] Augustine also said that "evil is the privation or corruption of the good." He says this also in his book *On 84 Questions*: "Perfect evil has no form, for it lacks all good, but a form is something good. And so evil does not exist, because it is contained in no species, and the whole meaning of evil is found in the privation of species."[5]—Also, in *On Ecclesiastical Dogmas*, it is said that "evil or wickedness was not created by God, but was discovered by the devil, who was created good himself."[6]—The same [Augustine], in the book *Against the Manichees*, also shows what it is to sin, saying: "What is it to sin, other than to err against the commands of truth, or against truth itself? And if they do not do this willingly, they are unjustly called sinners."[7] What, then, is to be held amid such great variety? What is to be said?

3. A TRUE VIEW ON SIN IS PROPOSED. It can well be said and it must be freely taught that sin is an evil action, interior and exterior, namely an

[5]1 Jn. 3, 4.
[6]Ps. 118, 119.
[7]Rather, Bede, *In I Ioannem*

[1]In c1 nn1-2.
[2]Jn. 1, 3.
[3]Augustine, *In Ioannem*, tr. 1 n13.
[4]Dist. 34 c4 n2.
[5]Augustine, *De diversis quaestionibus 83*, q6.
[6]Gennadius, *Liber seu diffinitio ecclesiasticorum dogmatum*, c27.
[7]That is, Evodius, *De fide contra Manichaeos*, c8.

evil thought, speech, and deed. Yet, sin exists primarily in the will, from which, like evil fruits from an evil tree, proceed evil deeds.[8]

4. THE RECEIVED OPINION OF SOME, WHO SAY THAT AN EVIL WILL AND ACTION, INSOFAR AS THEY ARE, ARE NATURES, AND SO THEY ARE GOOD; BUT INSOFAR AS THEY ARE EVILS, THEY ARE SINS. And some, diligently noting the words of Augustine, which he uses above[9] and on other places of Scripture, not unlearnedly teach that an evil will and evil actions, insofar as they are, or insofar as they are actions, are goods; but insofar as they are evils, they are sins. They say that every will and every action is a good nature of God insofar as it is an action or a will, and it is from God as author. But insofar as it is done in a disorderly manner and against the law and lacks a due end, it is a sin. And so, insofar as it is a sin, it is nothing, for it is no substance and no nature.

5. THEY PROVE BY AUTHORITIES THAT ALL WILLS AND ACTIONS ARE GOODS INSOFAR AS THEY ARE. And they prove that any will and action is a good insofar as it is, from what Augustine says in the book *On 84 Questions*: "God is the cause only of good: and so he is not the author of evil, because he is the author of all things that are, and these, insofar as they are, are good."[10]—The same, proving that nothing happens by chance in the world, says in the same: "Whatever happens by chance happens without design; whatever happens without design does not happen by providence. And so, if some things in the world happen by chance, the whole world is not administered by providence; if the whole world is not administered by providence, there is some nature or substance which does not pertain to the work of providence. But all that is, insofar as it is, is good. For that is the highest good by participation in which all other goods are; and all that is changeable, insofar as it is, is not good in itself, but by participation in that good, which we also call divine providence. And so nothing happens by chance in the world."[11]—By these testimonies, they strive to show that all that is, insofar as it is, is good. Hence the same Augustine, in *On Christian Doctrine*, book 1, says: "He most highly and primordially is who is entirely unchangeable; and all other things that are cannot exist apart from him, and they are good insofar as they have received that they be [from him]."[12]

6. WHAT FOLLOWS FROM THE AFORESAID. From the aforesaid, it is gathered and inferred that, if there is an evil will and an evil action, insofar as it is, it is good. But does anyone deny that an evil will and an evil action exist? And so an evil will or action, insofar as it is, is a good. And

[8]Cf. Mt. 7, 17-18; dist. 34 c2 n2, above.
[9]Here above, throughout dist. 34.
[10]Augustine, *De diversis quaestionibus 83*, q21.
[11]Ibid., q24.
[12]Augustine, *De doctrina christiana*, bk 1 c32 n35.

insofar as it is a will or an action, it is similarly a good; but it is evil from this vice; this vice is not from God, nor is it anything.

7. ON THE VICE OF THE WILL. Augustine appears to have noted this in the book *On 84 Questions*, saying: "It is by a vice of the will that man is made worse; this vice is far from God's will, as reason teaches."[13] From this text, they prove that the will, insofar as it is vicious, is not from God. And insofar as it is vicious, it is a sin. And it is a sin, they say, insofar as it has neither order, nor a due end. In the same way, an action, insofar as it proceeds from evil, does not have order and tends toward evil.

8. ANOTHER PROOF THAT EACH ACT, INSOFAR AS IT IS, IS GOOD. Also, they prove in another way that every act, interior or exterior, insofar as it is, is good, for there would not be an evil act, unless there were a good thing; for there is nothing which is evil, unless the same thing is good.—Hence Augustine in the *Enchiridion*: "Every nature is a good; nor would anything be evil, if the thing itself which is evil were not a nature, so there cannot be an evil, unless there is something good. And although this seems absurd in the telling, yet the inescapable conclusion of the argument compels us to say it."[14]

9. HE SUMMARIZES WHAT HAS BEEN SAID. From the above testimonies, they assert that all actions, insofar as they are, are good things; nor is anything evil, that is, a sin, unless the same thing is also in some respect a good. And they declare that God is the author of all things that are, insofar as they are, and that by his will are all things that are and that these, insofar as they are, are natures.

10. OBJECTION AGAINST THOSE WHO SAY THAT ALL ACTIONS, INSOFAR AS THEY ARE, ARE GOOD. This objection is made to them: If all things that are, insofar as they are, are good and are natures, then adultery, homicide, and suchlike, insofar as they are, are good and are natures, and happen with God's will. If this is so, then those who do such things do good things, which is entirely absurd.—THEIR RESPONSE. To these, however, they answer as follows: they say that adultery, homicide, and suchlike, do not denote simply actions, but the vices of actions; and the very actions of adultery and homicide, insofar as they are or insofar as they are actions, are from God and are good natures, but not insofar as they are adultery and homicide. And so they say that it does not follow that, if the actions which are homicides and adulteries are from God, then homicides and adulteries are from God.

11. ANOTHER OBJECTION OF THE OTHERS AGAINST THESE. Also, another objection is made to them: If something which is not a nature or a good thing is not evil, how then are not to believe in God, not to go to church,

[13]Augustine, *De diversis quaestionibus 83*, q3.
[14]Augustine, *Enchiridion*, c13.

and suchlike sins, since these are not natures, indeed are entirely without being? For it is not something or any thing not to go to church, or not to believe, and suchlike.—RESPONSE, WHERE THEY TEACH THAT WHAT IS SAID THROUGH NEGATION, AS NOT TO BELIEVE IN GOD AND SUCHLIKE, POSITS SOMETHING. To this they say that some things are in fact posited by these and similar expressions, which seem simply to denote privations and not to posit anything because they are said through negation, and that actions are signified through them. For they say that not to believe in Christ is unbelief, and that by the term unbelief an evil action of the mind is signified. In the same way, in the statement 'not to go to church is an evil,' the contempt of the one who does not go is signified, that is, his evil will or intention. For this is to fall away from a good, and so it is evil; similarly and conversely, to fall away from evil is a good. And so, just as the falling away from evil posits something, namely the will and intention of avoiding evil (for that which is nothing at all cannot be a good), so also the falling away from the good 'that is,' signifies [something], namely the will and intention to [do] evil. And according to this, that definition of mortal sin which Augustine set out above[15] is true and general.

Chapter 3 (233)

1. WHETHER AN EVIL ACTION, INSOFAR AS IT IS A SIN, IS A PRIVATION OR CORRUPTION OF THE GOOD. It can also be asked by them: since sin, as has been said above,[1] is a privation or corruption of the good, and every evil action is a sin, whether or not it is also a privation or corruption of the good insofar as it is a sin.—HE SETS OUT THE ARGUMENTS ON BOTH SIDES. For if, insofar as it is a sin, it is a corruption of the good, and since corruption or privation of the good is a punishment for man, then, insofar as it is a sin, it is a punishment. If it is so, then, insofar as it is a sin, it seems to be a good and to be from God. But if it is not a corruption insofar as it is a sin, then it is asked according to what is it a corruption. For if it is corruption—and not insofar as it is a sin, since it is nothing but a good, apart from that in which it is a sin—then it is corruption or privation of the good insofar as it is a good.

2. RESPONSE, WHERE IT IS SAID THAT, INSOFAR AS IT IS SIN, IT IS PRIVATION OR CORRUPTION OF THE GOOD, AND YET NOT A PUNISHMENT. To this too they say that an evil action is a privation or corruption of the good, not insofar as it is, nor insofar as it is a good, but only insofar as it is a sin; and yet, insofar as it is a sin, it is not a punishment or anything else which is from God. For as is gathered from the words of Augustine cited above,

[15]Above, c1 n1.

[1]Dist. 34 c4 n2.

sin is called a corruption or privation actively, not passively. Indeed, an evil or a sin is called a corruption of the good because it deprives a good nature "of some good; indeed, if it does not deprive it of any good, it does not harm it," as Augustine says above: "but it does harm it: and so it takes away the good."[2] And it does not harm it, except insofar as it is a sin; and so it deprives it of the good insofar as it is a sin; and so, insofar as it is a sin, it is a privation or corruption of the good.

Chapter 4 (234)

1. HOW, INSOFAR AS IT IS A SIN, IT CAN CORRUPT THE GOOD, SINCE IT IS NOTHING. But since it is nothing insofar as it is sin, how can it corrupt or destroy the good?—AUGUSTINE'S RESPONSE BY ANALOGY. Augustine teaches you this in the book *On the Nature of the Good*, saying: "To abstain from food is not some substance, and yet, if one abstains entirely from food, the substance of the body languishes and is weakened. In the same way, sin is not a substance"; and yet the nature of the soul is corrupted by it.[1]

2. THAT SIN IS PROPERLY A CORRUPTION OF THE SOUL, AND HOW. But sin, that is, fault, is properly a corruption of the soul. And if it is asked in what the soul can become corrupt, this becomes clear in the parable of the one who *fell among thieves*,[2] who robbed and wounded him. For man falls among thieves when he is drawn into the power of the devil through sin; and then, through sin, he is robbed of the freely-given goods, that is, the virtues, and he is wounded in his natural goods, which are reason or the intellect, memory, ingenuity, and suchlike, which are darkened and vitiated through sin. Through sin, he is also deprived of that good by participation in whom other things are good: he distances himself further from him, the more he is deprived of him.

Chapter 5 (235)

1. HOW MAN DISTANCES HIMSELF FROM GOD, NAMELY THROUGH THE UNLIKENESS WHICH SIN BRINGS ABOUT. And he distances himself from him through sin, not by distance of place, because God is entirely present everywhere to everyone and, as Augustine says in the book *On 84 Questions*, "all things are in him, and he is not a place. Indeed, God's temple is improperly called the place of God: not that he is contained in it, but that he is present and in-dwelling in it. But the clean soul is understood to be

[2]Dist. 34 c4 n2.

[1]Augustine, *De natura et gratia*, c20 n22.
[2]Cf. Lk. 10, 30; cf. also above, dist. 25 c7 n1.

that."[1] Thus, one becomes far from God through sin, and not according to place; and one becomes far because one departs from God's likeness, and the further one is, the more unlike one becomes.—As Augustine says in the book *On 84 Questions*: "And those things which are similar to God by participation are capable of unlikeness; but the likeness itself can in no way be unlike in any part. And so it is that, since the Son is the likeness of the Father, he cannot be unlike the Father in any part, by participation in whom all things that are like God are like him";[2] and they are capable of unlikeness. And there is nothing that makes man so unlike God as does sin.

2. THAT SIN IS ALSO THE PRIVATION OF THE GOOD OF THE BODY. And since sin is a corruption or privation of the good which is in the soul, it is also a privation or corruption of the good of the body, as was the case when it deprived the body of man of the benefit of that immortality and impassibility which it had before sin.

Chapter 6 (236)

WHETHER PRIVATION OF THE GOOD IS A PUNISHMENT. And it is usual to ask whether privation or corruption of the good is a punishment.—And this may be easily answered, if we recall to mind what has already been said. For we said above[1] that privation or corruption of the good is taken actively or passively, that is, according to its efficient cause or its effect. And so the privation or corruption of the good is called both sin and punishment: sin according to its efficient cause, because it deprives or corrupts the good, and punishment according to its effect, that is, according to the suffering which is the effect of sin. For fault is one thing, punishment another. The one is God's, that is, the punishment; the other is the devil's or man's, that is, the fault.[2]

DISTINCTION XXXVI

Chapter 1 (237)

1. THAT SOME THINGS ARE SINS AND PUNISHMENT OF SIN SIMULTANEOUSLY, SOME ARE SINS AND THE CAUSE OF SIN, BUT OTHERS ARE SINS AND THE CAUSE AND PUNISHMENT OF SIN. And yet it is to be known that some things are sins in such way that they are also punishments for sins. Hence Augustine, on that place of Psalm 57: *The fire fell over them and they did*

[1]Augustine, *De diversis quaestionibus 83*, q20.
[2]Ibid., q23.

[1]In c3 n2.
[2]See above, dist. 32 c3.

not see the sun,[1] says: "The fire of pride and concupiscence and anger" is meant. "Because few are able to see these punishments, the Apostle recalls them especially in the Epistle to the Romans,[2] and he enumerates many things which are sins and punishments for sin. For between the first sin of apostasy and the last punishment of eternal fire, there are middle things which are both sins and punishments for sin."[3]

2. Gregory too, in *On Ezechiel*, says: "Before a despiser who does not wish to repent, God places *a stumbling-block*,[4] namely an occasion to become more deeply mired. For a sin which is not quickly erased through penance is either a sin and the cause of sin, or a sin and a punishment of sin, or simultaneously a sin and a cause and punishment of sin. Hence Moses: *The sins of the Amorrhaeans are not yet complete*.[5] And David says: *Heap iniquity upon their iniquity*.[6] And another Prophet: *Blood touched blood*,[7] that is, sin was added to sin. Paul too says: *And so God handed them over to passions of ignominy*, etc.;[8] and also: *That they may always fill their sins*.[9] And to John too, the angel says: *As for the one mired in filth, let him continue to become filthy*."[10,11] From these testimonies, it is gathered that some sin is both a sin and a punishment of sin.

Chapter 2 (238)

1. A QUESTION ARISING FROM THE AFORESAID: NAMELY, WHETHER INSOFAR AS IT IS A SIN, IT IS PUNISHMENT OF SIN. And so it is deservedly asked whether insofar as it is a sin, it is punishment of sin.

2. THE REASON WHY IT IS NOT. This does not appear to be the case, since every punishment of sin is just; hence Augustine, in the book of *Retractations*: "Every punishment of sin is just, and is called a torment."[1] And so, if a sin which is [both] a sin and punishment of sin, insofar as it is a sin, is a punishment of sin, since all just punishment comes from God's justice, it seems that, insofar as it is a sin, it is just and comes from God.

3. THEIR RESPONSE, WHERE IT IS TAUGHT IN WHAT SENSE SIN IS CALLED A PUNISHMENT OF SIN OR A PUNISHMENT. To this they respond that sin is

[1]Ps. 57, 9.
[2]Cf. Rom. 1, 21-32.
[3]Augustine, *Enarrationes in Psalmos*, on Ps. 57, 9, nn18-19.
[4]Cf. Ezech. 3, 20.
[5]Gen. 15, 16.
[6]Ps. 68, 28.
[7]Hos. 4, 2.
[8]Rom. 1, 26.
[9]1 Thess. 2, 16.
[10]Apoc. 22, 11.
[11]Gregory, *In Ezechielem*, bk 1, hom. 11, nn23-25.

[1]Augustine, *Retractationes*, bk 1 c9 n5.

called a punishment of sin, because, through the sin into which a man falls out of guilt for a preceding sin, he is abandoned by God and his good nature is corrupted. Just as the punishment of the evil ones is called eternal fire, because they are tortured by it, and yet the torture itself of evildoers is not the fire, but it occurs in man through the fire, so through sin, nature is corrupted and the good of nature is diminished, and this very diminution and corruption of the good is a suffering and a punishment; and that through which this happens is not essentially sin itself, but it is called sin, as was said earlier, because through sin, as soon as man sins, that corruption occurs in man. Nevertheless, this happens with God as its author, for that punishment or suffering, which is the corruption of the good, is from God. Yet its matter and cause, so to speak, is sin, which is not from God.

4. AUGUSTINE. Augustine appears to have noted this and understood it in this sense, when he says in the book *On the Predestination of the Saints*: "By predestination, God foreknew those things which he would himself do; but God also foreknew those things which he would not himself do, that is, all evils. And although there are some things which are sins in such a way that they are also punishments for sin, according to the words of the Apostle: *God handed them over to passions*, etc.,[2] yet it is not the sin that is God's, but the judgement,"[3] namely the punishment. For in Scripture punishment is often understood by the term *judgement*.[4]—To those who diligently pay attention, he here seems to imply that those things which are sins and punishments for sin are of God, not insofar as they are sins, but insofar as they are punishments. Indeed, when he said that God would not do any evils, that is, sins, since the objection could have been made to him that some sins are also punishments for sin, and each punishment of sin is just and so from God, he added the rest, as if by way of determining in what respect God does them or in what respect he does not. But according to the aforesaid understanding, sins are correctly called punishments. Hence the Apostle calls them *passions of ignominy*,[5] because, as the authority says, "although there are some sins which delight, yet there are passions of nature which are not to be named,"[6] because nature is corrupted through them.

Chapter 3 (239)

1. THAT ALTHOUGH ANY SIN CAN BE CALLED A PUNISHMENT, NEVERTHELESS NOT EVERY ONE OF THEM IS A PUNISHMENT OF SIN. And although in

[2]Rom. 1, 26.
[3]Augustine, *De praedestinatione sanctorum*, c10 n19.
[4]Cf. e.g., Mt. 23, 33; Mk. 12, 40.
[5]Rom. 1, 26.
[6]Ordinary gloss, on Rom. 1, 26.

this sense any mortal sin can be called a punishment, nevertheless not every one of them can be called a punishment of sin. For a punishment of sin, as was said above,[1] is that whose cause is another preceding sin. Indeed, a sin is called a punishment of sin with respect to a preceding sin, just as it is called cause of sin in respect to an ensuing sin. It thereby follows that the same sin is cause and punishment of sin, but punishment of one sin and cause of another.

2. GREGORY. For as Gregory says in the *Moralia*, "a sin which is not erased by penance, by its weight soon draws to another sin; and so it happens that it is not only a sin, but also a cause of sin, for from it arises the subsequent fault. But the sin which arises from a sin is not only a sin, but also a punishment of sin; because by a just judgement, God clouds the heart of the sinner so that, out of guilt for the preceding sin, he also falls into other ones. For the one whom he did not will to free, he struck down by abandoning him."[2]—AUGUSTINE, IN *AGAINST JULIAN*: "Therefore," as Augustine says, "this is both the punishment of the preceding sin, and yet also itself a sin. For by the judgement of the most just God, as the Apostle says of some people, they have been handed over, either by being abandoned, or in some other explicable or inexplicable manner, *to the passions of ignominy*,"[3,4] "so that crimes are avenged with crimes, and the tortures of the sinners are not only torments, but also the increases of their vices."[5] "And those sins which the Apostle recalled,[6] because they are from pride, are not only sins, but also tortures."[7]

3. See, from these words it has already become very clear that some sins are also punishments and causes of sin; and that sin is a punishment of sin which has a preceding sin as its cause; and that sin is a cause of sin which has deserved the ensuing fault.

Chapter 4 (240)

1. FROM THE AFORESAID, IT APPEARS TO BE SIGNIFIED THAT THE VERY THINGS WHICH ARE THE SINS ARE ALSO THE PUNISHMENTS FOR SIN. But when he says, "crimes are avenged with crimes,"[1] he appears to indicate that the very things which are sins are essentially punishments for sin, that is, chastisements for sin.—But to this they say that these and similar

[1]In c2 n3.
[2]Gregory, *Moralia*, bk 25 c9 n22.
[3]Rom. 1, 26.
[4]Augustine, *Contra Iulianum*, bk 5 c3 n10.
[5]Augustine, *Contra adversarium Legis et prophetarum*, I c24 n51.
[6]Cf. Rom. 1, 24-32.
[7]Augustine, *Sermo 197*, n1.

[1]Above, c3 n2.

statements are in accordance with the reason mentioned above,[2] and so they are to be understood according to the above explanation. "For the meaning of statements is to be drawn from the reasons for speaking."[3]

2. THAT IT IS NOT CONTRARY TO THE TRUTH FOR ONE TO SAY THAT THE SINS THEMSELVES ARE ESSENTIALLY PUNISHMENTS FOR SIN. And yet it is not held to cause any prejudice to truth if one were to say that the very things which are sins are essentially, so to speak, punishments, that is, chastisements for preceding sins, which are just and are from God. Nevertheless, they are not from God insofar as they are sins; nor are they punishments for sin insofar as they are sins. And yet, insofar as they are sins, they are privations of the good; but, as was said above,[4] they are called privations causally and actively.

Chapter 5 (241)

HE PLAINLY SHOWS THAT SOME SINS ARE PUNISHMENT OF SIN, AND THE PUNISHMENT ITSELF IS JUST AND FROM GOD. And that some sins are a punishment, and the punishment itself is just and is from God, Augustine openly teaches in *Retractations*, book 1. There he says that some things which are evil are done by man by necessity, and these same things are a just punishment of sin. "Some reprovable things," he says, "are done by necessity, when man wants to act rightly and cannot. Otherwise, why would the Apostle say: *I do not accomplish the good which I will, but I do the evil which I hate*?[1] And also: *The flesh sets out its desires against the spirit, and the spirit against the flesh: these two struggle against each other, so that you cannot do the things that you will*?[2] But all these things are the result of that condemnation of death. Indeed, if this is not a punishment of man, but nature, then none of these things are sins. For if, in doing these things, one is not departing from the manner in which man was naturally made, then one does entirely the things which one ought. But if man is not good because this is the case, and does not have it in his power to be good, either because he does not see what he ought to be like, or because he sees it and is not able to be what he sees that he ought to be, who would doubt that this is a punishment? Now, all punishment, if it is punishment of sin, is just and is called a torment. If, however, the punishment is unjust, and no one doubts it to be unjust, then it has been imposed on man by some unjust tyrant. But since it is insane to doubt God's omnipotence and justice, this punishment is just and is imposed for some sin.

[2]Cf. above, c3 n1.
[3]Hilary, as above, Bk 1 dist. 25 c2 n1.
[4]Dist. 35 c6.

[1]Rom. 7, 15.
[2]Gal. 5, 17.

For it is not the case that some unjust tyrant either was able to steal man away, as it were, from an ignorant God, or to wrest him away, as it were, from an unwilling and weaker God, in order to torture man with an unjust punishment. And so it remains that this just punishment comes from the condemnation of man."[3] From these and many other testimonies, we are taught that some things are sins and punishment of sin.

Chapter 6 (242)

1. On some things which are without doubt sins and punishments, like anger, envy. Moreover, it is not at all to be doubted that some sins are most certainly punishments, like envy, which is "sorrow at another's good,"[1] and anger; these are sins even apart from their being punishments.

2. The same is also to be held regarding cupidity, fear, and others of this kind. Hence Augustine, in the book of *84 Questions*, says: "All emotion is passion; all cupidity is emotion; and so all cupidity is passion. But when any passion is in us, we suffer by that passion; and so, when any cupidity is in us, we suffer by that cupidity, and we suffer insofar as it is cupidity. But not every passion, insofar as we suffer it, is a sin. So it is with fear. It does not, however, follow that, if we suffer fear, therefore it is not a sin, because there are many sins which we suffer, but they are not sins insofar as we suffer by them."[2]

3. That a sentence of Jerome appears to contradict the words of Augustine cited above. But it is to be diligently noted that what Jerome says in his *Explanation of the Faith* appears to contradict the words of Augustine cited above, where he says that some reprovable and evil things are done by necessity.[3] And although Jerome's words were set out earlier above,[4] yet, in order that they may be known more thoroughly, we do not hesitate to repeat them. He says: "We execrate the blasphemy of those who say that something impossible was commanded by God to man, and that God's mandates cannot be observed by individuals, but [only] by all in common." And a little later: "And we say that those err who say with Manichaeus that man cannot avoid sin, just as much as those who assert with Jovinian that man cannot sin."[5]—See, here Jerome says that it is an error for anyone to say that a man cannot avoid sin. But one who says that some sins are done by necessity says that they cannot

[3] Augustine, *Retractationes*, bk 1 c9 n5.

[1] Interlinear gloss, on Rom. 1, 29.
[2] Augustine, *De diversis quaestionibus 83*, q77.
[3] At the beginning of the preceding chapter.
[4] Dist. 28 c4.
[5] That is, Pelagius, *Libellus fidei ad Innocentium Papam*, nn10 and 13.

be avoided. And so, since Augustine says that, it appears either that what he says is an error, or that what Jerome says is not true.

4. DETERMINATION REMOVING THE CONTRADICTION FROM BETWEEN THE SAINTS. To this it can be said that Augustine made that pronouncement according to the state of our [present] misery, to which pertain ignorance and difficulty, which came to us as a result of a just condemnation, as he says in the book *On Free Choice*; among which things, he included also venial sins. But Jerome speaks only of mortal sins, which anyone is able to avoid, if illuminated by grace; or he says that of man according to the state of free choice before sin.

5. HE COMPOSES AN EPILOGUE SO AS TO PASS ON TO OTHER THINGS. We have very diligently set out the view of those who say that all actions are good natures, and that, insofar as they are, they are good. We also interspersed some other things in this discussion which are not to be taken as being only their personal views because they are held without hesitation by all partakers of Catholic wisdom. And we have fortified these teachings with the testimonies of authorities and with the reasons of the same, who say that all actions are good by their essence, that is, insofar as they are; but some actions, insofar as they are done in a disorderly way, are sins.—HE REPEATS THE AFORESAID IN ORDER TO ADD TO IT. They also add that some actions are good not only by essence, but also generically, as to feed the hungry, which is an action of the genus [or category] of the works of mercy. Some actions, however, they call absolutely and perfectly good, which are commended not only by essence or genus, but also by cause and end, as are those actions which proceed from a good will and achieve a good end.

DISTINCTION XXXVII

Chapter 1 (243)

1. HE SETS OUT THE VIEW OF OTHERS, WHO SAY THAT EVIL ACTIONS ARE IN NO WAY FROM GOD, NOR ARE THEY GOOD, WHETHER IN THAT THEY ARE, OR IN ANY OTHER WAY. But there are many others who feel entirely otherwise concerning sin and action. For they assert that an evil will and evil action are sins, and on no account good; nor are they from God as their author according to any reason, because they are done without God.

2. WHY, ACCORDING TO THEM, SIN IS SAID TO BE NOTHING. And indeed, as the Evangelist says, *Without him, was made nothing*,[1] that is, sin; this is said to be nothing, not because it is not an evil action or will, which is

[1]Jn. 1, 3.

something, but because it separates men from true being and draws them to evil, and so leads them to non-being. For those who withdraw from participation in the highest good, which alone truly and properly is, are deservedly said not to be. And so Augustine says, in *On John*: "Sin is nothing, and men become nothing when they sin."[2]—And so, for this reason, they conclude that sin is nothing, because it distances man from true being. And they say that an evil will, and an evil action or speech, is a sin because these things are transgression and disobedience and are done against the law of God. And yet they exist, but from man or the devil, not from God. For they say that these things are in no way from God, whether insofar as they are, or in any other way.

3. HOW THEY DETERMINE THE WORDS OF AUGUSTINE CITED ABOVE, IN WHICH HE SAYS: ALL THAT IS, INSOFAR AS IT IS, IS GOOD. And as to those words of Augustine, in which he says that 'all that is, insofar as it is, is good and has God as its author,'[3] they teach that they are to be taken as concerning natures or substances. But by the term substance or nature, they say are signified the substances themselves and those things which they possess naturally, namely those things with which they are formed, as the soul naturally has intellect and ingenuity and will and suchlike. This is gathered from the words of Augustine above, where he calls man a nature, and an evil man an evil nature.[4]

4. ACCORDING TO THEM, EVIL ACTIONS ARE NOT NATURES OR SUBSTANCES. And so, according to this assertion or understanding, evil actions are not natures or substances, and neither are good actions. This, at any rate, Augustine appears to indicate in the book of *Retractations*, distinguishing between substances or natures, and good or evil actions. For in clarifying how something which he had handed down in the book *On True Religion*,[5] is to be understood, he says: "This was said of substances and natures, for that was then the subject of discussion, and not about good actions and sins."[6] Here, he seems to make a clear distinction between natures or substances and actions or sins. And so the aforesaid doctors assert that actions, whether interior or exterior, are not natures or substances; and if they are evil, they are sins, and are not from God.—Augustine, however, seems to signify that evil actions are not natures, saying in his first response against the Pelagians as follows: "The works of the devil, which are called vices, are actions, not things."[7] The same, in the fourth: "Each evil is not a nature, but an action accidental to some

[2]Augustine, *In Ioannem*, tr. 1 n13.
[3]*De diversis quaestionibus 83*, qq21 and 24; above, dist. 35 c2 n5.
[4]Above, dist. 34 c4 n3.
[5]Augustine, *De vera religione*, c41 nn77-78.
[6]Augustine, *Retractationes*, bk 1 c13 n8.
[7]Pseudo-Augustine, *Hypognosticon*, bk 1 c5 n7.

defect of the good. And so, because it is not a nature, God did not make it, because each thing which he has made is a nature."[8] Also: "All that is good by nature, God made from nothing, not the devil."[9]

5. ACCORDING TO THEM, THERE ARE SOME THINGS WHICH ARE NOT FROM GOD BY WHICH MEN ARE EVIL. From this one gathers that there are some things which are not from God, and that men are evil by these things. Indeed, they also grant this, finding support in the words of Augustine set out above, who, in the *Enchiridion*, determining those words of the prophecy: *Woe to those who call evil good*,[10] says that "this is to be understood of those very things by which men are evil, not of men."[11] And so there are some things by which men are evil.—And that by which man is made worse is not from God, because, as Augustine says in the book of *84 Questions*, "man does not become worse with God as author."[12] Therefore, God is not the author of the things by which man is made worse. But there are some things, as has been said, by which men are made evil; and so there are some things which are not from God, because these very things are sins. And so Scripture contends in many places that God is not the author of evils,[13] that is, of those things which are sins.

Chapter 2 (244)

1. ON THEIR PART, AN OBJECTION IS MADE TO THE FOREGOING STATEMENT, WHERE IT SAYS: GOD IS NOT THE AUTHOR OF EVILS. And in this statement[1] an objection is rightfully made to the view of those [mentioned] above, who say that God is not the author of the things which are evil insofar as they are evil, but [only] insofar as they are; and insofar as they are evil, they say that they are nothing. Indeed, what is strange about saying that God is not their author insofar as they are nothing, since no one can be the author of nothing? And so, when God is said to be the author of all things that are, these want it to be understood [only] of good things. And they call those things good which exist naturally; but they say that not only those things exist naturally which are substances or which form substances, as they accepted above,[2] but also all things which do not deprive a nature of the good. And so, according to them, there is a manifold meaning in the Scriptures when mention occurs of nature or substance, or of those things which are naturally.

[8]Pseudo-Augustine, *Hypognosticon*, bk 1 c1 n1.
[9]Ibid.
[10]Is. 5, 20.
[11]Augustine, *Enchiridion*, c19; see above, dist. 34 c5 n4.
[12]Augustine, *De diversis quaestionibus 83*, q3; see above, Bk 1 dist. 46 c7.
[13]Cf. Gen. 1, 31; Deut. 32, 4.

[1]Above, dist. 35 c2 nn4ff.
[2]In c1 n3.

2. AUGUSTINE. But Augustine, on that place of the Psalm: *There is no substance*,[3] discusses substance in a manner which seems to agree with the above statement, saying: "By substance is understood that which we are, whatever we are, man, beast, earth, sun; all these things are substances by the very thing by which they are. Natures themselves are called substances. Indeed, what is not a substance is entirely nothing. And so substance is some being. God made man a substance; but through iniquity, man fell from the substance in which he was made. Iniquity itself, to be sure, is not a substance, for iniquity is not a nature which God formed, but a perversion which man made. All natures were made by him; iniquity was not made by him because iniquity is not a substance. In that hymn of the three children,[4] every creature that praises God is recalled. For all things praise God, but [only] those which he made. The serpent there praises God, but avarice does not. All reptiles are named there, but not any vices, for we receive vices from ourselves and from our will, and vices are not a substance."[5]—Let the advocates of the sentences set forth above listen diligently to these words, and they will be able to perceive the reason and cause of the statements where Scripture makes mention of nature or substance.

3. But since we have given him full notice of both views,[6] we leave it to the reader to reach a judgement concerning them, hastening on to discuss those matters which still remain.

4. THAT WHEN GOD IS SAID NOT TO BE THE AUTHOR OF EVIL, THAT IT IS MEANT IN REGARD TO SIN, NOT TO PUNISHMENT. And so, although all Catholic authors agree in this, namely that God is not the author of evil things, you must nevertheless beware not to include punishments, like sins generally, under the term of evil things. For God is the author of punishments, as he himself says through the Prophet: *There is no evil in the city which God has not done.*[7] Also, elsewhere, in his own person, he says: *I am God, creating evil and making the good.*[8] See, here it is said that he created and made evil; but by the term evil, punishment is understood, not sin, as conversely, when it is said that 'God is not the author of evil things,' sins are understood by the term evil.

5. THAT THE PUNISHMENT OF EVIL PERSONS IS FROM GOD.—HOW IT IS SAID: GOD DID NOT MAKE DEATH. And so Augustine, who had said in the book of *84 Questions* that God is not the author of evil,[9] reveals in book 1

[3]Ps. 68, 3.
[4]Dan. 3, 52-90.
[5]Augustine, *Enarrationes in Psalmos*, on Ps. 68, sermon 1 n5.
[6]From the beginning of dist. 35.
[7]Amos 3, 6.
[8]Is. 45, 6-7.
[9]Augustine, *De diversis quaestionibus 83*, q21.

of the *Retractations* how that is to be understood, saying: "Beware not to misunderstand what I said: *God who is the author of all things that are is not the author of evil because, insofar as they are, they are good.* Do not hold from this that the punishment of evil persons, which is certainly an evil to those who are punished, is not from him. But I said this in the same way as it is said: *God did not make death,*[10] when it is written elsewhere: *Life or death is from God.*[11] And so the punishment of evil persons, which is from God, is certainly an evil to evil persons, but it is among the good works of God, because it is just that evil persons be punished, and all that is just is certainly good."[12] And so it is said that God did not make death because he did not make that for which death is inflicted, namely sin.—You have heard, reader, the cause of the statement; from this cause, a sound understanding is confirmed when it is said: *God is not the author of evil* and *God did not make death.*

DISTINCTION XXXVIII

Chapter 1 (245)

1. ON THE WILL, AND THE END FROM WHICH IT IS ITSELF JUDGED. After the aforesaid, we must discuss the will and its end. And so it is to be understood that, as Augustine says, it is known from its end whether the will is righteous or depraved.[1] And the end of a good will is blessedness, eternal life, God himself. But the end of an evil will is something else, namely an evil pleasure, or some other thing, in which the will must not rest.

2. WHAT A GOOD END IS, NAMELY CHARITY. The Prophet indicated the good end, saying: *I saw the end of every fulfilment*, etc.[2] And so charity, whose *command is broad, is* the end *of every fulfilment*, that is, of every good will and action; every mandate is to be referred to it. Hence Augustine, in the *Enchiridion*: "All divine mandates are referred to charity, of which the Apostle says: *The end of the precept is charity from a pure heart and a good conscience and a faith unfeigned.*[3] And so the end of every mandate is charity, that is, every mandate is referred to charity. But what is done either by fear of punishment, or by any other carnal intention, in such a way that it is not referred to charity, which is the love of God and neighbour, is not yet done as it ought to be done, even if it ap-

[10]Wis. 1, 13.
[11]Eccli. 11, 14.
[12]Augustine, *Retractationes*, c26.

[1]Augustine, *De Trinitate*, bk 11 c6 n10.
[2]Ps. 118, 96.
[3]1 Tim. 1, 5.

pears to have been so done. For the things that God commands, and those which he counsels, are then done rightly when they are referred to the love of God and neighbour."[4] By these words, it is plainly indicated what the right end of the will, or of action, is, namely charity, which is also God, as we show above.[5]

Chapter 2 (246)

THAT GOD IS THE END OF ALL GOOD ACTION, BECAUSE HE IS CHARITY; AND NOT THE HOLY SPIRIT ALONE, BUT ALSO CHRIST AND THE FATHER; NOR ARE THESE THREE ENDS, BUT ONE. And so, he who has charity as his end, has God as his end; that is why the Apostle says that *Christ* is *the end of the law for justification for anyone who believes*.[1] And rightly is Christ called *the end of the law for justification* because, as Augustine says in the book of *Sentences of Prosper*, "in Christ the law of justification is not destroyed, but fulfilled. For all perfection is from him, beyond whom there is none to whom hope may extend itself."[2] "The end and goal of the faithful is Christ; when the effort of the one who runs the race brings him to Christ, he has none by whom he may go further, but has that in which he must remain."[3] And so the right and highest end is God, namely Father and Son and Holy Spirit; nor are these three three ends, but one end, because God is one, and not three gods.

Chapter 3 (247)

1. THAT ALL GOOD WILLS HAVE ONE END, AND YET SOME GOOD WILLS ARE ALLOTTED DIFFERENT ENDS. But it is asked whether all good wills have only one end.—Concerning this, Augustine, in *On the Trinity*, book 11, speaks as follows: "All the many wills have their own ends, which nevertheless are referred to the end of that will by which we will to live blessedly, and to reach that life which is not referred to anything else, but suffices by itself for its lover. Similarly, the will to see has sight as its end, and the will to see the window has the sight of the window as its end; but the will to see passers-by through the window is something else, the end of which is the sight of the passers-by. To this also are referred the above-mentioned wills."[1]—Also: "All the interconnected wills are righteous, if that will is good to which they all are referred. But if that one is depraved,

[4]Augustine, *Enchiridion*, c121.
[5]Bk 1 dist. 17.

[1]Rom. 10, 4.
[2]Prosper of Aquitaine, *Sententiae ex Augustino delibatae*, n190.
[3]Ibid., n206.

[1]Augustine, *De Trinitate*, bk 11 c6 n10.

then they are all depraved. And so the connection of righteous wills is a kind of road for those ascending to blessedness, and it is travelled, as it were, by steps; but the entanglement of depraved and distorted wills is a bond by which is bound he who does his best *to be cast out into the outer darkness*."[2,3]—By these testimonies of authorities, it is plainly shown that there are many righteous wills in the faithful, [all] having their proper and different ends, and yet also one and the same, because they are all referred to the one, who is the end of ends, of which we spoke a little earlier.[4] So perhaps the converse is also true in evil people.

2. THERE SEEM TO BE SOME CONTRADICTIONS TO THIS VIEW. And yet, Augustine's warning elsewhere not to set two ends for ourselves appears to contradict this sentence in which it is said that some righteous wills of the faithful are allotted different ends, and yet are referred to one end. In the book *On the Lord's Sermon on the Mount*, he says as follows: "We must not preach the Gospel in order to eat, but eat in order to preach the Gospel, so that food is not a good which is desired, but a necessity which is added, in order to fulfil that text: *Seek first the kingdom of God, and all these other things will be added to you*."[5,6] "He did not say: *Seek first the kingdom of God*, and then seek these things, although they are necessary; but he says: *all these other things will be added to you*, that is, these will follow, if you seek those, lest, as you seek one, you turn away from the other, or lest you set two ends, so that you seek both the kingdom for its own sake, and these necessary things for the sake of the kingdom. And so we must do all things only for the sake of the kingdom of God, and not consider the temporal reward, either by itself or with the kingdom of God."[7]—See, he here says plainly that we must not set two ends for ourselves, but only one, that is, the kingdom of God, even though he had said above that all the many good wills have their proper ends.

3. HERE IT IS SHOWN HOW THE ABOVE ARE NOT CONTRADICTORY, EVEN THOUGH THEY APPEAR TO BE SO. But one who attends to the above words diligently and with a simple eye understands that they are not in opposition. For the one who said that we must not set two ends for ourselves, but do all things for the sake of the kingdom, also said earlier that we must eat in order to preach the Gospel. And when we do these things in this way, we set the Gospel as the end of that action, but we also refer this end to the kingdom of God. For we eat for the sake of the Gospel, and we eat and preach the Gospel for the sake of the kingdom of God.

[2]Cf. Mt. 22, 13.
[3]Augustine, *De Trinitate*, bk 11 c6 n10.
[4]In c2.
[5]Mt. 6, 33.
[6]Augustine, *De sermone Domini in monte*, bk 2 c16 n54.
[7]Ibid., bk 2 c17 n56.

And so we set two ends for ourselves in eating; but do we sin by doing these things? Far be it. Indeed, [Augustine] himself persuades us to do so, if we examine his words with diligence.

4. HOW THE PHRASE IS TO BE UNDERSTOOD: WE MUST NOT SET TWO ENDS FOR OURSELVES. Therefore, when he says that 'we must not set two ends for ourselves,' he wished it to be understood of ends tending toward different things, namely one of which is not referred to the other. And so, when he says that all things are to be done for the sake of the kingdom of God alone, nor is temporal reward to be considered with it, it is to be understood in this way: that we not consider temporal reward with the kingdom by desiring it in such a way that we desire it not for the kingdom, but for its own sake, namely so that we desire the kingdom for its own sake, and these other things for the sake of the kingdom, as he teaches.[8] For if we ask for eternal life, and we also ask for temporal things from God, but we ask for these things for the sake of eternal life, we do not offend, nor does *the left hand* then know *what the right hand is doing*,[9] because we do not consider temporal reward for its own sake, but for the kingdom of God, so that the left hand is under the head, while the right one embraces.[10] Otherwise, if we seek these temporal things for their own sake, just as we do eternal things, then the left hand is joined to the right. And so, when the Lord said: *Beware not to perform your justice before men so as to be seen by them*,[11] he says elsewhere: *Let your good works so shine before men that they may give glory to your Father who is in heaven.*[12] And so all things are to be done for the sake of God, so that we refer all that we do and the ends of all that we do to him.

Chapter 4 (248)

1. ON THE DIFFERENCE OF WILL AND INTENTION AND END. It is also usual to ask what difference there is among will and intention and end.

2. WHAT THE WILL IS, WHAT THE END. To this it can be said, to distinguish in a sure and clear manner between will and end, that the will is that by which we will something; but the end of the will is either that which we will, through which the will itself is fulfilled, or rather something else for the sake of which we will what we will.—HOW INTENTION IS TAKEN. Intention, however, is sometimes taken for the will, sometimes for the end. Let the diligent and pious reader take care to discern which is meant when these terms occur in Scripture.

[8]Above, in n3.
[9]Cf. Mt. 6, 3.
[10]Cf. Song 2, 6.
[11]Mt. 6, 1.
[12]Mt. 5, 16.

3. WHAT THE END IS. And the end of the will is the good or evil pleasure which each strives to reach. Hence Augustine, on that place of the Psalm: *God searches hearts and reins*,[1] speaks as follows: "God alone searches *hearts*, that is, what each one thinks; and *reins*, that is, what gives pleasure to each, because the end of care and thought is pleasure, which each strives to reach by care and thought."[2] And a little later: "Men can see our works, which consist in words and deeds, but God alone sees in what spirit they are done and what they desire to reach. And when God sees that our heart is in heaven, and we do not delight in the flesh, but in the Lord, that is, when our thoughts and their ends are good, *he directs the just one*."[3,4]—The same, on a text of another Psalm, namely: *In the very snare which they set, their foot is caught*,[5] says: "The foot of the soul is love, which, if it is depraved, is called cupidity or lust; if it is righteous, it is called charity. The soul is moved by it, as if to the place to which it tends, that is, to good or evil pleasure; having reached this through love, it rejoices."[6]

4. HE REPEATS THE AFORESAID, ADDING AN EXAMPLE. And so, the end of the will, as was said earlier,[7] is said to be both that which we will and that for the sake of which we will it; and intention looks to that for the sake of which we will, and the will to that which we will. For example, if I will to feed the hungry in order to have eternal life, my will is that by which I will to feed the hungry, whose end is the feeding of the hungry; but my intention is that by which I will to attain to [eternal] life in this manner; and the highest end is that life itself, to which even the other end is referred.

5. WHETHER THAT INTENTION IS THE WILL. But one asks whether such an intention is also a will and, if it is a will, whether in this work the will by which I will to have eternal life and by which I will to feed the hungry is one and the same.

6. HERE, THAT INTENTION IS CALLED A WILL. Such an intention certainly appears to be a will, for just as there is a will by which I will to feed the hungry, so too there is a will by which, through this means, I will to have eternal life.

7. WHETHER THE LATTER IS A DIFFERENT WILL FROM THE FORMER. And the will by which I will to have eternal life seems to be one thing, and that by which I will to help the poor another, but the latter is referred to

[1]Ps. 7, 10.
[2]Augustine, *Enarrationes in Psalmos*, on Ps. 7, 10, n9.
[3]Cf. Ps. 7, 10.
[4]Augustine, *Enarrationes in Psalmos*, on Ps. 7, 10, n9.
[5]Ps. 9, 16.
[6]Augustine, *Enarrationes in Psalmos*, on Ps. 9, 16, n15.
[7]In n2.

the former.—AUGUSTINE, *ON THE TRINITY.* Indeed, "although the latter is so pleasing that the will rests in it with some delight, nevertheless it is not yet that to which one tends, but it is referred to something else, so that one is regarded as the native country of a citizen, but the other as a place of refreshment or rest for a traveller."[8] And these wills are dispositions or movements of the mind by which, as if by degrees or steps, one tends toward one's native country. Therefore, just as the will to see windows is one thing, as we learned above with Augustine as our teacher, and the will to see passers-by through the windows is another, which is born from the first, similarly, it seems to some that the will to give alms to the poor is one thing, and the the will to have eternal life another.—But others hold that there is only one will both here and there, but because of the multiplicity of subjects, a diversity of wills is mentioned.—But whichever of these may be true, no one doubts that the will is weighed by its ends, whether it is righteous or depraved, sin or grace; and that by the term intention, sometimes the end is understood, and sometimes the will.

DISTINCTION XXXIX

Chapter 1 (249)

1. SINCE THE WILL IS ONE OF THE THINGS WHICH MAN HAS NATURALLY, WHY IS IT SAID TO BE A SIN, WHEN NONE OF THE OTHER NATURAL GIFTS IS A SIN. And here arises a very necessary question, which draws its origin from what was said above. For it has been said above that the will is naturally in man, as are intellect and memory.[1] But these are natural gifts in man and, however vitiated they may be, they nevertheless do not cease to be goods because vice is not able to consume entirely the goodness in which God made them. For example, intellect and reason and ingenuity and memory, although they become clouded and corrupted by vices and sins, are nevertheless goods and are not called sins. In *On the Trinity*, book 15, Augustine clearly shows this to be so with regard to reason, which is the image of God in which we have been made; he says: "This is the image in which men were created and by which they rule over the animals. This creature, the most excellent of created things, when it is justified by God, is changed from a deformed form to a beautiful one. For its nature was good even in the middle of vices."[2] And this image is reason or the intellect. Therefore, since the will is one of the natural gifts, why is it not always a good, even though it is sometimes subject to vices?

[8]Augustine, *De Trinitate*, bk 11 c6 n10.

[1]Dist. 37 c1 n3.
[2]Augustine, *De Trinitate*, bk 15 c8 n14.

2. RESPONSE, ACCORDING TO SOME. To this, it is easy for those to respond who say that all things that are, insofar as they are, are good. As we set out above, they assert that the will too, insofar as it is, or insofar as it is the will, is good, but insofar as it is disordered, it is evil and a sin.

3. Here it may reasonably be asked of them: If the will, insofar as it is disordered, is a sin, why then are the intellect, reason, ingenuity, and suchlike, not sins when they are disordered? Like the will, they are disordered when they do not tend to the right end and their actions are transgressions.—To this they say that, by the term will, sometimes the force, or natural power of willing, is signified, and sometimes an action of the same force. And the force itself, which is naturally in the soul, is never a sin, as is neither the force of memory or intellect; but an action of this force, which is also called the will, is a sin when it is disordered.

Chapter 2 (250)

1. WHY AN ACTION OF THE WILL IS A SIN, IF THE ACTIONS OF THE OTHER POWERS ARE NOT SINS. But now it is asked why an action of this natural power is a sin, if the actions of the other powers are not sins, namely of the power of memory, whose action is to remember, and of the power of the intellect, whose action is to understand.—RESPONSE. To this the same persons answer that an action of the will is of a different kind from the actions of memory or intellect. For here the action is to obtain or not to commit something,[1] which cannot exist with regard to evil without the action itself being evil. For to will evils is an evil, but to understand or remember evils is not evil; (THAT THEY SAY THAT EVEN ACTIONS OF THE MEMORY OR INTELLECT ARE SOMETIMES EVIL) although some of them assert, not without sound reason, that even these actions are at times evil. For at times one remembers an evil in order to do it, and seeks to understand the truth in order to oppose it.—See, this is how the above question is resolved by those who teach that all things are good, insofar as they are.[2]

2. RESPONSE, ACCORDING TO SOME. But those who say[3] that evil wills are sins and in no way goods, answer more briefly, saying that an action of the will is not among the natural gifts, but only the force and power of willing, which is always a good, and is in everyone, even in little children, in whom an act of the will does not yet exist.

[1]Cf. above, dist. 26 c2 n1.
[2]The solution begins above, c1 n2.
[3]Concerning whom, see above, dist. 37 c1.

Chapter 3 (251)

1. IN WHAT SENSE THE STATEMENT: EVEN A MAN WHO IS A SLAVE TO SIN NATURALLY WILLS THE GOOD, IS TO BE UNDERSTOOD. Moreover, it is usual to ask how is to be understood what Ambrose says in his exposition of that phrase of the Apostle: *For I do not accomplish what I will; but I do what I do not will.*[1] For he says that "a human being subject to sin does what he does not will, because he naturally wills the good, but this will is ever deprived of effect, if God's grace"[2] does not aid and free it. If man is subject to sin, he wills and works evil because he is the slave of sin, and, as Augustine said above, he willingly does his [master's] will;[3] how, then, does he naturally will the good?

2. WHETHER OR NOT IT IS BY THE SAME WILL THAT MAN NATURALLY WILLS THE GOOD AND WILLINGLY SERVES SIN. Is it the same will, that is, the same movement, by which he freely serves sin and by which he naturally wills the good? If it is not the same will, then which of them is it that is freed from servitude to sin when man is justified? For as we discussed earlier,[4] God's grace frees and aids man's will; it prepares the will of man to be aided and aids it when it is prepared. But which will is it? Is it that which naturally wills the good, or that which freely serves sin, if indeed there are two wills?

3. HE PURSUES THE QUESTION WHICH HE HAS POSED, FIRST ACCORDING TO THOSE WHO SAY THAT THERE ARE TWO MOVEMENTS. The question which has been posed is a deep one, which is resolved differently by different people. For some say that there are two movements, by the first of which man naturally wills the good. But why do they say naturally, and why natural? Because such was the movement of human nature at its first establishment, in which we were created without vice, and which is properly called nature; for man was created righteous in his will.[5]—GENNADIUS. Hence, in *On Ecclesiastical Dogmas*, it is written: "Hold most firmly that the first human beings were created good and righteous, with free choice, by which they were able, if they willed, to sin by their own will; and that they sinned not by necessity, but by their own will."[6] And so it is rightly said that man naturally wills the good, because he was established in a good and righteous will; for the higher spark of reason, which, as Jerome says, even in Cain could not be extinguished, always wills the

[1]Rom. 7, 19.
[2]Cf. Ambrosiaster on Rom. 7, 15.
[3]Dist. 25 c8 n5.
[4]Dist. 26 c1.
[5]Cf. Eccl. 7, 30.
[6]Rather, Fulgentius, *De fide ad Petrum*, c25 n66.

good and hates evil.[7]—And they say that there is a second movement of the mind by which the mind, after relinquishing the law of higher things, subjects itself to sins and takes pleasure in them. This movement, they say, before grace is present in one, dominates and rules in man, and presses down the first movement; and yet each of them is from free choice. With the coming of grace, however, the evil movement is crushed, and the naturally good one is freed and aided so as to will the good efficaciously. But before grace, although man naturally wills the good, yet it is not suitable to grant absolutely that he has a good will, but rather an evil one.

4. ACCORDING TO OTHERS, THE WILL IS SAID TO BE ONE. But others say that there is [only] one will, that is, one movement, by which man naturally wills the good, and it is on account of vice that he wills evil and finds delight in it; and insofar as he wills the good, he is naturally good; insofar as he wills evil, he is evil.

DISTINCTION XL

Chapter 1 (252)

1. WHETHER ALL ACTIONS ARE TO BE WEIGHED BY THEIR END SO THAT THEY MAY BE SAID TO BE SIMPLY GOOD OR EVIL. After these matters, it appears that we must add [something] concerning actions, and whether they too, like the will, are to be judged good or evil from their end. For although, according to some,[1] all actions are good, insofar as they are, yet not all are to be called good absolutely, nor are all worthy of reward; but some are called simply evil, as others are called good.

2. WHICH ACTIONS ARE TO BE CALLED SIMPLY GOOD, AND WHICH SIMPLY EVIL. Indeed, those actions are simply and truly good which have a good cause and intention, that is, which are accompanied by a good will and tend to a good end. But those actions are to be called simply evil which have a perverse cause and intention.—Hence Ambrose says: "Your disposition gives a name to your deed."[2] And Augustine, on Psalm 31: "Let no one count his works before faith as good. For they seem to me to be like great efforts and a very fast race off the track; because when there was no faith, there was no good work, for it is intention that makes a work good, and it is faith which directs the intention. Do not pay attention so much to what a man does, but to what he has in view as he does it, to which he directs with the greatest skill all his efforts."[3]

[7]Jerome, *In Ezechielem* 1, 7.

[1]On whom see above, dist. 35 c2 n4.
[2]Ambrose, *De officiis*, bk 1 c30 n147.
[3]Augustine, *Enarrationes in Psalmos*, exp. 2 on Ps. 31, n4.

3. By these testimonies, it appears to be indicated that works are good or evil from their intention and end. Consonant with this is what Truth says in the Gospel: *A good tree cannot bear evil fruits, nor can an evil tree bear good fruits.*[4] By the term tree is to be understood not the nature of the human mind, but the will which, if it is evil, bears evil deeds, and not good ones; but if it is good, it bears good deeds, not evil ones.

4. WHETHER ALL THE WORKS OF MAN ARE GOOD AND EVIL FROM AFFECTIVE DISPOSITION AND END. But it is asked whether all the works of man are good or evil from affective disposition and end.

5. THE OPINION OF SOME WHO SAY THAT THEY ARE ALL INDIFFERENT. This seems to be the case to some, who say that all actions are indifferent, so that they are neither good nor evil in themselves, but that every action is good from a good intention and evil from an evil intention. According to them, any action can be good, if it is done with a good intention.

6. THE OPINION OF OTHERS, WHO DRAW A THREEFOLD DISTINCTION AMONG ACTIONS. But it seems to others that some actions are evil in themselves, so that they cannot be anything other than sins, even if they have a good cause; and some are good in themselves, so that, even if they have an evil cause, nevertheless they do not cease to be good.—They confirm this by the testimony of Augustine, who says that the good is sometimes not done well.[5] For one does not do well what one does unwillingly or by necessity, because one does not do it with a good intention, as Augustine says, in *On John*: "A servile *fear is not in charity*;[6] in such fear, although one believes God, yet one does not believe in God, and although one does a good thing, yet one does not do it well."[7] "For no one does well what one does unwillingly, even though what one does is a good thing."[8]—See, you have here that one does not do well that which is good; therefore, one does what is good with an intention which is not good. Hence they assert that there are some works which are so good that they cannot be evil, no matter how they are done, just as, conversely, some are so evil that they cannot be good, for whatever cause they are done; but that there are other works which are good or evil from their end or from their cause. To this last group alone the testimonies of the Saints[9] refer, in which they say that the judgement of works is to be weighed from disposition or intention. These argue for a threefold distinction of actions.

7. AUGUSTINE APPEARS TO FEEL OTHERWISE; HE SAYS THAT THE WORKS OF MAN ARE GOOD OR EVIL FROM INTENTION AND CAUSE, EXCEPT THOSE

[4]Mt. 7, 18.
[5]Augustine, *Confessiones*, bk 1 c12 n19.
[6]1 Jn. 4, 18.
[7]Augustine, *De spiritu et littera*, c32 n56.
[8]Augustine, *Confessiones*, bk 1 c12 n19.
[9]See above, n2.

WHICH ARE SINS IN THEMSELVES. But Augustine most clearly teaches in the book, *Against Lying*, that all actions are to be judged good or evil according to intention and cause, except for some which are so evil that they can never be good, even if they seem to have a good cause. He says: "It is always relevant for what cause, to what end, with what intention something is done. But those things which we know to be sins are not to be done with any claim of a good cause, for any apparent good end, with any allegedly good intention. For those works of men which are not in themselves sins are now good, now evil, according to whether they have good or evil causes. And so, to give food to the poor is good, if it is done because of mercy with right faith; and conjugal intercourse too, when it is done for the cause of procreating and if it is done with the trust that their offspring will be born again. But these same things are evils if they have evil causes, as, for instance, if a poor person is fed for the sake of boasting of it, or one sleeps with one's wife because of lust, or children are begotten to be nurtured not for God, but for the devil. But when the works themselves are sins, like thefts, rapes, blasphemies, who would say that they are to be done for good causes, or are not sins, or, what is more absurd, that they are righteous sins? Who would say: Let us steal from the rich, so that we may have something to give to the poor; or let us bear false witness, not so the innocent may be harmed by it, but rather so that they may be saved? For there are two goods here: that a needy person be fed, and an innocent one not be punished. Or who would say that an adultery is to be committed so that a man may be saved from death through the woman with whom it was committed? Likewise, why do we not suppress true testaments and submit forged ones so that those who help the needy may receive inheritances, rather than those who do nothing good? Why should these evil things not be done for the sake of those good ones, if for the sake of these good ones, those are not evil at all? Why should a good man not steal the riches of unclean prostitutes, who enrich pimps, in order to distribute them to the needy, since no evil is evil if it is done for the sake of the good?"[10]

8. NOT ONLY WHY, BUT ALSO WHAT IS DONE IS TO BE WEIGHED. "Who would say this, other than one who strives to subvert human affairs and morals and laws? For of what crime would it not be said that it can be done righteously, and not only with impunity, but even gloriously, so that no punishment should be feared in its commission, but there should even be hope of reward, if we have once granted that in the case of evil actions what is to be asked is not what is done, but why it is done, so that whichever ones have been done for good causes should not be judged to be evils? But justice deservedly punishes him who says that he took super-

[10]Augustine, *Contra mendacium*, c7 n18.

fluous things from a rich person to give them to a poor one; and the forger who falsified someone else's will so that he who would give large alms should be the heir, and not he who would give none; and also the one who declares that he committed adultery to free a man from death through the woman with whom he committed it."[11]

9. ONE WHO STEALS OUT OF COVETOUSNESS IS WORSE THAN ONE WHO STEALS OUT OF COMPASSION. But "someone will say: And so a thief who steals with a will of mercy is to be equated with any other thief? Who has said so? But of these two, one is not good because the other is worse: for the one who steals out of covetousness is worse than the one who does so out of compassion. But if all theft is sin, we must abstain from all theft. For who would say that we ought to sin, even though one sin is greater, the other lighter? Now, however, we are asking which action is or is not a sin, not which is graver and which lighter."[12]

10. Attend, reader, to the words here set out with the whole consideration of your mind because they contain an exercise which is far from useless; and you will recognize which action is a sin, namely one which has an evil cause; and not only that one, because there are some actions which, although they have a good cause, are nevertheless sins, as is set out above.

11. From this it seems to follow that a will or action is not always judged to be evil from its end, as is the case with those things which are sins in themselves. For when one has done these things for some good cause, they appear to have a good end; and the will is not evil as a result of the end, nor is the action made evil as a result of the will, but the will is made depraved as a result of the action.—AMONG THOSE WHICH ARE EVIL IN THEMSELVES SOME PLACE THE ACTION OF THE JEWS. Among these, some place the action of the Jews, who, in crucifying Christ, judged that *they were paying homage to God*;[13] because they say that the Jews set a good end for themselves, namely homage to God, and yet they claim that their will and action were perverse.

12. But no exception is made concerning good things in the above words of Augustine that every good will is good from its end and every good action is good from its end and will. But not every evil will is evil from its end, and not every evil action is evil from its end and will; and each one which has an evil cause is evil, but not each one which has a good cause is good. And so, when it is said that the name is given to the deed from the disposition,[14] this rule is generally true as to good works, but, as to evil ones, those are excepted which are evil in themselves. And

[11] Augustine, *Contra mendacium*, c7 n18.
[12] Ibid., c9 n19.
[13] Cf. Jn. 16, 2.
[14] Cf. above, n2.

so all the works of man are judged good or evil according to intention and cause, except for those which are evil in themselves, that is, which cannot be done without transgression.

13. SOME SAY THAT THE AFORESAID CANNOT BE DONE WITH A GOOD END. Nevertheless, some contend that such things never have a good cause. He who steals another's goods to give them to the poor does not, they say, steal rightly, for it is not good to give another's goods to the poor. Indeed, one who *offers a sacrifice* to God out of what he has stolen, as authority says,[15] does the same *as one who sacrifices a son in his father's presence*, or offers the sacrifice of a dog to God.[16] The offering of the impious is surely abominable to God.[17] They also say it is evil to free a man from death through adultery, for even if it is good to free a man from death, nevertheless they assert it is evil to free him in such a way.

14. THEY FIND IN THE WORDS OF AUGUSTINE CITED ABOVE THAT THOSE THINGS ARE NOT DONE WITH A GOOD END. They say that is why Augustine, above, tempered his speech and spoke cautiously where he says: "But those things which we know to be sins are not to be done for any *apparent* good end, with any *allegedly* good intention."[18] For he did not simply say 'good end' and 'good intention,' but added *apparently* and *allegedly*; because such things are not done with a good end and a good intention, but with an intention which is alleged to be good and an end which appears to be good, but is not so. And Augustine, they say, did not single these out as not having evil causes, but because they have causes which appear to be good, and yet are evil.

DISTINCTION XLI

Chapter 1 (253)

1. WHETHER EVERY INTENTION AND ACTION OF THOSE WHO LACK FAITH IS EVIL. And since, as was said above,[1] the intention makes a work good, and faith directs the intention, it is not irrelevant to ask whether every intention and every work of those who do not have faith is evil. For if faith directs the intention and the intention makes a work good, where there is no faith, it appears that there is neither good intention nor good work.

2. SOME SAY THAT ALL THE ACTIONS OF MAN, WHICH ARE GOOD WITHIN FAITH, ARE EVIL WITHOUT FAITH. This is not unreasonably concluded by

[15]Eccli. 34, 24.
[16]Cf. Is. 66, 3; Deut. 23, 18.
[17]Cf. Prov. 15, 8; 21, 27.
[18]Above, in n7.

[1]Dist. 40 n2.

some people, who say that all those actions and wills of man, which are good if one has faith, are evil without faith.

3. THEY SUPPORT THEIR OPINION WITH AUTHORITIES.—AUGUSTINE, IN THE BOOK OF *SENTENCES OF PROSPER*. Hence the Apostle says: *All that is not from faith is a sin.*[2] Expounding this, Augustine says: "The entire life of unbelievers is a sin, and nothing is good without the highest good. Where the acknowledgement of eternal truth is lacking, there is false virtue, even with the best of morals."[3]—And James, in the canonical Epistle, says: *The man who has offended against one point*, namely charity, *has become guilty against all of them.*[4] And so every action of one who does not have faith and charity is a sin because it is not referred to charity. For whatever is not referred to charity, as Augustine recalled above,[5] is not done as it ought to be done, and so is evil.

4. THAT THE COMMANDMENTS ARE NOT KEPT WITHOUT CHARITY. And so one who lacks charity does not keep the commandments because none of the commandments is kept without charity. Hence Augustine, in *On the Epistle to the Galatians*, says: "The Apostle calls it 'the keeping of the law' not to kill, not to commit adultery, and others of this kind pertaining to good morals, which cannot be fulfilled without charity and hope."[6] And so, one who does not have faith and charity fulfils none of the commandments, and does no good work. For *it is impossible*, as the Apostle says, *without faith to please God* in anything.[7] And so, because every good pleases God, those things which are done without faith are not good.

5. FROM THE WORDS OF AUGUSTINE, SOME OBJECTIONS ARE MADE TO THE FOREGOING. But to these statements is objected what Augustine said above, namely that "although one does a good thing in servile fear, nevertheless one does not do it well: no one does well what one does unwillingly, even though what one does is a good thing."[8] Here he says that one who does not have charity does a good thing, but not well. For one who fears in a servile way lacks charity, and yet it is said of him here that he does a good, but not well. On that place of the Psalm: *The turtledove finds for herself a nest in which to put her young*,[9] he also says that "Jews and heretics and pagans do good works, because they clothe the naked, and feed the poor, and suchlike; but they do not do this in the nest of the Church, that is, in faith, and so their young are crushed."[10]

[2]Rom. 14, 23.
[3]From Prosper of Aquitaine, *Sententiae ex Augustino delibatae*, n106.
[4]James 2, 10.
[5]Above, dist. 38 c1 n2.
[6]Augustine, *In Epistolam ad Galatas*, n62.
[7]Hebr. 11, 6.
[8]Dist. 40 n6.
[9]Ps. 83, 4.
[10]Augustine, *Enarrationes in Psalmos*, on Ps. 83, 4, n7.

6. HOW THEY REPLY TO THESE WORDS. To these words, they reply by saying that works of this kind, which are done without charity, are called good not because they are good when they are so done, which Augustine clearly taught above, but because they would be good if they were done otherwise. Also, such things are good in their kind, but they become evil from the [doer's] disposition.

7. THE VIEW OF OTHERS ON THE ABOVE QUESTION, IN WHICH IT WAS ASKED WHETHER EVERY ACTION OF THOSE WHO LACK FAITH IS EVIL. But others, who draw a threefold distinction of actions,[11] conclude that all works which come to the support of nature are always good.

8. HE DETERMINES THE ABOVE WORDS OF AUGUSTINE. But what Augustine says concerning their being evil 'if they have evil causes,'[12] is not to be taken as if they were themselves evil, but that those who do them for an evil end sin and are evil.—Also, as for that other text, namely 'intention makes a work good and faith directs the intention,'[13] they determine it by saying that there that is called 'good' which is worthy of reward for life; not that that work alone is good, for there are also many others, although they are not good for the same reason as that one.

Chapter 2 (254)

IN WHAT WAYS [SOMETHING] IS CALLED GOOD. For good is taken in many senses, namely for useful, for worthy of reward, for a sign of the good, for a species of the good, for lawful, and perhaps in other ways. And that intention alone is worthy of reward for life which faith directs; but it is not the only one which is good, they say. For if a Jew or a bad Christian, driven by natural piety, has relieved the need of a neighbour, he has done a good thing, and the will by which he did that was good.

Chapter 3 (255)

HERE ARE SET OUT SOME CHAPTERS OF AUGUSTINE WHICH HE RETRACTED, NOT AS IF THEY HAD BEEN WRONGLY SAID, BUT IN ORDER TO INDICATE IN WHAT SENSE HE HAD SAID THEM.—FIRST CHAPTER. After these matters, it is suitable to investigate how what Augustine says in the book *On True Religion* is to be understood : "To such a degree is sin a voluntary evil that it would in no way be a sin, if it were not voluntary."[1]—RETRACTATION CONTAINING A DOUBLE DETERMINATION. Revealing the reason for this statement, in the book of *Retractations*, Augustine says:

[11]On whom see above, dist. 40 n6.
[12]Above, dist. 40 c1 n7.
[13]Above, dist. 40 c1 n2.

[1]Augustine, *De vera religione*, c14 n27.

"This definition may seem false; but if it is diligently examined, it is found to be most true. For that is to be regarded as a sin which is only a sin, and not that which is also punishment of sin"— namely the first sin of man, which was sin and cause of sin, but not punishment of sin—"although even those sins which are not undeservedly called involuntary, since they are perpetrated in ignorance or compulsion, cannot be committed entirely without the will, because even he who sins in ignorance does entirely willingly that which he holds ought to be done, even though it ought not to be done. And he who is caught in the desire of the flesh against the spirit, does not do what he wills and desires unwillingly, and in that regard does not do what he wills; but if he is overcome, he consents willingly to concupiscence, and in that regard he does not do other than what he wills. And that which is an original sin in little children was contracted from the first evil will of man. And so what I said is not false: 'To such a degree is sin a voluntary [evil],' etc."[2]—See how that statement is to be taken, namely either concerning the first sin of man, or of all mortal sins generally. And although some of the latter are called involuntary, namely those which are done through ignorance or weakness, nevertheless they can be called voluntary by reason of the fact that they are not committed without the will.

Chapter 4 (256)

ANOTHER CHAPTER. The meaning ought also be sought of that which he published in the book *On the Two Souls*, saying: "Sin is nowhere other than in the will."[1]—RETRACTATION. This also he clearly determines in the book of *Retractations*, saying: "This opinion may be thought to be false, in which we said, 'Sin is nowhere, other than in the will,' since the Apostle says: *What I do not will, this I do*,"[2] etc. "But the sin which 'is nowhere other than in the will' is to be understood particularly to be the one which was followed by a just condemnation,"[3] that is, the first sin of man.

Chapter 5 (257)

ALSO, ANOTHER CHAPTER. Also in the same book *On the Two Souls*, he teaches something else worthy of consideration. For he says: "There is no sinning apart from the will"; and he defined the will itself, saying: "The will is a movement of the spirit, under no compulsion, either toward not committing or toward obtaining something."[1]—AUGUSTINE, RETRACTA-

[2]Augustine, *Retractationes*, bk 1 c13 n5.

[1]Augustine, *De duabus animabus*, c10 n12.
[2]Rom. 7, 16.
[3]Augustine, *Retractationes*, bk 1 c15 n2.

[1]Augustine, *De duabus animabus*, c10 n14.

TION. Revealing the cause of this statement and explaining its meaning, in the book of *Retractations*, he says: "Moreover, this was said so that the definition might serve to distinguish the willing from the unwilling, and that in this way intention would referred to those who, in paradise, committed the original evil by sinning under no one's compulsion, that is, by a free will because they acted knowingly against [God's] command, and their tempter persuaded them to do so, but did not compel them. For one who has sinned unknowingly can not unsuitably be said to have sinned 'unwilling,' although he too, nevertheless did willingly what he did unknowingly. (THE WILL TO DO A DEED WHICH IS A SIN IS NOT ALWAYS THE WILL TO SIN BECAUSE ONE WILLS THAT WHICH IS A SIN, AND YET NOT THE SIN.) And so such a sin could not occur without the will; but [what was] there was the will to do the deed, not the will to sin. And yet, the deed was a sin, for that which ought not to have been done was done. And anyone sins knowingly, if he is able, without sin, to resist another who compels him to sin, and yet he does not do it; such a one certainly sins willingly because one who can resist is not compelled to yield. For these reasons, it is very true that there cannot be sinning apart from the will."[2] From these words is made clear how the above are to be taken.

Chapter 6 (258)

THAT AN EVIL WILL IS A VOLUNTARY SIN. And if every mortal sin is voluntary, since an evil will is a mortal sin, it is clear that it is a voluntary sin.—AUGUSTINE, IN THE BOOK *ON FREE CHOICE*. As Augustine says: "For what is as much in the will as the will itself?"[1] And so an evil will is rightly called a voluntary sin because it resides in the will. As Augustine says in the same: "The will is certainly the first cause of sinning, or no sin is the first cause of sinning. Nor is there anyone to whom sin may rightly be imputed, other than the sinner; and so there is nothing to which it may rightly be imputed, other than the will."[2]—And this is to be understood of actual and mortal sin. As Augustine himself says in the *Retractations*, with these words, he did not wish to show anything other than that "the will is that by which one sins and lives righteously."[3]

[2]Augustine, *Retractationes*, bk 1 c15 n3.

[1]Augustine, *De libero arbitrio*, bk 1 c12 n26.
[2]Ibid., bk 3 c17 n49.
[3]Augustine, *Retractationes*, bk 1 c9 n4.

DISTINCTION XLII

Chapter 1 (259)

1. WHETHER AN EVIL WILL AND ACTION IN THE SAME MAN CONCERNING THE SAME THING ARE ONE SIN OR SEVERAL. But since an evil will and action are sinful, it is usual to ask whether, in the same man and concerning the same thing, these two are one sin or several. If someone willingly steals, he has an evil will, which is sinful, and an evil action, which is also sinful. And these are two different things, namely will and action; but are they different sins, or one sin?

2. OBJECTION AGAINST THOSE WHO SAY ONE SIN. Some say that there is one sin. But others say that there are different sins because, since it is clear that there are two different things, either they are called two different sins, or two different things, but not two sins.—RESPONSE. To them others respond that there are two different things, and not two sins. For they are not two sins, but one sin, because the same transgression or disobedience is committed in both, either when he wills, or when he acts. And the contempt there shown is also one, but it is less when the sin is contained only in the will, and greater when the deed is added to the will. And so the sin becomes greater, but not plural, when the will is given over to the deed.

3. ANOTHER OBJECTION AGAINST THE SAME. But another objection is made to the same: If these two are only one sin, how is it that one who had first conceived the will to do evil, and afterwards accomplished the deed, is not liable for anything other than that for which he was liable before the deed, when the sin consisted only in the will. For no one is liable to eternal death other than for sin. But the sin committed by the action is none other than that which was first admitted by the will. And so, by the sinful action, such a person does not make himself condemnable to anything other than that to which he had been before, when he offended with the will alone.—RESPONSE. And to this too they respond and say that a thief is rendered liable by that sin alone. And although his will and action are one sin, yet he is rendered liable for something else by the action of sinning than he was before, when he offended by the will alone; he is now liable also for the action, which is something other than the will, although not another sin.

4. ANOTHER OBJECTION AGAINST THE SAME. Still pressing on with the question, they also say that these are two different sins because they are transgressions of different commandments of the Law. For the action of stealing is forbidden by one commandment of the Law, namely: *You shall not steal*;[1] the will to steal by another, namely: *You shall not covet what*

[1]Exod. 20, 15; Deut. 5, 19.

belongs to your neighbour.[2] And since these are two different commandments, by which those two things are forbidden, it is clear that there are two different transgressions, and so [two] different sins.—RESPONSE. To this the others also reply that the commandments are indeed different by which those two things are forbidden distinctly, as Augustine teaches, in *On Exodus.*[3] And yet, in the failure to observe them, only one transgression is incurred and only one sin is contracted, even though two different things are forbidden by the commandments. Similarly and conversely, there are two commandments of charity, by which two are commanded to be loved [i.e. God and one's neighbour],[4] and yet one charity is commended to us by means of them.

Chapter 2 (260)

1. WHETHER A SIN COMMITTED BY SOMEONE REMAINS IN HIM UNTIL HE REPENTS. Moreover, it is usual to ask: when a sin has been voluntarily committed by someone, and the will to commit it and the action have ceased, and yet he has not yet had true penance, whether that sin is in him until he repents. This appears not to be the case, because the will, which was before, is no longer, and neither is the action, because he does not [now] will or do that which he willed and did before.

2. RESPONSE DETERMINING THE QUESTION. But it is not to be ignored that sin is said to be in someone and to cease in two ways, namely by action and by liability. It is in someone by action while the very thing which is a sin, such as an action or a will, is in the sinner; but it is in him by liability when, because of it, whether it has ceased or is still present, the mind of man is polluted and corrupted, and the whole man is bound to perpetual pains. Apart from the original one, no sin is ever in anybody by action without being there also by liability, but sometimes it is there by liability after it has ceased in respect to action.

Chapter 3 (261)

1. IN WHAT WAYS LIABILITY IS SPOKEN OF IN SCRIPTURE. And liability in Scripture is taken in several ways, namely for fault, for punishment, for the obligation of temporal or eternal punishment. If it is mortal, it obliges us to eternal punishment; if venial, it binds us to temporal punishment.

2. WHAT MORTAL SIN IS, WHAT VENIAL IS. For there are two kinds of sins, namely mortal and venial. A mortal sin is that through which man deserves eternal death; "for," as Augustine says, " it is a crime which is

[2]Exod. 20, 17; Deut. 5, 21.
[3]Augustine, *Quaestiones in Heptateuchum*, bk 2 q71.
[4]Cf. Mt. 22, 37-39.

worthy of indictment and condemnation,"[1] but a venial one is that which does not burden man to the point of liability to eternal death, and yet deserves punishment, but is easily forgiven.

Chapter 4 (262)

1. ON THE MODES OF SINNING, WHICH ARE DESCRIBED IN A VARIETY OF WAYS.—FIRST DISTINCTION. And the modes of sinning are distinguished in a variety of ways in Scripture; in it, it is said that sin is committed in two ways, namely by cupidity and by fear, as Augustine teaches on that place of the Psalm: *Burned with fire and cut from below*.[1] For he says that all mortal sins are included in these two ways. He calls those sins *burned* which arise from an evilly smouldering cupidity; and he calls those *cut from below* which come from an evilly humiliating fear.[2] This is when one desires what is not to be desired, or fears what is not to be feared.

2. SECOND DISTINCTION. But elsewhere, sin is said to be committed in three ways, namely in thought, word, deed. Hence Jerome, in *On Ezechiel*: "There are three general crimes to which humankind is subject; for we sin either in thought, word, or deed."[3] Sometimes, a fourth way is added to these three, namely that of habituation, which is signified by Lazarus lying dead for four days.[4]

3. THIRD. Man is also said to sin against God, against himself, and against his neighbour. Against God, when he thinks wrongly concerning God, as does a heretic; or when he dares to usurp things which are God's, as by participating unworthily in the sacraments; or when he holds God's name in contempt by swearing. He sins against his neighbour when he harms his neighbour unjustly; but against himself when he harms himself, but not anyone else.

Chapter 5 (263)

IN WHAT DO FAULT AND SIN DIFFER. It also has different names, for it is called both sin and fault. And, as Augustine says in his *Questions on Leviticus*, "perhaps fault is to fall away from the good, and sin is to do evil. For to fall away from the good is one thing, and to do evil is another. And so sin is the perpetration of evil, fault the abandonment of the good. And even the name itself shows it. For what else does fault sound like, if not fall? And from what does he fall away, the one who fails, if not from the

[1]Augustine, *In Ioannem*, tr. 41 n9.

[1]Ps. 79, 17.
[2]Augustine, *Enarrationes in Psalmos*, on Ps. 79, 17 n13.
[3]Jerome, *In Ezechielem* 43, 23-25.
[4]Cf. Jn. 11, 39; Augustine, *In Ioannem*, tr. 49 n3.

good? Or fault is what is done in ignorance, and sin is what is committed knowingly. And yet sin is indiscriminately called fault, and fault sin."[1]

Chapter 6 (264)

ON THE SEVEN PRINCIPAL VICES. Moreover, it is to be known that there are seven capital or principal vices, as Gregory says on Exodus, namely vainglory, anger, envy, sloth or sadness, avarice, gluttony, lust.[1] As Chrysostom says, these are signified in the seven nations who held the land of the promise made to Israel.[2] From these, as if from seven springs, all the deadly corruptions of souls emanate. And these are called capital because from them arise all evils. For there is none which does not derive its origin from one of these.

Chapter 7 (265)

1. ON PRIDE, WHICH IS THE ROOT OF ALL EVILS. And yet all evils, both these and others, arise from pride; because, as Gregory says, "pride is the root of all evil, of which it is said: *Pride is the beginning of all sin*";[1,2] and it is "the love of one's own excellence."[3]

2. ON THE FOUR KINDS OF PRIDE. And there are four kinds of pride, as Gregory says: "The first is when someone attributes to himself the good which he has; the second, when he believes that the good is given by God, and yet for his own merits; the third, when he boasts that he has what he does not have; the fourth, when he has contempt for all others and wishes to seem unique."[4] Deservedly, then, pride is called the root of all evil.

3. THAT CUPIDITY IS THE ROOT OF ALL EVILS. But what the Apostle says: *The root of all evils is cupidity*,[5] seems to contradict this because, if cupidity is the root of all evils, then it is also the root of pride. How, then, is pride the root and beginning of all sin?

Chapter 8 (266)

IN WHAT SENSE EACH, NAMELY PRIDE AND CUPIDITY, IS CALLED THE ROOT OF ALL EVILS. But each of these is understood to be rightly described, if each term is understood to include types of individual sins, and not the

[1]Augustine, *Quaestiones in Heptateuchum*, bk 3 q20.

[1]Ordinary gloss, on Exod. 23, 22; from Gregory, *Moralia*, bk 31 c45 n87.
[2]Ordinary gloss, on Exod. 23, 23; John Cassian, *Conlationes*, coll. 5, cc16 and 23.

[1]Eccli. 10, 15.
[2]Ordinary gloss, on Exod. 23, 22; from Gregory, *Moralia*, bk 31 c45 n87.
[3]Augustine, *De Genesi ad litteram*, bk 11 c14 n18.
[4]Ordinary gloss, on Job 32, 8; from Gregory, *Moralia*, bk 23 c6 n13.
[5]1 Tim. 6, 10.

individual sins themselves. Certainly, there is no type of sin which, at some time, does not come from pride; and also, there is none which does not sometimes descend from cupidity. For there are some men who become proud from cupidity, and others who become covetous from pride. "For," as Augustine says, "there is a kind of man who would not be a lover of money, if he did not think he would be more excellent through it";[1] and so he is covetous of riches in order to excel. From such pride arises cupidity. And there is another who would not desire to excel, if he did not think that he would have greater riches through this; and so he labours in the pursuit of excellence because he loves to have riches. In such a person, pride, or the love of excellence, is born from cupidity. Therefore, it is evident that cupidity sometimes arises from pride, and pride sometimes from cupidity; and so, it is rightly said of each that it is the root of all evil.

DISTINCTION XLIII

Chapter 1 (267)

1. ON THE SIN AGAINST THE HOLY SPIRIT, WHICH IS ALSO CALLED THE SIN UNTO DEATH. Moreover, there is a kind of sin which is more grave and abominable than the others, which is called the sin against the Holy Spirit. Concerning it, Truth says in the Gospel: *Whoever* shall have sinned against *the Holy Spirit, it will not be remitted to him, neither* here, *nor in the future*;[1] and John in the canonical Epistle: *There is a sin unto death: I do not say that anyone pray for him.*[2] For if anyone sins against the Father, it will be remitted to him; and if anyone sins against the Son, it will be remitted to him; but *as for one* who has blasphemed against *the Holy Spirit, it will not be remitted to him, neither* here, *nor in the future*.

2. WHAT THAT SIN IS. THE OPINION OF SOME. But it is asked what that sin against the Holy Spirit or unto death is.—Some say that it is the sin of despair or obstinacy. Obstinacy is the pertinacity in wickedness of a hardened mind, through which a man is made impenitent. Despair is that by which one entirely lacks trust in God's goodness, reckoning one's own wickedness to exceed the greatness of divine goodness, like Cain, who said: *My iniquity is greater than the possibility of forgiveness.*[3]—Each of these is called a sin against the Holy Spirit, because the Holy Spirit is the love of the Father and the Son and the good pleasure by which they love

[1]Augustine, *De Genesi ad litteram*, bk 11 c15 n19.

[1]Mt. 12, 31-32; cf. also Mk. 3, 28-29; Lk. 12, 10.
[2]1 Jn. 5, 16.
[3]Gen. 4, 13.

each other and us; and it is so great that there is no end to it. And so they are rightly said to offend against the Holy Spirit who hold that their own wickedness exceeds God's goodness, and so do not accept penance, as also those who adhere to iniquity with such pertinacity of mind that they never propose to relinquish it, nor ever to return to the goodness of the Holy Spirit, abusing God's patience and presuming too much on God's mercy. Wickedness pleases such people for its own sake, just as goodness pleases pious people.—AUGUSTINE, IN *ON THE WORDS OF THE LORD.* The former sin by excessive pertinacity and presumption, judging that God is not just; the latter, in their despair, do not judge God to be good, taking away, in this most turbulent sea of iniquities the harbour of divine forgiveness, where they might be welcomed from their perils. And so, in their very despair, they add sin to sin, saying: There is no mercy, and an unavoidable condemnation is owed to sinners.

3. WHETHER ALL OBSTINACY OR DESPAIR IS A SIN AGAINST THE HOLY SPIRIT. But it is asked whether all obstinacy of a mind obdurate in wickedness and all despair is a sin against the Holy Spirit.

4. THE OPINION OF SOME. Some say that all obstinacy and despair is a sin against the Holy Spirit. If this is so, then that sin is at times remitted because many, even of the most despairing and obstinate, are converted, as Augustine says on that place of the Psalm: *I will convert them from the depth of the sea*:[4] "That is, those who were most despairing";[5] and also: *He sends crystal like bread crumbs*:[6] that is, he makes obstinate those who would teach others.[7] And the conversion of such people is clearly shown where it says: *He leads out those bound in strength; as also that provoke, and who dwell in sepulchres.*[8]—According to them, that sin is called unremittable not because it is not at times remitted, but because it is forgiven sparingly, rarely, and with difficulty. For crystal is not dissolved without a very vehement effort of the spirit.

5. THE OPINION OF OTHERS. But others teach that not every obstinacy or despair is called a sin against the Holy Spirit, but only the one which is joined to impenitence. Indeed, these call impenitence the sin against the Holy Spirit, because Augustine says: "Impenitence is the sin against the Holy Spirit."[9]—But when someone is so obstinate that he does not repent, it is suitable to discuss whether obstinacy is one sin in him and impeni-

[4]Ps. 67, 23.

[5]Ordinary gloss, on Ps. 67, 23, from Augustine, *Enarrationes in Psalmos*, on Ps. 67, 23, n31.

[6]Ps. 147, 17.

[7]Ordinary and interlinear gloss, on Ps. 147, 17; from Augustine, *Enarrationes in Psalmos*, on Ps. 147, 17, n25.

[8]Ps. 67, 7.

[9]Augustine, *Sermo 71*, c12 n20.

tence another, or whether it is the same, but committed in different ways. —According to them, that sin is called unremittable because it is never forgiven. Hence Augustine too says that this sin alone cannot deserve forgiveness;[10] and Jerome says that one sinning in such a way "cannot worthily do penance."[11] And so John rightly says that *no one is to pray for him*,[12] because one who sins in this way cannot be helped by the prayers of the Church, either here or in the future, since he has a hardened *heart, as stone*, as we read of the devil.[13] Those who are exceedingly evil cannot be assisted by the merits of the Church after this life.

6. THAT THE SIN AGAINST THE HOLY SPIRIT IS TAKEN IN ANOTHER WAY. There is also another description of this sin. For in defining this sin in the book *On the Lord's Sermon on the Mount*, Augustine says: "The sin unto death occurs when someone, after knowing God through the grace of Christ, fights against the brotherhood and, gnawed by envy, is aroused against the very grace by which he was reconciled to God. This perhaps is to sin against the Holy Spirit; and this sin is said not to be remitted: not because the sinner will not be forgiven, if he repent, but because such is the shame of that sin, that he cannot submit to the humiliation of begging for forgiveness, even if he is compelled by his bad conscience to acknowledge and cry out his sin; and so Judas, after saying, *I have sinned*,[14] more easily ran in despair to his rope than sought forgiveness in humility. This happens to such people because they must believe that their sin, due to its great gravity, has already caused condemnation."[15]—See, some description of the sin against the Holy Spirit or unto death has been set out here, in which that sin is said to be an attack against the brotherhood after acceptance in it, and envy of grace after reconciliation; this can be understood to be a kind of obstinacy.

7. And yet, in the book of *Retractations*, Augustine recalls that definition and reveals that he had not made it by way of assertion and that something ought to be added to it. He says as follows: "I did not indeed assert this positively because I said that this was [merely] my opinion. But yet it ought to have been added: *if he should finish his life in this accursed perversity of mind*; because we ought not to despair even for the worst of sinners, while he is still in this life; nor do we pray imprudently for one of whom we do not despair."[16] By these words, it is indicated that the sin described in the above definition is only then to be called *unto death* or

[10]Augustine, *Sermo 71*, c6 n10.
[11]Interlinear gloss, on Mk. 3, 29.
[12]1 Jn5, 6.
[13]Cf. Job 41, 15.
[14]Mt. 27, 4-5.
[15]Augustine, *De sermone Domini in monte*, bk 1 c22 nn73, 75, 74.
[16]Augustine, *Retractationes*, bk 1 c19 n7.

against the Holy Spirit when it is not joined to penance; nor are we to despair of any sinner in this life, and so we are to pray for all.

8. Hence, it seems that that text of John, *I do not say that anyone pray for him*,[17] ought to be taken thus: that we do not pray for anyone who has sinned unto death or against the Holy Spirit after he has finished this life; but while he is in this life, we must neither judge his sin, nor despair of him, but pray for him.—Hence Augustine, in *On the Words of the Lord*, speaks as follows of impenitence, which is blasphemy against the Holy Spirit: "This impenitence, or this impenitent heart, cannot be judged for so long as one lives in this flesh. For we must despair of no one, so long as God's patience *invites to repentance*.[18] Today, he is a pagan; today, he is a faithless Jew; today, he is a heretic; today, he is a schismatic. What if tomorrow he embraces Catholic peace and follows Catholic truth? What if these, whom you find in every kind of error and condemn as most desperate, do penance before they finish this life and find true life in the future? *And so do not judge* anything *before it is time*."[19,20] From these words, it is shown that we must pray for all sinners in this life, and not lose hope concerning anyone, because anyone may be converted while he is in this life. For it cannot be known of anyone whether he has sinned unto death or against the Holy Spirit, except when he has departed from this life; or unless perhaps it were miraculously revealed to someone through the Holy Spirit.

9. From what has been said above, it can be grasped somewhat how the sin against the Holy Spirit is taken: namely envy of grace which impenitently attacks the brotherhood; this certainly appears to be obstinacy as well as the obstinacy and despair of every impenitent person. But it is to be noted that not everyone who does not do penance can be called impenitent, because impenitence properly belongs to the obstinate and, as some would have it, even to the despairing.

10. ANOTHER DESCRIPTION OF THE SIN AGAINST THE HOLY SPIRIT. Discussing this sin against the Holy Spirit, Ambrose too, in the book *On the Holy Spirit*, hands down a definite description, saying: "Attend with diligence to why the Lord said: *Whoever has blasphemed against the Son of man, it will be remitted to him; but whoever has blasphemed against the Holy Spirit, it will not be remitted to him, neither here, nor in the future*.[21] Is there, then, one offense against the Son, another against the Holy Spirit? Just as there is one dignity, there is one injury. But if someone, perhaps deceived by the form of Christ's human body, thinks something

[17]1 Jn. 5, 16.
[18]Cf. Rom. 2, 4.
[19]1 Cor. 4, 5.
[20]Augustine, *Sermo 71*, c13 n2.
[21]Mt. 12, 32.

rather less than what is worthy about Christ's flesh, he is at fault, and yet he is not excluded from forgiveness. But if one denies the eternal dignity, majesty, and power of the Holy Spirit, and holds that *demons* are not cast out *through the Spirit of God*, but *through Beelzebub*,[22] there cannot then be an exhortation to forgiveness when there is a fullness of sacrilege."[23] Here is explained clearly enough what the sin against the Holy Spirit is.—This seems to be in keeping with the description of Augustine, in which that sin is said to be an envy of grace attacking the brotherhood. For one who, after knowing the truth, denies the truth of the Holy Spirit and says that his works are Beelzebub's, is not doubted to envy the power, goodness, and grace of God.

11. And so that distinction of words[24] is not to be so taken as if offenses against the three persons are being separated; rather, it is the types of sins which are there being distinguished. For that sin is understood to be against the Father which is done through weakness, because Scripture frequently attributes power to the Father; the sin against the Son is that done through ignorance, because wisdom is attributed to the Son; and the third has been expounded.[25] And so, the one who sins through weakness or through ignorance easily obtains forgiveness, but not the one who sins against the Holy Spirit. But although the power, wisdom, goodness of the three is one, why power is more often assigned to the Father, wisdom to the Son, goodness to the Holy Spirit has been said earlier above.[26]

DISTINCTION XLIV

Chapter 1 (268)

1. ON THE POWER TO SIN, WHETHER IT COMES TO MAN OR THE DEVIL FROM GOD. After the aforesaid, it seems worth considering whether the power to sin comes to us from God or from ourselves.

2. THE OPINION OF SOME THAT IT IS NOT FROM GOD; BUT THAT IS FALSE BY ANALOGY. Some hold that the power to act righteously comes to us from God, and that the power to sin does not come from God, but from ourselves or from the devil, just as an evil will does not come to us from God, but from ourselves or from the devil, and a good will comes to us from God alone.—ARGUMENT TO PROVE THAT A GOOD WILL DOES NOT COME TO MAN OTHER THAN FROM GOD.—AUGUSTINE, IN THE BOOK *ON*

[22]Cf. Mt. 12, 24-28.
[23]Ambrose, *De Spiritu sancto*, bk 1 c3 n54.
[24]See above, n1.
[25]In nn2 and ff.
[26]In Bk 1 dist. 34 c4 n2.

FAITH TO PETER: "Indeed, the beginning of a good will and thought is not born in man from his own self, but is divinely prepared and granted: God clearly shows this to be the case by the fact that neither the devil, nor any of his angels, from the time when they were cast out into this darkness, was able or could be able to take on again a good will. Because if it were possible that human nature, after turning away from God and losing the goodness of the will, could have it again from its own self, it would be much more possible that the angelic nature would have this, since the less burdened it is by the weight of an earthly body, the more it would be endowed with this faculty."[1]—And so a man or angel cannot have a good will from his own self, but [only] an evil one. They speak similarly of power, discussing the power of good and evil by analogy with the will, that the first is from God, but not the second.

3. BY AUTHORITIES, HE CONCLUDES THAT THE POWER TO SIN IS FROM GOD. But it is indubitably shown by many testimonies of the Saints that the power of evil is from God, from whom is all power. For the Apostle says: *There is no power unless from God*;[2] this must be understood not only of the power of good, but also of the power of evil, since Truth says to Pilate: *You would not have power over me, if it had not been given to you from above*.[3]—AUGUSTINE, ON PSALM 85: As Augustine says: "The wickedness of men certainly has the desire to harm through itself. But it does not have the power, if God does not give it. And so the devil, before taking anything from Job, said to the Lord: *Put forth your hand*,[4] that is, give the power";[5] "because even the power of those who do harm does not exist other than from God, as Wisdom says: *Kings rule through me, and tyrants hold the earth through me*.[6] Hence Job too says of the Lord: *He makes the hypocrite to reign because of the perversity of the people*.[7] And God says of the people of Israel: *I gave them a king in my anger*."[8,9]—AUGUSTINE, IN *ON GENESIS*: "For the will to do harm may be from the spirit of man, but the power is from none but God, and this by a hidden and just justice";[10] "indeed, through the power given to the devil, God makes the righteous his own."[11]—Of this, Gregory too, in the *Moralia*, says: "In crime, there is the bloatedness of pride, not the order of power. God

[1]Fulgentius, *De fide ad Petrum*, c3 n32.
[2]Rom. 13, 1.
[3]Jn. 19, 11.
[4]Job 2, 5.
[5]More accurately, Augustine, *Enarrationes in Psalmos*, on Ps. 32, sermon 2 n12.
[6]Prov. 8, 15-16, Septuagint.
[7]Job 34, 30, Septuagint.
[8]Hos. 13, 11, Septuagint.
[9]Augustine, *De natura boni*, c3.
[10]Augustine, *De Genesi ad litteram*, bk 11 c3 n5.
[11]Augustine, *De natura boni*, c32.

grants the power, but it is the wickedness of our mind that brings about the bloatedness of power. And so let us remove what is our own, because it is not a just power that is condemned, but a depraved action."[12]—By these authorities and many others, it is clearly shown that the power of good or evil does not come to anyone other than from the equitable God, even if his equity is hidden from you.

Chapter 2 (269)

1. WHETHER POWER IS SOMETIMES TO BE RESISTED. Here arises a question which is not to be passed over in silence. For it was said above that the power to sin and to do harm does not come to man or to the devil other than from God. And the Apostle says that *he who resists power, resists the ordinance of God*.[13] And so, since the power of evil belongs to the devil by God's ordinance, it seems that his power is not to be resisted.

2. THAT POWER IS SOMETIMES TO BE RESISTED. But it is to be known that the Apostle there speaks of secular power, namely a king and prince or suchlike; these are not to be resisted in those things which God commands to be given to them, namely tributes and suchlike.[14]—But if any prince or devil commanded or suggested anything against God, then he is to be resisted. Hence Augustine, determining when power is to be resisted, says in the book *On the Nature of the Good*: "If power commands that which you ought not to do, in this regard you do well to disregard power, fearing a greater power. Consider the very degrees of human affairs. If a curator has commanded something, is it still to be done, if his command is contrary to that of the proconsul? And again, if the proconsul commands one thing and the emperor commands another thing, does anyone doubt that the first is to be disregarded and the second is to be served? And so, if the emperor commands one thing and God another, the first is to be disregarded and God is to be obeyed."[15] Let us then resist the power of devil or man, when it has suggested something against God; in this, we do not resist God's ordinance, but conform ourselves to it, for God so commanded that we obey no power in evil things.

HERE ENDS THE SECOND BOOK

[12]Gregory, *Moralia*, bk 26 c26 n48.
[13]Rom. 13, 2.
[14]Cf. Rom. 13, 6-7; Mt. 22, 2.
[15]Rather, Augustine, *Sermo 62*, c8 n13.

Bibliography

English translations, in print or on-line, of works cited in Book 2.[1]

AMBROSE, SAINT, BISHOP OF MILAN, D. 397.

DE FIDE = "Exposition of the Christian Faith" in *Ambrose: Select Works and Letters*. Nicene and Post-Nicene Fathers: A Select Library of the Christian Church, 2nd ser., v. 10. Edited by Philip Schaff and Henry Wace. New York: Christian Literature Publishing Co., 1890-1898. Rpt. Peabody, MA: Hendrickson Publishers, 1994.
<http://www.ccel.org/ccel/schaff/npnf210.iv.iv.html>
<http://www.newadvent.org/fathers/34041.htm>

DE OFFICIIS. Trans. by Ivor J. Davidson. 2v. The Oxford Early Christian Studies. Oxford; New York: Oxford University Press, 2001.

"Three Books on the Duties of the Clergy" in *Ambrose: Select Works and Letters.* Nicene and Post-Nicene Fathers, 2nd ser., v. 10.
<http://www.ccel.org/ccel/schaff/npnf210.iv.i.ii.html>
<http://www.newadvent.org/fathers/3401.htm>

DE PARADISO = "Paradise" in *Hexameron, Paradise and Cain and Abel*. Trans. by John J. Savage. The Fathers of the Church, A New Translation, v. 42. Washington, DC: Catholic University of America Press in association with Consortium Books, 1977.

DE SPIRITU SANCTO = "The Holy Spirit" in *Saint Ambrose: Theological and Dogmatic Works*. Trans. by Roy J. Deferrari. The Fathers of the Church, v. 44. Washington, DC: Catholic University of America Press, 1963.

"On the Holy Spirit" in *Ambrose: Select Works and Letters*. Nicene and Post-Nicene Fathers, 2nd ser., v. 10.
<http://www.ccel.org/ccel/schaff/npnf210.iv.ii.html>
<http://www.newadvent.org/fathers/34021.htm>

EPISTOLA 49 (ad Sabinum) = "Letter 26 (49) To Sabinus" in *Letters 1-91*. Trans. by Mary Melchior Beyenka. The Fathers of the Church, A New Translation, v. 26. New York: Fathers of the Church, Inc., 1954.

IN PSALMUM 118, 25, sermon 4 = *Homilies of St. Ambrose on Psalm 118 (119)*. Trans. by Ide Ni Riain. Dublin: Halcyon Press, 1998.

[1]The notes to the translation use the Latin names for the works cited; this bibliography provides a list of available translations arranged alphabetically by author and Latin title so that the text of the authority may be found in any translation which reproduces the accepted divisions of the original texts.

APULEIUS

DE DEO SOCRATIS = "On the God of Socrates" in *Rhetorical Works*. Trans. by Stephen Harrison. Oxford; New York: Oxford University Press, 2001.

AUGUSTINE, SAINT, BISHOP OF HIPPO, 354–430.

CONFESSIONES =*Confessions*. Trans. by Garry Wills. New York: Penguin Books, 2006.

The Confessions of Saint Augustine. Trans. by Edward B. Pusey. New York: Modern Library, 1999.
<http://www.ccel.org/ccel/augustine/confess.html>

The Confessions. Trans. by Maria Boulding, The Works of Saint Augustine: A Translation for the 21st Century, pt. 1, v. 1. Hyde Park, NY: New City Press, 1997.

The *Confessions* of Augustine: An Electronic Edition. Text and Commentary Copyright (c) 1992. James J. O'Donnell.
<http://www.stoa.org/hippo/>

Confessions. Trans. by Vernon J. Bourke. The Fathers of the Church, v. 21. Washington, DC: Catholic University of America Press [1966, c1953].

Confessions and Enchiridion. Trans. by Albert C. Outler. Philadelphia: Westminster Press [1955].
<http://www.ccel.org/ccel/augustine/confessions.i.html>

The Confessions of St. Augustin. Nicene and Post-Nicene Fathers, 2nd ser., v. 1.
<http://www.ccel.org/ccel/schaff/npnf101.vi.html>
<http://www.newadvent.org/fathers/1101.htm>

CONTRA ADIMANTUM = "Answer to Adimantus, A Disciple of Mani" in *The Manichean Debate*. Trans. by Roland Teske. The Works of Saint Augustine: A Translation for the 21st Century, pt. 1, v. 19. Hyde Park, NY: New City Press, c2006.

CONTRA ADVERSARIUM LEGIS ET PROPHETARUM = "Answer to an Enemy of the Law and the Prophets" in *Arianism and Other Heresies*. Trans. by Roland Teske. The Works of Saint Augustine: A Translation for the 21st Century, pt. 1, v. 18. Hyde Park, NY: New City Press, 1995.

CONTRA FAUSTUM= "Reply to Faustus the Manichæan" in *The Writings Against the Manichæans and Against the Donatists*. Nicene and Post-Nicene Fathers, 1st ser., v. 4. Also in *Writings in Connection with the Manichæan Heresy*. The Writings of Aurelius Augustinus, Bishop of Hippo, v. 5. Edinburgh: T. & T. Clark, 1872.
<http://www.ccel.org/ccel/schaff/npnf104.iv.ix.html>
<http://www.newadvent.org/fathers/1406.htm>

CONTRA IULIANUM= "Answer to Julian" in *Answer to the Pelagians, II*. Trans. by Roland J. Teske. The Works of Saint Augustine: A Translation for the 21st Century, pt. 1, v. 24. Hyde Park, NY: New City Press, 1997.

Against Julian. Trans. by Matthew A. Schumacher. The Fathers of the Church, A New Translation, v. 35. New York: Fathers of the Church, Inc., 1957.

Contra Maximinum = "Debate with Maximinus" and "Answer to Maximinus" in *Arianism and Other Heresies*. Trans. Teske. The Works of Saint Augustine: A Translation for the 21st Century, pt. 1, v. 18.

Contra mendacium = "Against Lying." Trans. by H.B. Jaffee. In *Treatises on Various Subjects*. The Fathers of the Church, A New Translation, v. 16. Washington, DC: Catholic University of America Press [1965, c1952].

"To Consentius, Against Lying" in *On the Holy Trinity; Doctrinal Treatises; Moral Treatises*. Nicene and Post-Nicene Fathers, 1st ser., v. 3. Also in *Seventeen Short Treatises of S. Augustine, Bishop of Hippo*. Oxford: John Henry Parker, 1847.
<http://www.ccel.org/ccel/schaff/npnf103.v.vi.html>
<http://www.newadvent.org/fathers/1313.htm>

Contra secundam Iuliani responsionem opus imperfectum = "Unfinished Work in Answer to Julian" in *Answer to the Pelagians, III*. Trans. by Roland J. Teske. The Works of Saint Augustine: A Translation for the 21st Century, pt. 1, v. 25. Hyde Park, NY: New City Press, 1999.

De civitate Dei = *Concerning the City of God against the Pagans*. Trans. by Henry Bettenson. London; New York: Penguin Books, 2003.

The City of God. Trans. by Marcus Dods. New York: Modern Library, 2000.
<http://www.ccel.org/ccel/schaff/npnf102.iv.html>
<http://www.newadvent.org/fathers/1201.htm>

The City of God against the Pagans. Trans. by R.W. Dyson. Cambridge; New York: Cambridge University Press, 1998.

The City of God. Trans. by Demetrius B. Zema and Gerald G. Walsh. The Fathers of the Church, vv. 8, 14, 24. Washington, DC: Catholic University of America Press [1977, c1950].

De continentia = "Continence." In *Marriage and Virginity*. Trans. by Ray Kearney. The Works of Saint Augustine: A Translation for the 21st Century, pt. 1, v. 9. Hyde Park, NY: New City Press,1999.

"Continence." Trans. by M.F. McDonald. In *Treatises on Various Subjects*. The Fathers of the Church, A New Translation, v. 16.

"On Continence" in *On the Holy Trinity; Doctrinal Treatises; Moral Treatises*. Nicene and Post-Nicene Fathers, 1st ser., v. 3. Also in *Seventeen Short Treatises of S. Augustine*.
<http://www.ccel.org/ccel/schaff/npnf103.v.i.html>
<http://www.newadvent.org/fathers/1308.htm>

De correptione et gratia = "Rebuke and Grace" in *Answer to the Pelagians, IV*. Trans. by Roland J. Teske. The Works of Saint Augustine: A Translation for the 21st Century, pt. 1, v. 26. Hyde Park, NY: New City Press, 1999.

"Admonition and Grace" in *Christian Instruction; Admonition and Grace; The Christian Combat; Faith, Hope and Charity.* Trans. by John Courtney Murray. The Fathers of the Church, A New Translation, v. 2.Washington, DC: Catholic University of America Press [1950, c1947].

"A Treatise on Rebuke and Grace" in *Anti-Pelagian Writings,* Nicene and Post-Nicene Fathers, 1st ser., v. 5.
<http://www.ccel.org/ccel/schaff/npnf105.xx.i.html>
<http://www.newadvent.org/fathers/1511.htm>

DE DIVERSIS QUESTIONIBUS. 83 = *Eighty-three Different Questions.* Trans. by David L. Mosher. The Fathers of the Church, v. 70. Washington, DC: Catholic University of America Press, c1982.

DE DOCTRINA CHRISTIANA = *On Christian Teaching.* Trans. by R.P.H. Green. Oxford; New York: Oxford University Press, 1997.

Teaching Christianity. Trans. by Edmund Hill. The Works of Saint Augustine: A Translation for the 21st Century, pt. 1, v. 11. Hyde Park, NY: New City Press, 1996.

On Christian Doctrine. Trans. by D.W. Robertson. New York: Macmillan, 1987, c1958.

"Christian Instruction" in *Christian Instruction; Admonition and Grace; The Christian Combat; Faith, Hope and Charity.* Trans. by John Gavigan. The Fathers of the Church, v. 2.

"Christian Doctrine" in *City of God, Christian Doctrine.* Nicene and Post-Nicene Fathers, 1st ser., v. 2.
<http://www.ccel.org/ccel/augustine/doctrine.iv.html>
<http://www.newadvent.org/fathers/1202.htm>

DE DUABUS ANIMABUS = "The Two Souls" in *The Manichean Debate.* Trans. Teske. The Works of Saint Augustine: A Translation for the 21st Century, pt. 1, v. 19.

"On the Two Souls, against the Manichæans" in *The Writings against the Manichœans and against the Donatists.* Nicene and Post-Nicene Fathers, 1st ser., v. 4.
<http://www.ccel.org/ccel/schaff/npnf104.iv.vi.html>
<http://www.newadvent.org/fathers/1403.htm>

DE GENESI AD LITTERAM = "The Literal Meaning of Genesis" in *On Genesis: A Refutation of the Manichees. Unfinished Literal Commentary on Genesis. The Literal Meaning of Genesis.* Trans. by Edmund Hill. The Works of Saint Augustine: A Translation for the 21st Century, pt. 1, v. 13. Hyde Park: New City Press, 2002.

The Literal Meaning of Genesis. Trans. by John Hammond Taylor. Ancient Christian Writers, vv. 41-42. New York: Newman Press, c1982.

DE GENESIS CONTRA MANICHEOS = "A Refutation of the Manichees" in *On Genesis: A Refutation of the Manichees. Unfinished Literal Commentary on Genesis. The Literal Meaning of Genesis.* Trans. Hill. The Works of Saint Augustine: A Translation for the 21st Century, pt. 1, v. 13.

"Two Books on Genesis against the Manichees" in *On Genesis: Two Books on Genesis against the Manichees; and, On the Literal Interpretation of Genesis, an Unfinished Book.* Trans. by Roland J. Teske. The Fathers of the Church, v. 84. Washington, DC: Catholic University of America Press, 1991.

DE GRATIA ET LIBERO ARBITRIO = "Grace and Free Will" in *The Teacher. The Free Choice of the Will. Grace and Free Will.* Trans. by Robert P. Russell. The Fathers of the Church, A New Translation, v. 59 Washington, DC: Catholic University of America Press [c1968].

"On Grace and Free Will" in *Anti-Pelagian Writings.* Nicene and Post- Nicene Fathers, 1st ser., v. 5.
<http://www.ccel.org/ccel/schaff/npnf105.xix.i.html>
<http://www.newadvent.org/fathers/1510.htm>

DE HAERESIBUS = "Heresies" in *Arianism and Other Heresies.* Trans. Teske. Works of Saint Augustine: A Translation for the 21st Century, pt. 1, v. 18.

De haeresibus. Trans. by Liguori G. Müller. Patristic Studies, v. 90. Washington, DC: Catholic University of America Press, 1956.

DE LIBERO ARBITRIO = *On Free Choice of the Will.* Trans. by Thomas Williams. Indianapolis: Hackett Pub. Co., c1993.

"The Free Choice of the Will" in *The Teacher. The Free Choice of the Will. Grace and Free Will.* Trans. Russell. The Fathers of the Church, v. 59.

On Free Choice of the Will. Trans. by Anna S. Benjamin and L.H. Hackstaff. Indianapolis: The Bobbs-Merrill Co., 1961.

The Problem of Free Choice. Trans. by Mark Pontifex. Westminster, MD: The Newman Press; London: Longmans, Green and Co., 1955.

DE NATURA BONI = "The Nature of the Good" in *The Manichean Debate.* Trans. Teske. The Works of Saint Augustine: A Translation for the 21st Century, pt. 1, v. 19.

"The Nature of the Good" in *Earlier Writings.* Trans. by John H.S. Burleigh. Library of Christian Classics, v. 6. Philadelphia: Westminister Press [1953].

"Concerning the Nature of the Good, against the Manichees" in *The Writings against the Manichæans, and Against the Donatists.* Nicene and Post-Nicene Fathers, 1st ser., v. 4.
<http://www.ccel.org/ccel/schaff/npnf104.iv.x.html>
<http://www.newadvent.org/fathers/1407.htm>

DE NATURA ET GRATIA = "Nature and Grace" in *Answer to the Pelagians.* Trans. by Roland J. Teske. The Works of Saint Augustine: A Translation for the 21st Century, pt. 1, v. 23. Hyde Park, NY: New City Press, 1997.

"On Nature and Grace" in *Four Anti-Pelagian Writings.* Trans. by John A. Mourant. The Fathers of the Church, v. 86. Washington, DC: Catholic University of America Press, c1992.

"A Treatise on Nature and Grace" in *Anti-Pelagian Writings.* Nicene and Post-Nicene Fathers, 1st ser., v. 5
<http://www.ccel.org/ccel/schaff/npnf105.xii.html>
<http://www.newadvent.org/fathers/1503.htm>

DE NUPTIIS ET CONCUPISCENTIA = "Marriage and Desire" in *Answer to the Pelagians, II.* Trans. Teske. The Works of Saint Augustine: A Translation for the 21st Century, pt. 1, v. 24.

"On Marriage and Concupiscence" in *Anti-Pelagian Writings.* Nicene and Post-Nicene Fathers, 1st ser., v. 5.
<http://www.ccel.org/ccel/schaff/npnf105.xvi.i.html>
<http://www.newadvent.org/fathers/1507.htm>

DE PECCATORUM MERITIS ET REMISSIONE ET DE BAPTISMO PARVULORUM = "The Punishment and Forgiveness of Sins and the Baptism of Little Ones" in *Answer to the Pelagians.* Trans. Teske. The Works of Saint Augustine: A Translation for the 21st Century, pt. 1, v. 23.

"A Treatise on Merit and the Forgiveness of Sins, and the Baptism of Infants" in *Anti-Pelagian Writings.* Nicene and Post- Nicene Fathers, 1st ser., 5.
<http://www.ccel.org/ccel/schaff/npnf105.x.i.html>
<http://www.newadvent.org/fathers/1501.htm>

DE PERFECTIONE IUSTITIAE HOMINIS = "The Perfection of Human Righteousness" in *Answer to the Pelagians.* Trans. Teske. The Works of Saint Augustine: A Translation for the 21st Century, pt. 1, v. 23.

"A Treatise concerning Man's Perfection in Righteousness" in *Anti-Pelagian Writings.* Nicene and Post-Nicene Fathers, 1st ser., 5.
<http://www.ccel.org/ccel/schaff/npnf105.xiii.i.html>
<http://www.newadvent.org/fathers/1504.htm>

DE PRAEDESTINATIONE SANCTORUM = "The Predestination of the Saints" in *Answer to the Pelagians, IV.* Trans. Teske. The Works of Saint Augustine: A Translation for the 21st Century, pt. 1, v. 26.

"On the Predestination of the Saints" in *Four Anti-Pelagian Writings.* Trans. Mourant. The Fathers of the Church, v. 86.

"A Treatise on the Predestination of the Saints" in *Anti-Pelagian Writings.* Nicene and Post-Nicene Fathers, 1st ser., v. 5.
<http://www.ccel.org/ccel/schaff/npnf105.xxi.html>
<http://www.newadvent.org/fathers/15121.htm>

DE QUANTITATE ANIMAE = "The Magnitude of the Soul" trans. by John J. Mc-Mahon in *The Immortality of the Soul: The Magnitude of the Soul: On Music: The Advantage of Believing: On Faith in Things Unseen.* The Fathers of the Church: A New Translation, v. 4. Washington, DC: Catholic University of America Press in association with Consortium Books, 1977, c1947.

The Greatness of the Soul. The Teacher. Trans. by Joseph M. Colleran. Ancient Christian Writers: The Works of the Fathers in Translation, v. 9. Westminster, Md., Newman Press, 1950.

De quantitate animae; The Measure of the Soul. Trans. by Francis E. Tourscher. Philadelphia: The Peter Reilly Company; London: B. Herder, 1933.

DE SERMONE DOMINI IN MONTE = *Commentary on the Lord's Sermon on the Mount: with Seventeen Related Sermons*. Translated by Denis J. Kavanagh. The Fathers of the Church: A New Translation, v. 11.Washington, DC: Catholic University of America Press in association with Consortium Books, 1977, c1951.

The Lord's Sermon on the Mount. Translated by John J. Jepson. Ancient Christian Writers: The Works of the Fathers in Translation, v. 5. Westminster, MD: Newman Press, 1948.

"Our Lord's Sermon on the Mount" in *Sermon on the Mount; Harmony of the Gospels; Homilies on the Gospels*. Nicene and Post-Nicene Fathers, v. 6. <http://www.ccel.org/ccel/schaff/npnf106.v.html> <http://www.newadvent.org/fathers/1601.htm>

DE SPIRITU ET LITTERA = "The Spirit and the Letter" in *Answer to the Pelagians*. Trans. Teske. The Works of Saint Augustine: A Translation for the 21st Century, pt. 1, v. 23.

"The Spirit and the Letter" in *Later Works*. Trans. by John Burnaby. Library of Christian Classics, v. 8. Philadelphia, Westminister Press [1955].

"A Treatise on the Spirit and the Letter" in *Anti-Pelagian Writings*. Nicene and Post-Nicene Fathers, 1st ser., v. 5. <http://www.ccel.org/ccel/schaff/npnf105.xi.html> <http://www.newadvent.org/fathers/1502.htm>

DE TRINITATE = *The Trinity*. Trans. by Edmund Hill. The Works of Saint Augustine: A Translation for the 21st Century, pt.1, v. 5. Hyde Park, NY: New City Press, 1991.

The Trinity. Trans. by Stephen McKenna. The Fathers of the Church, v. 45. Washington, DC: Catholic University of America Press [1970, c1963].

"The Trinity" in *Later Works*. Trans. Burnaby. Library of Christian Classics, v. 8.

"On the Trinity" in *On the Holy Trinity, Doctrinal Treatises, Moral Treatises*. Nicene and Post-Nicene Fathers, 1st ser., v. 3. <http://www.ccel.org/ccel/schaff/npnf103.iv.i.html> <http://www.newadvent.org/fathers/1301.htm>

DE VERA RELIGIONE = "True Religion" in *On Christian Belief*. Trans. by Edmund Hill. Works of Saint Augustine: A Translation for the 21st Century, pt. 1, v. 8.

Of True Religion. Trans. by J.H.S. Burleigh. Chicago: Regnery, c1959; also in *Earlier Writings*. Library of Christian Classics, v. 6.

ENARRATIONES IN PSALMOS = *Expositions of the Psalms*. Trans. Maria Boulding. The Works of Saint Augustine: A Translation for the 21st Century, pt. 3, vv. 15-20. Hyde Park, NY: New City Press, 2000-2004.

St. Augustine on the Psalms. Trans. by Scholastica Hebgin and Felicitas Corrigan. Ancient Christian Writers, vv. 29-39. Westminster, MD: Newman Press, 1960– .

Expositions on the Book of Psalms. Nicene and Post-Nicene Fathers, 1st ser., v. 8. <http://www.ccel.org/ccel/schaff/npnf108.ii.html> <http://www.newadvent.org/fathers/1801.htm>

Expositions on the Book of Psalms. Trans. by J.H. Parker. The Fathers of the Holy Catholic Church, vv.8-13. Oxford: 1847-1857.

ENCHIRIDION = *The Augustine Catechism: The Enchiridion on Faith, Hope, and Love*. Augustine Series, v. 1. Hyde Park, NY: New City Press, 1999.

"Enchiridion" in *On Christian Belief*. Trans. by Bruce Harbert. The Works of Saint Augustine: A Translation for the 21st Century, pt. 1, v. 8.

Confessions and Enchiridion. Trans. by Albert C. Outler. Library of Christian Classics, v. 7. Philadelphia, Westminster Press [1955]. <http://www.ccel.org/ccel/augustine/enchiridion.i.html>

Enchiridion, or, Manual to Laurentius concerning Faith, Hope, and Charity. Trans. by Ernest Evans. London, S.P.C.K., 1953.

"Faith, Hope and Charity" in *Christian Instruction; Admonition and Grace; The Christian Combat; Faith, Hope and Charity*. Trans. by Bernard M. Peebles. The Fathers of the Church, v. 2.

"The Enchiridion" in *Basic Writings of Saint Augustine*, v. 1. Trans. by J. Shaw. New York: Random House, 1948. <http://www.newadvent.org/fathers/1302.htm>

Faith, Hope and Charity. Trans. by Louis A. Arand. Ancient Christian Writers, v. 3. Westminster, MD: Newman Bookshop, 1947.

EPISTOLAE = *Letters*. Trans. by Roland Teske. The Works of Saint Augustine: A Translation for the 21st century, pt. 2, vv. 1-4. Hyde Park, NY: New City Press, 2001-2005.

Letters 1–29**. Trans. by Robert B. Eno. The Fathers of the Church, v. 81. Washington, DC: Catholic University of America Press, 1989.

Letters. Trans. by Sister Wilfrid Parsons. The Fathers of the Church, vv. 12, 18, 20, 30, 32. Washington, DC: Catholic University of America Press, c1951-c1964. <http://www.newadvent.org/fathers/1102.htm>

IN EPISTOLAM AD GALATAS = *Augustine's Commentary on Galatians*. Trans. by Eric Plumer. Oxford; New York: Oxford University Press, 2003.

IN EPISTOLAM AD ROMANOS QUAEDAM PROPOSITIONES = *Augustine on Romans: Propositions from the Epistle to the Romans, Unfinished Commentary on the*

Epistle to the Romans. Trans. by Paula Fredriksen Landes. Early Christian Literature Series, v. 6. Chico, CA: Scholars Press, c1982.

In Ioannem = *Tractates on the Gospel of John.* Trans. by John W. Rettig. The Fathers of the Church, vv. 78, 79, 85, 88, 90, 92. Washington, DC: Catholic University of America Press, c1988-1995.

"Tractates (Lectures) / Homilies on the Gospel of John" in *Homilies on the Gospel of John, Homilies on the First Epistle of John, Soliloquies.* Nicene and Post-Nicene Fathers, 1st ser., v. 7. <http://www.ccel.org/ccel/schaff/npnf107.iii.html> <http://www.newadvent.org/fathers/1701.htm>

Retractationes = *The Retractations.* Trans. by Mary Inez Bogan. The Fathers of the Church, v. 60. Washington, DC: Catholic University of America Press [1968].

Sermones = *Sermons.* Trans. by Edmund Hill. The Works of Saint Augustine: A Translation for the 21st Century, pt. 3, vv. 1-11. Hyde Park, NY: New City Press, c1990-1997.

Sermons. Trans. by Mary Sarah Muldowney. The Fathers of the Church, v. 81. Washington, DC: Catholic University of America Press, 1959.

Sermons on Selected Lessons of the New Testament. Trans. by J.H. Parker. Fathers of the Holy Catholic Church. Oxford: J.H. Parker, 1844-1875. <http://www.newadvent.org/fathers/1603.htm>

BEDE, THE VENERABLE, SAINT, 673-735.

In Acta = *Commentary on the Acts of the Apostles.* Trans. by Lawrence T. Martin. Cistercian Studies Series, v. 117. Kalamazoo, MI: Cistercian Publications, 1989.

In 1 Ioannem = "Commentary on 1 John" in *The Commentary on the Seven Catholic Epistles of Bede the Venerable.* Translated by David Hurst. Cistercian Studies Series, v. 82. Kalamazoo, MI: Cistercian Publications, 1985.

Libri quatuor in principium Genesis = *On Genesis.* Trans. by Calvin B. Kendall. Liverpool: Liverpool University Press, 2008.

BOETHIUS, D. 524.

In libro Aristotelis De interpretatione, editio secunda seu maiora commentaria = "Second Commentary" in *On Aristotle's On Interpretation 9. Boethius: First and Second Commentaries.* Trans. by Norman Kretzmann. Ancient Commentators on Aristotle. Ithaca, NY: Cornell University Press, 1998.

CASSIAN, JOHN, CA. 360–CA. 435.

Conlationes = *The Conferences.* Trans. by Boniface Ramsey. Ancient Christian Writers: The Works of the Fathers in Translation, v. 57. New York: Paulist Press, c1997.

Conferences of John Cassian. Nicene and Post-Nicene Fathers, 2nd ser., v. 11.
<http://www.ccel.org/ccel/cassian/conferences.i.html>
<http://www.newadvent.org/fathers/3508.htm>

PSEUDO-DIONYSIUS, THE AREOPAGITE

DE CAELESTI HIERARCHIA = "The Celestial Hierarchy" in *Pseudo-Dionysius:The Complete Works*. Trans. by Colm Luibhéid. The Classics of Western Spirituality, v. 54. New York: Paulist Press, c1987.

The Works of Dionysius the Areopagite. Trans. by John Parker. London: James Parker & Co., 1897-1899. Rpt. Merrick NY: Richwood Pub. Co., 1976.

The Mystical Theology and the Celestial Hierarchies of Dionysius the Areopagite. Fintry, Brook, near Godalming, Surrey: Shrine of Wisdom, 1965. <http://www.esoteric.msu.edu/VolumeII/CelestialHierarchy.html>

FULGENTIUS, SAINT, BISHOP OF RUSPA, 468-533.

DE FIDE AD PETRUM = "To Peter on the Faith" in *Selected Works*. Trans. by Robert B. Eno. The Fathers of the Church, v. 95. Washington, DC: Catholic University of America Press, c1997.

GREGORY I, POPE, CA. 540-604.

DIALOGI = *Dialogues.* Trans. by Odo John Zimmerman. The Fathers of the Church, A New Translation, v. 39. New York: Fathers of the Church, Inc., c1959.

IN EVANGELIA = *Forty Gospel Homilies*. Trans. by David Hurst. Cistercian Studies Series, v. 123. Kalamazoo, MI: Cistercian Publications, 1990.

IN EZECHIELEM = *The Homilies of St. Gregory the Great on the Book of the Prophet Ezekiel*. Trans. by Theodosia Gray. Etna, CA: Center for Traditionalist Orthodox Studies, 1990.

MORALIA = *Morals on the Book of Job*. Oxford: J.H. Parker, 1844-1850.

GREGORY, OF NYSSA, SAINT, CA. 335–CA. 394.

DE VITA MOYSI = *The Life of Moses*. Trans. by Abraham J. Malherbe and Everett Ferguson. The Classics of Western Spirituality. New York: Paulist Press, c1978. Rpt. HarperCollins Spiritual Classics. [San Francisco]: HarperSan Francisco, c2006.

HUGH, OF SAINT-VICTOR, 1096?-1141.

DE SACRAMENTIS = *On the Sacraments of the Christian Faith* (*De sacramentis*). Trans. by Roy J. Deferrari. Mediaeval Academy of America, v. 58. Cambridge, MA: Mediaeval Academy of America, 1951.

ISIDORE, OF SEVILLE, SAINT, D. 636

ETYMOLOGIAE = *The Etymologies of Isidore of Seville*. Trans. by Stephen A. Barney [et al.]. Cambridge; New York: Cambridge University Press, 2006.

JEROME, SAINT, D. 419 OR 420.

ADVERSUS JOVINIANUM = "Against Jovinianus" in *Letters and Select Works.* Nicene and Post-Nicene Fathers, 2nd ser., v. 6.
<http://www.ccel.org/ccel/schaff/npnf206.vi.vi.html>
<http://www.newadvent.org/fathers/3009.htm>

HEBRAICAE QUAESTIONES IN LIBRO GENESIS = *Saint Jerome's Hebrew Questions on Genesis.* Trans. by C.T.R. Hayward. Oxford Early Christian Studies. Oxford, England: Clarendon Press; New York: Oxford University Press, 1995.

JOHN CASSIAN. *SEE* CASSIAN, JOHN

JOHN CHRYSOSTOM, SAINT, D. 407

IN EPISTOLAM AD HEBRAEOS = *Homilies on the Gospel of Saint John and the Epistle to the Hebrews.* Nicene and Post-Nicene Fathers, 1st ser., v. 14.
<http://www.ccel.org/ccel/schaff/npnf114.v.html>
<http://www.newadvent.org/fathers/2402.htm>

The Homilies of S. John Chrysostom, Archbishop of Constantinople, on the Epistle of S. Paul the Apostle to the Hebrews. The Fathers of the Holy Catholic Church, v. 44. Oxford: James Parker, 1877.

ORIGEN, 185–254.

IN IOSUE = *Homilies on Joshua.* Trans. by Barbara J. Bruce. The Fathers of the Church, A New Translation, v. 105. Washington, DC: Catholic University of America Press, c2002.

IN LUCAM = *Homilies on Luke; Fragments on Luke.* Trans. by Joseph T. Lienhard. The Fathers of the Church, A New Translation, v. 94 Washington, DC: Catholic University of America Press, c1996.

Index of Scriptural and Patristic Authorities[1]

[1]This index is keyed to the continuous series of chapters and paragraphs within each distinction.